Praise for The e-HR Advantage

"This is a timely topic with potential that very few companies have fully explored. With this book, Waddill and Marquardt offer a comprehensive and practical guide to HR leaders who are ready to embrace the myriad of possibilities technology offers. With their sage guidance and optimism, Waddill and Marquardt will convert even the Luddites among us."

    —Shannon Banks, Senior HR Business Partner, Microsoft Corporation

"I found reading this book entirely enticing, as it captures both the logic and spirit of connecting leadership development with available technology support. This book serves as a road map to continually expand your organization's capability to grow and sustain excellence."

    —Richard G. Milter, Professor, The Johns Hopkins Carey Business School

"More than ever, technology is influencing how we function in the workplace. This well organized, scholarly book serves IT and HR professionals, business executives, and laypersons alike as a guide for leveraging current and emerging IT in this new age. Knowing how to apply IT effectively for e-learning, communicating, transferring knowledge, and managing and developing all aspects of HR, has never been more critical. This cutting edge book shows us the way."

    —Thomas J. Dembeck, Health Innovation Consultant, Noblis

"This is a comprehensive resource. It will benefit not only the HR practitioner, but any leader who is keen to leverage technology to addr issues and achieve business goals."

    —Peng Soon Lim, President, Learning & Performance Systems

"*The e-HR Advantage* is a powerful book that offers practical tips and guidelines on real HR issues in the new environment."

    —Dr. Mohd Effendy Rajab, Executive D
    (SSA); Associate Faculty, Singapore I
    (UNISIM); and Former Adult Resource Director of the World Organization
    of the Scout Movement (

The e-HR Advantage

THE COMPLETE HANDBOOK FOR TECHNOLOGY-ENABLED HUMAN RESOURCES

Dr. Deborah D. Waddill and
Dr. Michael J. Marquardt

nb

NICHOLAS BREALEY
PUBLISHING

BOSTON · LONDON

This book is dedicated to Bill and Kelsey.

There are those who contributed mightily to the quality and substance of this text; these individuals should be acknowledged. They include the many authors whose research enriched and informed our writing, thank you; we stand on your shoulders. Others directly involved include: Erika Heilman, Jennifer Delaney, Nancy Prehn, Eric Anderson, Ryan Watkins, Howie Southworth, Craig and Stephanie Graby. The supporting cast includes: C. William Waddill, Jr., Robert and Liz DeWolfe, Jack DeWolfe (deceased), Lauren Lozowski, Paula Inglis, Nancy Lundgren, Dr. Teresa Klansek, Janice Befus, Cynthia Mazanec, Marjorie Veiga, Thomas Murray. Thank you.

This edition first published by Nicholas Brealey Publishing in 2011.

20 Park Plaza, Suite 1115A	3–5 Spafield Street, Clerkenwell
Boston, MA 02116 USA	London, EC1R4QB, UK
Tel: 617-523-3801	Tel: +44-(0)-207-239-0360
Fax: 617-523-3708	Fax: +44-(0)-207-239-0370

www.nicholasbrealey.com

© 2011 Deborah D. Waddill & Michael J. Marquardt

Printed in the United States of America

15   14   13   12   11   1   2   3   4   5

ISBN: 978-1-90483-834-0

Library of Congress Cataloging-in-Publication Data
Waddill, Deborah DeWolfe.
The e-HR advantage : the complete handbook for technology-enabled human resources / Deborah DeWolfe Waddill and Michael Marquardt.
        p. cm.
Includes bibliographical references.
ISBN 978-1-904838-34-0
  1. Personnel management—Technological innovations. 2. Personnel management—Information technology.   I. Marquardt, Michael.   II. Title.
HF5549.5.T33W33 2011
  658.300285—dc23

2011019148

Contents

SECTION 2

Learning Systems   27

3   Technologies That Enable Learning   29

4   e-Learning Technology Selection, Design, and Implementation: What Makes Sense   46

8   e-Recruiting   110

9   Handling HR Functions with an HRIS and/or Specialty Software   126

10   Electronic Performance Support Systems   143

SECTION 4

Communication Technologies 157

11 Groupware for Collaboration 159

12 Social Networks and Organizations 169

Purpose and Uses of This Book

Welcome to the world of technology-enabled Human Resources (e-HR). You are embarking on the path toward understanding the technologies available to you for HR functions.

The e-HR Advantage will allow you to be conversant with HR technology terms and related topics and to understand, most importantly, the valuable contributions you can make in the selection, design, implementation, and evaluation of technology *without* being a technology expert.

The technologies discussed in this book are those that will be of significance to anyone with human resource development (HRD) or human resource management (HRM) responsibilities. We will provide you with resources that you can use to manage technology-related activities, and we will clearly delineate areas of responsibility for the HR manager. In addition, we'll address some of the legal and regulatory issues associated with the technologies. Finally, we will provide direction regarding books, articles, and other resources if you want to examine a given topic in more depth.

Who Will Benefit from This Book?

Those who have people care responsibilities and who are unfamiliar with the full range of technologies available to HR professionals will benefit from this book. Readers may include business owners, executives, managers, and information technology and HR professionals. The text uses layman's terms for all descriptions.

How to Use This Book

Each chapter stands on its own and includes definitions, discussions of technology applications, graphics demonstrating major concepts, an explanation of the role of human resources relative to the technology, legal/regulatory/policy considerations, examination of cross-cultural issues HR professionals may encounter, related texts, examples, and current case studies.

All technology terms are italicized and described at first use, usually in the words of a leading expert in the field. "Tips and Tools" boxes provide recommendations to assist you with selection, implementation, and evaluation of the technology as well as "open-source" (free) or shareware (trial version) examples of the tool (when available), which you may use to try out the technology. "HR-Intersect" is a feature that indicates other units, divisions, and functional groups that can inform your decisions and with which you should collaborate. The "Case Study" boxes contain real-life examples offered by technology experts, executives, Human Resource managers, and professionals just like you. The case studies are used with the permission of the authors and their organizations. At the end of the book is a section entitled "Digging Deeper," which offers you a list of resources that you may use to research beyond the text.

We provide very few vendor names for the major technology groupings. Because each geographical region offers a variety of vendors too numerous to list comprehensively, we suggest that you join a local or regional HR association or community of practice. Trust your colleagues and results of local research for a list of reliable vendors, consultants, subcontractors, and so on available where you work. We will emphasize best practices rather than promote specific organizations or products.

It is very important to find a regional HR association or community of practice (CoP) in which you can participate. These groups will benefit you both intellectually and professionally. Further, your connections may provide much-needed support for your technology-related decisions.

You may read this book from cover to cover, but more likely you will read selectively in the areas most relevant to your needs and then keep the book available as a desktop reference to use when you encounter a new term or technology-related question. We hope you will turn to this guide again and again as you participate in and contribute to technology decisions in your workplace!

Introduction

CHAPTER 1

Technology and Its Impact on the Human Resources Professional

In the twenty-first century, we are constantly inundated with new ideas, new processes, and new products. The overwhelming onslaught of advertising messages, technical advances, and organizational policy changes influence our choices and behaviors; while these changes generally promise improved quality of life, they don't always deliver on that promise. Amidst the deluge—and contributing to it—is technology.

Technology permeates every aspect of our lives, and it changes constantly. It seems that "work-saving" technologies emerge almost daily, and, if adopted, they affect organizational policies, practices, and workflow.

There is no denying that technology can impact all facets of society. In the last century we saw radical economic, social, and work-life changes from:

- Machine/Industrial Age to the Technology/Informational Era
- National economies to global economies
- The physical to the virtual workplace
- Manufacturing to "Mentofacturing" (the production of ideas)
- Face-to-face interactions to online interactions (Schwandt and Marquardt 2000)

Another obvious fact is that technology contributed to these shifts.

In some ways, technology simplifies work, and in other ways it makes the workplace more complex. Technology offers both obstacles to success (the inevitable computer crashes) and increased opportunities (connections with people to whom we would not normally have access). Technology is neither bad nor good, but neutral. The way in which we use technology increases or decreases its positive net effect on us. Technology is, after all, nothing more than a tool. However, before proceeding any further, let's define the term.

What Is Technology?

Technology includes any innovation humans have developed, any tool that aids us in extending and interacting with our environment. Each generation has a different tool that qualifies as technology. For example, the primary technological invention of the fifteenth century was arguably the printing press; it revolutionized publishing, communication, and the distribution of knowledge. The key technological advancement of the twentieth century was—undeniably—the computer. Computers forever altered business, leisure, personal lives, and public platforms. Both the printing press and modern-day computers are technologies that radically changed societies. When we talk about technology, then, we are referring to any tool, technique, or system that enables us to control and adapt to our environment.

In the twenty-first century, the emergence of Web 2.0 extends the impact of computer technology. In some measure, our environment is controlled, supported, and influenced by the Internet; businesses, public places, and homes are all affected by the Internet, in developed and developing countries. Whether scientists use Web 2.0 to obtain high-resolution radar images. Based on Web 2.0, we have developed new ways of caring for the old and sick. Trust communities use this secure framework for accessing an unlimited number of online resource providers while maintaining privacy. Business operations require automation and customization, which are enhanced by Web 2.0. It enables vivid images and smooth business videoconferencing, and it supports the use of sophisticated simulations, including *avatars*, computer-generated graphics that look like people (Steele 2007). The Internet is so pervasive and powerful globally that you could call the twenty-first century the "Internet century" (Doherty 2001).

Human Resources and Technology

In the field of *Human Resources* (HR)—the learning and human development arm of most organizations—technology has completely altered business processes. This occurred in spite of the fact that HR departments tend to change more slowly than other departments and tend to be reluctant to use technology. It may be HR professionals' emphasis on workers, rather than the tools used by the workers, that in some cases dampens their enthusiasm for technology.

Typically, if you are in Human Resources, you care about people more than about things. There is a reason for that predisposition.

When Leonard Nadler coined the term *human resource development*, he cited Human Resource professionals' role within organizations as helping individuals to grow and learn. The role became more sophisticated as human resource development (HRD) became more clearly defined to include the three-fold notion of training, education, and development. In the twenty-first century, Human Resource responsibilities surpassed a focus on individual and organizational development to encompass oversight of learning at the individual, team, and organizational levels.

An interesting phenomenon in this century has been the redistribution of conventional HR functions into the hands of non-HR managers. In this case, the care of employees becomes the responsibility of the employees' direct supervisors rather than someone in the HR department. In such cases, the "people care" shifted from HR to managers. It is important to note this migration of responsibilities. Consequently, many HR roles and responsibilities appear under the job descriptions of supervisors and managers rather than a bona fide HR department. The impetus for this change can in part be attributed to cost efficiencies offered by HR technologies.

This migration of responsibilities may explain why non-HR professionals often make many of the technology decisions that impact the Human Resource department. As technology has gained in importance, it has begun to support many of the people-care functions that HR professionals previously handled themselves.

Traditionally, HR professionals have performed several key functions, including: HR strategic advisor, HR systems designer and developer, organization change consultant, organization design consultant, learning program specialist, instructor/facilitator, individual development and career consultant, performance consultant, and researcher.

In the past, each of these functions contributed significantly to an organization's well-being. Interestingly, however, in the twenty-first century the functions have morphed to a new set of competencies, many of which can be enhanced or entirely performed using technology. In a study performed by the RBL Group and the Ross School at University of Michigan (assisted by the Society for Human Resource Management), a new set of competency domains were identified for the HR professional. These include:

- Credible activist
- Culture and change steward

- Strategic architect
- Talent manager and organization designer
- Business ally
- Operational executor (Society for Human Resource Management 2007)

Technology underpins all of these HR competencies and can, at very least, increase the effectiveness of the HR department. In fact, HR-related technologies offer many attractions. In short, technology can be used to enhance performance, quicken decision making, handle *administrivia* (excessive administrative detail), enable the exchange of knowledge, offer learning to a broader audience, and provide cost savings (Gueutal and Stone 2005).

The Society of Human Resource Management offers current advice on important HR matters in its journal, *HRMagazine*. Rita Zeidner states, in *HRMagazine*: "Core administrative responsibilities as diverse as recruitment, oversight of legal and regulatory compliance, benefits administration, and the safeguarding of confidential employee info *cannot* be carried out effectively without high-tech tools" (2009, 49). Organizations that reject emerging HR technologies are likely to find themselves at a severe disadvantage.

Riding the Wave of Internet-Enabled Technologies

Peter Vaill wrote in his book *Learning as a Way of Being* (1996) that society is in a perpetual state of turbulence similar to "white water," which Merriam-Webster's dictionary defines as a "frothy water (as in breakers, rapids, or falls)." Experience demonstrates that tumultuous, surprising, novel, ill-structured, and obtrusive events that simulate the chaos of "white water" in our everyday lives often involve—or are related to—technology.

Whereas some simply avoid the water—rejecting technology entirely—others participate and become fully engaged. Yet there is a third option: learning survival techniques. There are strategies for coping with technological change that enable the businessperson to find safe harbor amid technology chaos. The key is this: one must prepare, use the appropriate tools, and seek assistance in order to deal with each new technology wave.

The first order of business is to differentiate the technology gimmicks from the effective tools. This requires an understanding of the selection process, the audience, the business, the existing technologies, and the future plans of the organization. Human Resource (HR) professionals must have the technology acumen to participate in and contribute to technology research, selection, and implementation. HR managers must understand technology so that they can gauge its potential impact on the workforce. And Human Resource, managers and leaders must help prepare others for technology-generated change that is occurring in the field of Human Resources.

Technology presents tremendous advantages. Global economies, countries, and organizations can realize cost efficiencies from investments made in Internet-enabled technologies. At the personal level, those who understand Internet-enabled technologies have a business advantage, especially in terms of higher wages (The U.S. Bureau of Labor Statistics 2003). Technology expertise can be a fast track to promotion. In fact, technology may be the key for organizational success, allowing HR staff to manage vast quantities of information and handle the pace of change while maintaining a leading edge. Consequently, to lead at this time in history, the HR professional must understand the technologies that impact HR functions and responsibilities.

Technology and Opportunity

In spite of solid evidence to the contrary, there are those who remain unconvinced of the importance of technology and the Internet. There is even a term for these people: *neo-Luddites*, a term used to describe those who mistrust or fear the inevitable changes brought about by new technology. The original *Luddites* were named after Ned Lud, an English laborer who was reported to have destroyed weaving machinery around 1779; the Luddites destroyed technological devices that they felt threatened their livelihoods.

Let's be honest now … Have you ever wanted to take a bat to your computer? We thought so. This negative response, as you know, is ineffective against the advances of technology. Neo-Luddites are unable to halt technological progress, yet they cannot be convinced that the proactive approach of embracing technology is the more sensible plan.

When HR professionals reject technology, they force others—who may or may not understand the responsibilities of Human Resources management—to make decisions about the technology selection appropriateness. Often, those who fill in are not the stakeholders; rather they are information technology (IT) experts. While IT professionals have technical knowledge of hardware and software, they may not know the characteristics and workflow of the target audience; when those who will use the technology are not represented in the decision, they become disgruntled and sometimes frustrated. HR professionals should serve as the liaison.

The sensible, happy medium is for HR professionals to examine proposed technologies for whether or not they will satisfy the stakeholders' workplace needs. Technology can positively impact organizational, team, and individual development in a variety of areas. There are many instances where technology enhances the learning, effectiveness, and communication within an organization. Consider the examples of online learning, workplace collaboration tools, employee time-tracking technology, and communication by e-mail. These technologies render more efficient everything from internal communication to knowledge management. Technology can streamline employee surveys and certification; assistive technology increases opportunities for those with physical disabilities; and HR information systems and self-service sites enable the free flow of compensation, healthcare, and retirement information. Collaboration increases through the use of listservs, social networking sites, and groupware. Opportunities for new efficiencies in the technology-enabled workplace are endless.

Organizational Readiness

As with any business decision, good sense, research, and an understanding of the organizational climate must prevail when making technology decisions. Technology selection must take into account the business environment and organizational disposition toward new technologies. The organization's mission and organizational climate indicate its readiness to adopt a new technology; its readiness to accept new technology influences both the type of technology selected and ultimately the technology's success in that environment.

HR's Changing Role

Corporate leaders around the world care very much about the integration of technology, learning, and organizational life. In the case of HR functions, it should be the HR executive and her HR managers who select, implement, and evaluate technology options that affect their work. Even those HR professionals who are not technology-savvy can—and should—have significant input. At the very least, HR managers, as stakeholders, should be aware of and research technological improvements that impact the workplace in order to participate in technology decisions. This is a recent change to the role of the HR professional.

Other ways in which technology changes the role of the HR professional include:

- Assessing the effectiveness of new technologies
- Knowing when and where to apply new technologies
- Integrating existing technologies with new technologies
- Redesigning business processes to incorporate the new technology
- Securing appropriate buy-in on technologies from the user groups

Typically, the HR professional knows the business environment and understands the employees within the organization—information that is invaluable to those making technology decisions. The HR leader must assess the readiness of the organization to implement new technologies; HR and people-care managers should play a significant role in every major technology decision that impacts workers and the flow of work within their organization.

The Competitive Edge

HR-related decisions must not be made in a vacuum. The Human Resources Department and those with human resource responsibilities have important information and contacts that can inform the process. HR professionals also should involve the target audience in the HR technology selection process.

Further, technology-related functions in which HR professionals should participate include:

- Gathering system requirements
- Acting as the gatekeepers of the technology
- Establishing operating principles
- Establishing standards for secure information
- Performing electronic onboarding processes for new hires
- Directing employee benefit contributions
- Generating reports from HR systems
- Evaluating workers
- Conducting employee surveys
- Providing e-learning
- Conducting computer-based testing
- Enabling workplace collaboration and other efficiency-producing operations (Zeidner, 2009)

These are all important ways for HR professionals to add value to the technology decision-making process.

Still unconvinced of your need for technology expertise? For the Human Resources Department, there are many benefits to using the current technologies. For instance, the HR manager who assists in implementing knowledge management technologies promotes organizational learning. Learning technologies can generate learning transfer, while document sharing and database technologies can increase information availability for those who need it just-in-time. Groupware technologies facilitate team and individual learning as well as promote communities of practice. And, as stated previously, technologies such as HR systems can increase efficiency and accuracy as well as reduce the time HR professionals spend on administrative tasks.

From the viewpoint of the organization, the new technologies allow an organization to keep pace with, and meet the demands of, a complex environment. Knowledge management allows an organization to collect, analyze, and organize information in a way that provides a competitive edge to the organization. Customer relationship management (CRM) systems can gather valuable information about clients that informs the marketing team about client needs. New techniques, information, and processes can be disseminated using e-learning technologies. These are just a few examples of how technology benefits an organization.

In the field of human resources, many technology opportunities offer a competitive advantage. HR departments that do not adapt to the sophisticated technologies around them will languish and become irrelevant. Further, they do a disservice to the population they are designed to serve. In order to deal with the twenty-first-century business environment, HR departments, HR managers, and those with HR responsibilities must have the internal capabilities to adapt to new technologies. Human resource professionals must be involved in analyzing, selecting, designing, implementing, and evaluating new technologies, especially those that impact the domain of human resources.

Individually, HR professionals must understand HR-related technologies in order to have credibility. Professionals cannot lead when they do not understand the tools of their trade. This does not mean that HR professionals must program instruction, design websites, or manage technology implementation efforts. Rather, HR leaders must understand the new technologies well enough to make informed decisions about them, to abide by regulatory and legal requirements, to establish policies regarding the technologies, to understand how they will impact business processes, and to redesign workflow to accommodate the technologies. All of these functions fall within the domain of HR.

HR professionals must be knowledgeable about technologies that can benefit the practice of HR in their organizations. This lends credibility to the HR department and earns it a more prominent role in strategizing and making executive decisions.

Conclusion

Technology changes rapidly. Some professionals resist this change. Human resource professionals are among those who tend to flout technology because their interest is in humans rather than technology. However, it is beneficial to the organization, the HR professional, and the employees they serve for HR professionals to become involved in the technology selection and implementation process. In so doing, HR professionals can take advantage of the new, sophisticated, labor-saving hardware and software, represent employees' best interests in the technology selection process, and add to their own credibility by being knowledgeable about this important business area. Ultimately an HR professional's understanding of technology positions her at a strategic level, as a decision-maker.

CHAPTER 2

Technology in Workplaces around the World

The adoption and acceptance of technology—or the lack of acceptance—depends in part on the characteristics and environment of the culture into which it is introduced. Often, those managers and workers directly affected by technology are neither taken into account nor consulted when new systems are launched. Ignoring the culture of the target audience, the organizational culture, and the workers within the organization can spell failure for a technology implementation effort. Whether an organization is putting into place an entirely new technology system, upgrading an existing system, or implementing a new module in a system, those employees who will use the technology should be considered.

Because of their understanding of organizational culture, even nontechnical HR professionals are crucial to the selection, implementation, and adoption of new technology. Those who focus on the care and development of employees have vital information about the audience and the organizational context. Further, HR professionals typically have the skills to identify the ways in which the technology will impact workflow, jobs, training, benefits, organizational policies, the quality of work life, and so on. It is satisfying to most HR professionals to help those who are going to be affected by changes in technology. Insights from HR professionals can determine whether or not the new system, machine, or program is actually used. You can really make a difference!

When a new technology is introduced, there is a ripple effect through the entire organization. Depending on how well the organization considers its culture and prepares its staff for the change, the ripple may result in tiny waves or it may cause a tsunami. So let's start with culture in the workplace. Then we will address the interplay between technology and culture, technology and the organization, and technology and the worker. Finally we will outline your important role as an HR professional.

Culture and the Workplace

In today's rapidly globalizing marketplace, understanding cultural differences is critical for both employee satisfaction and corporate success. Managers and HRD professionals who have worked internationally have long recognized that people live and learn differently because of culture; employees are managed and motivated differently, and they think and react differently because of culture. In truth, culture shapes every aspect of the workplace. Why? Because culture teaches each of us specific "correct" ways to think and act, which are different from every other culture's way of thinking and acting. These cultural differences affect how we do our work.

Culture and How We Do Things

Culture influences the way in which groups of people behave and the belief systems that they develop to justify and explain these behaviors.

Geert Hofstede, an influential organizational psychologist, has written extensively about culture. We will use his framework, which features six dimensions for analysis of culture, including power distance, individualism, masculinity versus femininity, uncertainty avoidance, long-term/short-term avoidance, and indulgence versus restraint (Hofstede, Hofstede, and Minkov 2010). Each dimension is defined below:

- Power distance focuses on the degree or the extent to which the less powerful members of organizations and institutions (like the family) accept and expect that power is distributed unequally.
  - Small power distance is the extent to which people want a say in how they are led.
  - Large power distance indicates acceptance by the followers of relations that are autocratic or paternalistic.
  - The distribution of power is defined from below, not from above, and is endorsed by the followers as much as by the leaders.
- Individualism versus collectivism concentrates on the degree to which society reinforces the achievements of an individual or those of the collective.
  - Individualist societies are those in which everyone looks after self and immediate family.

- Collectivist societies are those in which people belong to strong, cohesive ingroups, such as extended families, where protection is exchanged for loyalty.
- Masculinity versus femininity revolves around the distribution of roles between the genders.
    - Masculinity embraces assertiveness and competitiveness.
    - Femininity values modesty and caring.
    - The assertive pole has been called "masculine" and the modest, caring pole "feminine."
- Uncertainty avoidance focuses on the acceptance of uncertainty and ambiguity within the society, such as tolerance for unstructured situations.
    - High uncertainty avoidance indicates the culture has little tolerance for uncertainly and ambiguity, resulting in a rule-oriented society that institutes controls in order to reduce uncertainty.
    - Low uncertainty avoidance implies that the culture has more tolerance for a variety of opinions, readily accepts change, and takes more risks.
- Long-term versus short-term orientation focuses on the degree to which society accepts or rejects long-term devotion to traditional, forward-thinking values, based on Confucian heritage.
    - Long-term focus indicates appreciation of long-range commitments and respect for tradition, including a strong work ethic in which long-term rewards are expected as a result of hard work.
    - Short-term orientation indicates that the culture accepts that change can occur rapidly, and believes that traditions and long-term commitments should not become impediments to change. This orientation embraces the future and change.
- Indulgence versus restraint
    - Indulgent societies support open gratification of basic and natural human desires necessary to enjoying life.
    - Restrained cultures suppress gratification of desires and regulate it using social norms.

Another view on the same topic of culture is presented by Dean Foster, former director of the global leadership and training company Berlitz International. He describes culture by categorizing the way it addresses these three questions:

- What is the best way for people to relate to one another?
- What is the best way to view time?

■ What is the best way for society to work with the world at large? (Foster 2002)

Culture provides people with a meaningful context in which to meet other people, to think about themselves, and to face the outer world. It is important to realize that culture is logical and rational to the members of the culture but often appears irrational or illogical to those outside it.

Several factors impact a culture and, in turn, are influenced by the culture. These include religion, language, education, economics, politics/law, family, class structure, history, and geography/natural resources. What distinguishes one culture from another is not the presence or absence of these factors, but rather the patterns and practices found within and between these factors (Marquardt and Engel 1992). Importantly—and directly related to this book—each of these factors can and does influence the ways in which a cultural group responds to technology.

Cultural attributes can be categorized into three major groups of cultural orientations, and within those groups are three subgroups of cultural preferences (Foster 2002). Because culture is so critical to technology selection and implementation, let's look at these attributes a bit more closely.

Culture and the Best Way for People to Relate to Each Other

Each culture has its own unique way of describing the best way for people to relate to each other. As mentioned earlier, power distance focuses on the degree to which the less powerful members of organizations and institutions accept and expect that power is distributed unequally. Within this context, consideration should be given to whether the culture is other-independent or other-dependent. Other-*independent* is a characteristic that allows people within the culture to act autonomously, with individuality and without constant reference to family, clan, or other membership group. Other-*dependent* is the opposite, and emphasizes the group (collectivism) rather than the individual (individualism). This is enabled through collaboration and harmony rather than competition and winning.

Structure in everyday life can be presented as either hierarchical or egalitarian in nature. Within a hierarchy-oriented society, respect for elders, rulers, and religious leaders plays a pivotal role; whereas in an egalitarian society, social status and hierarchy have little influence. The relationship-oriented society is highly dependent on loyalty toward a person who is deemed to have power and authority and with whom there is a relationship. Conversely, in the rule-oriented culture, objective rules are the ultimate authority, and there is an emphasis on equality where each individual's opinions count.

Culture and the Best Way to View Time

Another aspect of culture is the group's perspective on the best way to view time, with respect to certain categories. Is the time system, within the society, monochronic (things are done one at a time) or polychronic (many things are done at once, often called multitasking)? Is the culture past-oriented, with an emphasis on tradition, or future-oriented, embracing change? These questions represent the opposite ends on a scale of how to view time. This also relates to Hofstede's view of constraint versus indulgence, where constraint suppresses desires and indulgence requires immediate gratification (2010).

Culture and the Best Way for Society to Work with the World at Large

With regard to the best way for society to work with the world at large, there are three major continuums to examine. One continuum can be summarized with this question: is the communication high-context indirect or low-context direct? *High-context indirect* is a communication style in which context has ultimate importance. High-context indirect communication uses nonverbal elements such as voice tone, facial expression, gestures, and eye movements to convey a message. One talks around the point and embellishes it. Communication is seen as an art form, a way of engaging someone. *Low-context direct* refers to communications in which the individual pays more attention to the literal meanings of words than to the context surrounding them. The message is carried more by words than by nonverbal methods. The verbal message is direct; one spells things out exactly. Communication is seen as a way of exchanging information, ideas, and opinions. Disagreement is depersonalized and focuses on rational solutions, not personal ones.

The next question to ask is whether the culture is process-oriented or result-oriented. Process orientation depends more on analogous reasoning with an interest in human beings more than the task, often considered feminine characteristics. In contrast, result-oriented thinking relies upon proving and disproving the logic in a systematic way.

Formal or informal behavior is another cultural differentiator. Formal societies are ritualized and predicated upon honoring hierarchies and status as well as a respect for elders, and saving face. In informal societies, competence and results take precedence over respect for status or age.

THE CULTURE SPECTRUM

What's the best way for people to relate to one another?

Other-Independent	←——————————————→	*Other-Dependent*
Individualism		Collectivism/Group
Winning		Collaboration/Harmony
Egalitarian-Oriented	←——————————————→	*Hierarchy-Oriented*
Equality		Chain of command
Equal distribution of power		Unequal distribution of power
Rule-Oriented	←——————————————→	*Relationship-Oriented*
Equal under law		Relationships supersede law
Internal control		External control

What's the best way to view time?

Polychronic	←——————————————→	*Monochronic*
Time is money		Time is life
Multi-tasking		Doing one thing at a time
Action/Doing		Being/Acceptance
Future-Oriented	←——————————————→	*Past-Oriented*
Short-term focus		Long-term focus
Future/Change		Traditions/History
Immediate Gratification		Restraint

What's the best way for society to work with the world at large?

Low Context	←——————————————→	*High-Context*
Direct communication		Indirect communication
Demonstrate pride		Save face
Use clear speech and facts		Emphasize analogies/ precedents
Emphasize achievement		Demonstrate modesty
Result-Oriented	←——————————————→	*Process-Oriented*
Systematic/Mechanistic		Humanistic
Masculine		Feminine
Informal	←——————————————→	*Formal*
Respect for competence		Respect for elders
Respect for results		Respect for status

FIGURE 2-1   Culture Spectrum

One way to view cultural issues is to examine them using the cultural mores spectrum. Merging Hofstede's and Foster's approaches provides us with the illustrated view of the spectrum of cultural dimensions.

The cultural characteristics shown above provide a mirror, as well as a window, into the reasons people may react differently in the workplace.

Cultural Adaptations

Understanding that people's cultures influence their behaviors is highly relevant to the modern workplace. In order to adapt to situations involving other cultures, HR professionals, and organizations in general, must apply some basic guidelines. They must:

- Be cognizant of cultural differences in business settings.
- Discuss cultural differences in a nonjudgmental manner.
- Be open and willing to learn.
- Realize that the business goal is not to elevate one culture's way over another's—rather to find the best way/approach for a project (Zweifel 2010).

Technology and Culture

How does culture relate to technology? Anytime a new technology is under consideration, those with HR responsibilities must realize that culture may have an impact on how it is accepted and integrated into the workplace. There are technologies that may be particularly offensive to some cultures. For instance, some cultures value face-to-face encounters and do not appreciate technologies that replace in-person interaction. The simulated world, with its avatars (which are computer-simulated beings that can be controlled by the user) and undisclosed personalities, can be highly offensive to those who are accustomed to more formal relationships based upon hierarchy and status.

A new technology can be received negatively or positively, but rarely is the response neutral. It is, therefore, important to analyze the culture, organizational context, and impact on workers before adopting a new technology. If the cultural predisposition toward a technology makes it difficult for employees from that culture to use it, then the HR professional must get involved to help find alternatives. Perform an audience analysis before instituting any new technology within another culture, and include members of the target audience in the technology selection process in order to get their feedback. When selecting a technology, consider cultural values, and choose a technology that aligns with these. Use culturally appropriate visuals and terminology in your communication. Conform to the most conservative legal and regulatory technology policies, whether they originate in the country of the organization's headquarters or the country hosting the technology.

Globalization and Culture

Over the past one hundred years, companies have undergone a corporate evolution from domestic markets toward globalization. As they evolved from the domestic to the international phase, companies began freely importing and/or exporting parts and products. In the multinational phase, occurring within the past twenty years, companies have become global, operating as if the entire world were a single, borderless entity. These global companies have been made possible by technology. However, the success of a company's globalization process depends largely upon the effectiveness of the technology it has chosen and on how that technology works with the employees' cultural capacities. To the extent that the technology maximizes the strengths of various cultures, the organization benefits. This capability leads to multiple perspectives, the development of a wider range of options and approaches, the heightening of creativity and problem-solving skills, and increased flexibility in addressing culturally distinct clients and partners. Thinking and operating globally are critical to organizational survival and growth in the twenty-first century.

Globalization does not erase culture, however. In fact, employees of global companies may hold onto their cultural beliefs and practices more tightly than employees of domestic companies. Although some values transcend nationalities and can operate on a worldwide scale (such as the value of teamwork, continuous learning, respect for individuals), culturally unique principles and ideals do not disappear. Thus, embracing aspects of other cultures such as food, clothes, and entertainment represents a superficial behavioral change rather than a change to core cultural values and basic assumptions.

Cultural differences affect all global organizations: there is no global or multinational organization that operates devoid of culture's influence. In fact, every organization is immersed, at the very least, in the culture of the region. The tools we use—right down to our writing implements—are impacted by culture. Organizations cannot separate themselves from the culture of their location. As organizations broaden their reach, they must also consider and adapt to the cultures that they encounter.

Tips for Aligning Technology with Culture

Following are some tips about culture and technology:

- Culture impacts the way people learn and communicate; therefore, technology-enhanced events and products must be altered for different cultural settings.
- When selecting a technology, consider cultural values and choose a technology that aligns with these.
- Use culturally appropriate visuals and terminology in your communication.
- Conform to the most conservative legal and regulatory technology policies, whether they originate in the country of the organization's headquarters or in the country hosting the technology.

Organizational Readiness for Technology

Organizational culture is most evident in the artifacts of the organization (such as buildings, logos, and signs), basic guiding assumptions (about human nature, human relations, and the environment), and the organization's values and beliefs as shown by the actions of the organization (Schein 1992). The organizational culture impacts both the adoption of and adaptation to technology. Some organizations are predisposed to embrace technology; others are not. The organizational context and the disposition of an organization toward technology should be identified before implementing new technology. After such an analysis, the message and implementation approach can be adapted for the audience.

Electronic medical records management was introduced in the United States as a government initiative in 1996 but was not adopted until the American Recovery and Reinvestment Act (ARRA) of 2009. Other nations, including England, Australia, Canada, and Estonia, adopted the electronic medical record system as early as 2005. Why did it not take root earlier in the United States? One answer is that healthcare organizations were not ready for the technology and the broad changes that would attend its implementation. Additionally, it is possible that cultural perceptions needed to shift.

Is the Organization Ready for Technology?

Gauging organizational readiness is an important and necessary task. Jeffrey Liker, Carol Haddad, and Jennifer Karlin provide insight into how one can assess an organization's preparedness for a new technology (1999). Elements like the organization's vision and mission, management philosophy, the tone of labor–management interactions, and the degree of shared agreement about the technology all impact organizational readiness for a new technology. These are some of the contextual inputs that should contribute to technology selection and implementation.

The following visual (see Figure 2-2: Organizational Readiness for Technology) categorizes an organization's views of technology along two axes. At one end of the horizontal continuum is the technology focus. An organization whose primary focus may be on technology embraces and encourages use of new technologies, and much of its success depends upon technology. For example, institutions in information technology, telecommunications, or research industries quickly adapt to new technologies because the mechanics of the programs are similar to their business offerings. On the other end of the continuum is the environment focus. An organization at this end of the spectrum typically emphasizes human interactions. Examples of institutions that

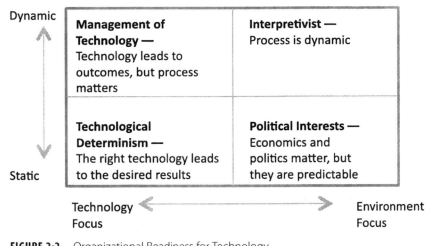

	Dynamic	
Management of Technology — Technology leads to outcomes, but process matters		**Interpretivist —** Process is dynamic
Technological Determinism — The right technology leads to the desired results		**Political Interests —** Economics and politics matter, but they are predictable

Dynamic

Static

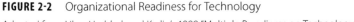

Technology
Focus

Environment
Focus

FIGURE 2-2   Organizational Readiness for Technology

Adapted from Liker, Haddad, and Karlin's 1999 "Multiple Paradigms on Technology Impacts."

prefer to make people a priority include nonprofit organizations and those that emphasize people-provided skills. Typically, political organizations, counseling organizations, and educational institutions all rely heavily on their workers rather than on the benefits of technology.

On the vertical axes are the static and dynamic views of technology's impact. The static view is deterministic, equivalent to "if this then that" linear thinking. Organizations on this end of the continuum are typically bound by regulations and processes that make outcomes foreseeable. Static organizations believe that the right technology leads to desired results, or traditional engineering thinking. The dynamic view, on the other hand, considers a more complex interplay of technology and the organization; while technology design is important, process matters. The organization with a dynamic view of technology considers technology implementation to be a complex process that may have major social transformation qualities. However the processes for technology design and implementation must be followed—changing management is important, and user involvement is key. In this paradigm, organizational innovations may precede technology.

Human Resources and Organizational Readiness for Technology

Assessing the host organization's readiness for technology is important. Those organizations that are more focused on the context and the people involved rather than on the technology itself may be more difficult to convince of the need for technology. Conversely, when an organization's technology focus outweighs the contextual influence, the organization is usually more inclined toward technology adoption.

When it is time to make a technology decision, it is the HR professional who knows the organizational environment best. An assessment of the organization's readiness for technology may help to forecast acceptance—or rejection—of a new technology. An HR professional has the interpersonal and communication skills to help introduce new technology in a way that increases the likelihood that the change will work for the employees.

The Worker and Technology

The worker should influence the selection and implementation of technology. The worker's interface with technology occurs at the business process, workflow level. The degree to which technology affects workflow and business process matches the degree of discomfort that you can expect from employees working with the new technology.

Intersects between Workers and Technology

While technology use varies, we can identify four common areas of interaction between technology and the worker. The first area involves interaction with computer-based equipment such as electronic cash registers or bar-code scanners, robotic or computer-controlled machine tools, computerized diagnostic devices, and various office machines. In this area, people interact directly with hardware but usually not with software, so workers generally need little understanding of the technology. They can operate the equipment by following a specific set of procedures or steps. This type of human interface with equipment is typical of service and manufacturing jobs, as well as tasks done by the general public.

The second area of interaction between workers and technology is with one or more proprietary application programs. This includes any system for processing transactions (e.g., customer orders, billing, reservations), completing or checking records in a database (e.g., medical, insurance, law enforcement, inventory), or specialized decision making (e.g., loan appraisals, budgeting, transportation routing). The information processing activities of almost every organization are heavily dependent upon such proprietary software, and millions of clerical jobs revolve around their use. Learning to use such a system typically requires formal training delivered by internal staff or contractors. The duration and extent of this training can range from a few hours to many weeks, depending upon the complexity and stability of the software application.

The third area of technology interaction involves the use of commercially available application software such as word processing, spreadsheets, databases, project management, or telecommunications programs. While organizations may use these programs in unique or specialized ways (including accessing proprietary systems), the software usually comes with its own, off-the-shelf performance support or training materials, including manuals, online help/ tutorials, and even workshops.

The fourth area of interaction entails knowledge of computer systems or networks themselves. This is the domain of information or technology specialists who plan, design, procure, install, or maintain hardware and software. These specialists may be programmers, technicians, engineers, system analysts, project managers, or senior administrators. The range of specific skills or knowledge about technology required in these positions can be very extensive and diverse. It is also likely to be transient, as the hallmark of technology is the rapid speed at which everything changes.

HR's Role, the New Technology, and the Worker

Each area of interaction presents its own training challenges and learning needs in which the HR professional should participate. Additionally, with technology comes an impact on the workflow and the individual work processes. The design of the organization, labor relations, and the implementation process will have the most dramatic effect at the individual level. If the HR professional manages the interface between the worker and the technology, that will assist with the technology implementation. To facilitate the transition, identify the impact on workflow early and communicate changes in business processes. Then determine the target audience/user's skills, knowledge, abilities, location, expectations, attitudes, and culture (audience characteristics) to identify gaps that can be addressed using training, job aids, or performance support. Doing this analysis beforehand will ensure a comfortable transition to the new technology.

Preparation for Technology Implementation in Global Organizations

How can organizations possibly avoid the potential pitfalls inherent in the varied and sometimes competing priorities of a multicultural organization? Once organizational readiness for technology has been determined, external culture has been assessed, and the target group has been analyzed for receptivity and readiness, then the HR professional must answer some critical questions about the best technology to implement given the profile of the organization and its cultural context. Without the critical information gained by examining these overarching issues, any technology initiative is bound to suffer setbacks and possible derailment.

In order to be of optimum assistance, HR professionals must do their research and examine different elements contributing to the technology decision.

The following questions can be used to analyze conditions and prepare for new technology. This preparation will mitigate the cultural, organizational, and individual issues. Before implementing new technology, HR professionals should gather this information and use it in the decision-making process. The questions to ask prior to technology selection are:

- What is the organization's mission and how does the technology align that mission?
- How would you describe the organization's position relative to technology (organizational readiness)?
- What is the larger cultural context for the region where the technology will be implemented and for the target audience?
- How will this new technology be received by the organization as a whole and the target audience in particular?
- What are the proposed technology's capabilities?
- Why is this technology better than the other options?
- What existing technology infrastructure will the new technology replace or enhance?
- What are the client/customer needs (nature of learning, nature of the course)?
- How would you describe the audience/user's skills, knowledge, abilities, location, expectations, and attitudes (audience characteristics)?
- How will the new technology impact business processes?
- Will there need to be training before the audience is able to use this technology?
- What are the costs and benefits of this technology?
- How will this technology contribute to learning transfer?
- What support for the technology use will be provided?
- How will the technology be maintained and updated?
- Are there any ethical issues regarding the use of this technology?
- Do the capabilities for development and implementation reside in-house or will you need to outsource this technology development and implementation?

These questions span instructional, logistical, and management considerations, all of which play a role in technology decisions. These questions can and should be asked by the HR professional. Conforming to the above process of analysis reinforces the critical role of HR.

Regulatory and Legal Issues Regarding Technology and Global Organizations

Not only can the HR professional impact the selection of technology, but he should have input regarding legal and regulatory compliance. A key to successful technology implementation is to have reviewed and identified the intersection between the regulatory issues of the host country and the technology in use. Always err on the side of the more conservative interpretation of the law. Whether the prevailing law is that of the host country or the organization's home country, ensure that your organization carefully follows all guidelines that have legal ramifications. For example, some countries have relatively vague copyright laws, whereas U.S. copyright laws are clearly outlined. Consequently, when designing courseware for an international audience, if the organization's headquarters are in the United States, abide by U.S. copyright laws. Or, for instance, if the workday for the host country includes time for midday prayers, but the country in which the organization is headquartered does not, abide by the guidelines of the host country, and don't schedule conference calls or synchronous communications that interfere with that cultural provision.

As cybercrime rises, the issues of laws of the host country versus the organization's home country become increasingly important. On this topic, Jennifer Schramm of *HR Magazine* says, "Combating cybercrime has become increasingly challenging for law enforcement agencies everywhere, so individuals and organizations—and HR professionals in particular—must continue to take steps to protect themselves and the data they collect" (2004, 152). Because developing countries often have fewer laws addressing cybercrime, and law enforcement tends to focus on nontechnology-related crimes, cybercriminals operate more freely. In failing to legislate and/or enforce laws related to technology, less-developed countries may inadvertently provide safe haven to cybercriminals. Keep these issues in mind and follow best practices in order to protect confidential data and sensitive information.

These examples demonstrate the expediency of knowing the technology-related laws of the host countries. Additionally, an understanding of the cultural mores for each of the countries touched by a global organization plays a critical role in the success of the organization's technologies. Analyzing the specific culture within the organization and the impact the new technology will have on the target audience will also prepare the HR professional for the response to technology initiatives. Finally, answering the list of technology questions before choosing the technology and offering that important information to inform decision making can have a positive impact on the process.

Conclusion

HR professionals can and should contribute to technology decisions, especially ones that involve the HR department and the people it serves. HR professionals bring a unique perspective to bear on any technology selection effort. It is their job to ensure that specific issues are addressed. They provide invaluable input about the culture, business processes, employee disposition toward the technology, and the readiness of the organization for new technologies. HR professionals add value when they are informed, and they can become irreplaceable members of the technology team.

Learning Systems

CHAPTER 3

Technologies That Enable Learning

A wide variety of technologies are available to support organization, team, and individual learning. Online learning is an effective venue for distributing learning. Other supplemental technologies, such as audio and video components, discussion boards and chats, simulations, and virtual worlds, enhance online learning. This chapter begins with a description of various online learning tools. Next, we will address the cost benefits, in particular, of online learning. Case studies provide real-life examples of how these technologies can be used.

e-Learning

E-learning is one of the most-talked-about tools available in the area of education. For the purposes of this book, *e-learning* is defined as "any type of learning situation in which instructional context is delivered through the use of computer-networked technology, primarily over an intranet or through the Internet" (Bondarouk and Ruel 2010, 149). E-learning may be designed by programmers using programming code such as Hypertext Markup Language (HTML), Dreamweaver MX, Flash, Authorware, Javascript, etc., and hosted on a server, or it may be authored and hosted within a larger system called a learning content management system (LCMS). E-learning hosted on a server and e-learning delivered using an LCMS both rely upon the Internet. This commonality earns it the name of "web-based instruction" (WBI) or "e-learning."

Why Use e-Learning?

E-learning quickly emerged as the delivery medium of choice in the late twentieth century. Many aspects of e-learning appeal to organizations and learners alike; however, legitimate shortcomings also exist.

Advantages of e-Learning

E-learning offers significant benefits to any organization that has the technology to support it and the wherewithal to invest in e-learning design. E-learning is well suited to providing standardized training to an entire dispersed audience concurrently. Those who perform much of their work on the computer can use the computer for learning events, resulting in learning transfer. The materials on an e-learning website or LCMS are easily updated, so they can remain current, and well-designed e-learning can be highly interactive and collaborative. E-learning gives learners access to experts online—people they might not ordinarily meet.

Asynchronous e-learning, commonly facilitated by e-mail and discussion boards, has a built-in lag time that encourages reflection and thoughtfulness, so that students can think about and refine their online contributions. Additionally, asynchronous e-learning offers flexible learning so the learner may work on the course whenever it is convenient.

Synchronous e-learning occurs immediately, in real time. It is often supported by media such as video conferencing and chat. Synchronous e-learning encourages relationships and the formation of communities of learning (CoLs) because learners participate in real time and experience the synergy that results from immediate, substantive interactions.

Limitations of e-Learning

E-learning also has some limitations. In chapter 2 we discussed the impact of culture on technology selection, and culture can influence employees' success with e-learning as well. The impersonal aspect of e-learning creates challenges for learners who are accustomed to—or have a cultural preference for—face-to-face interaction with an instructor. Poorly designed materials impact learner participation. When PowerPoint slides are uploaded to the Internet to masquerade as courseware, there is no learning value. Many organizations do this as a cost-effective alternative to face-to-face training; however, mediocre materials can cause learners to lose interest. Off-the-shelf e-learning that is not customized to meet the learners' needs may also diminish the power and appeal of e-learning. Simplified courseware that eliminates higher-level thinking skills and the reflection necessary to perform management-level tasks makes e-learning unpopular among those who perform complex tasks that require judgment and evaluation. Organizations that use e-learning when they are not ready to support it often experience technology problems, which can undermine learning and cause the audience to react negatively (Frankola 2001;

Osberg 2002; Rossett 2000). At worst, e-learners will drop out; in fact, the high dropout rate for e-learning is an issue in itself (Rossett 2000).

In light of these challenges, one might question the reason organizations have converted entire training programs to e-learning. Why the big rush? Perhaps the biggest selling point for e-learning is this: e-learning can offer significant cost benefits.

Cost Benefits of e-Learning—An Advantage

When comparing the development and administration costs associated with e-learning to the costs for face-to-face coursework, e-learning inevitably impresses. The exceptions to the savings are some programmed simulations or other labor-intensive e-learning products.

Many different cost-benefit models exist, but they all boil down to a comparison of the standard costs associated with delivering the training in a face-to-face mode versus the costs of delivering the training online (Phillips, Phillips, and Hodges 2004). To calculate the cost benefits, assign a dollar value to the many effects of a program, as well as to the costs for the program. Compare the costs of one approach to the costs of another.

There are standard cost components that facilitate comparison of face-to-face versus online training (Philips, Philips, and Hodges 2004). A list of the costs for a course delivered in a face-to-face environment typically includes the following:

- Course design and preparation
- Facilities costs
- Incidentals and materials
- Equipment rental
- Instructor fees
- Travel costs
- Salaries at an hourly rate for time away from work (using 2080 hours in a work year)
- Evaluation

In the context of e-learning technologies, the initial and ongoing expenditures for hardware and software, as well as the design and development of course materials, comprise the majority of the costs. There are also labor costs for the delivery and implementation of courses; instructors, administrative and technical staff, and consultants all contribute to the cost.

Let's compare the costs for a management training course with two trainers delivering the course face-to-face over two days to the same course facilitated by two instructors using a leased learning content management system (LCMS) and including a video produced in-house. We will call the LCMS version web-based instruction or WBI. This case provides a good opportunity to analyze some of the key components of a training cost benefit. Figure 3-1 details the comparison.

In Figure 3-1, you have sixty out-of-state and thirty local management and upper-level trainees attending the management training course. The course was offered over two days, with a third day reserved for travel, resulting in a total of three workdays away from the office. The cost for this two-day course face-to-face was $170,352, which included delivery by two external instructors for two days each ($8,000), travel for sixty trainees (airfare for 60 students = $18,000; per diem for 60 students = $9,720; hotel for 60 students at $90 per night = $10,800; salaries for time off the job = $78,422) with refreshments on site ($360), facilities rental ($12,000), as well as audiovisual (AV) equipment rental ($400).

Now examine, on the right, the same course delivered as WBI. In this example, all of the trainees already have laptop computers with broadband Internet access. The development costs ($30,000) for face-to-face or online delivery and the evaluation costs ($2,500) are the same. The two instructors

Face-to-Face Data Elements versus Web-Based Instruction (WBI)

- **Face-to-Face Data Elements**
  - Preparation: Course development = $30,000
  - Facilities = $12,000
  - Refreshments = $360
  - A/V equipment = $400
  - Two outside instructors = $8,000
  - Incidentals and copying costs = $150
  - Airfare (60 trainees) = $18,000
  - Per diem total=$9,720
  - Hotel (for 60 trainees), two nights @ $90 per night = $10,800
  - Salaries (hourly rate of $38.46 for 60 trainees, three days) = $55,382
  - Salaries, local (hourly rate of $48 for 30 trainees, two days) = $23,040
  - Cost of evaluation = $2,500
  - TOTAL COST= $170,352

- **Web-Based Instruction Data Elements**
  - Preparation: Course development = $30,000
  - Technology = Lease of LCMS: $10,000
  - Facilities cost = 0
  - Video development and conversion = $7,000
  - Two outside instructors @ flat rate of $2,500 per instructor = $5,000
  - Conference call kick-off = $150
  - Trainee costs, for 60 trainees, eight hours (hourly rate of $38.46 per hour) = $18,461
  - Trainee costs, local, for 30 trainees, eight hours (hourly rate of $48 per hour) = $11,520
  - Cost of evaluation = $2,500
  - TOTAL COST= $84,631

FIGURE 3-1 Cost Benefits of e-Learning

handle the WBI, eight-hour course at a lower fee ($5,000) because it requires less time. To offer the same training online as an eight-hour course spread over two weeks, leasing space on a learning content management system (LCMS) at a set fee of $10,000 results in significantly lower costs even when including a video ($7,000) and hosting a conference call for the kickoff session ($150).

For the face-to-face training effort, consider the course development costs, plus the salaries and employee benefits for trainees for three workdays (divide each employee's salary by the work year hours of 2080 to get the hourly rate— this will differ by country—then multiply by the total number of hours out of the office for training). In Figure 3-1, the thirty local upper-level managers at headquarters earn, on average, $100,000-per-year, and the sixty managers coming in from the field earn approximately $80,000-per-year so use that pay divided by a total of 2080 work hours per year to calculate hourly rates. You will find the hourly rate is $38.46 for the $80,000-per-year employees and $48 for the $100,000-per-year employees. Then use those rates to find the total cost for the two separate groups of employees to attend a two-day session plus one travel day if the workday is eight hours. Add to that the per diem for meals and incidental expenses, travel costs, training facility costs, instructors' fees, refreshments per attendee, AV equipment rental, and, finally, the cost of evaluation. Refer again to Figure 3-1 for rough calculations. Clearly, the major savings offered by the web-based instruction (WBI) occurs when travel and facilities costs are eliminated and training hours reduced (Murray 2002).

The level of sophistication of the online courseware increases the e-learning development costs; nevertheless, the savings can still be significant. Based on this analysis, the evidence weighs in favor of e-learning for delivery of instruction. Remember that the cost benefits of e-learning are realized only if the learning outcomes are the same or better than for the face-to-face class. Analysis of the literature on that topic clearly indicates that there is no significant difference of learning outcomes between online and face-to-face courses (Bernard, Abrami, Lou, and Borokhovski 2004).

This example clearly demonstrates the savings offered by online instruction. For face-to-face training, the travel and hotel expenses alone increase the face-to-face course costs exponentially. It is no wonder so many organizations adore online training; the savings would convince anyone to switch!

Tips and Tools for Calculating Cost Benefits

Many free and shareware (meaning a demo is available for trial) online tools exist to help you conduct your analysis. One such tool, a free cost-benefit calculator, is offered by AADM Enterprises, Inc. Using this online calculator, you can get a rough estimate of the cost comparison points for e-learning versus face-to-face course offerings. The website is *www.aadm.com/ROICalc.htm*

Blended Learning

While the cost benefits of e-learning are impressive, remember that the best practices in e-learning design involve combining the online and face-to-face approaches to create a blended offering (Bonk and Graham 2006; Masie 2002). *Blended learning* combines instructor–student in-person interactions with online instruction. Typically, the face-to-face session takes place first, with time spent familiarizing students with the layout of the online course. This makes the transition from the in-person classroom experience to online learning easier and less stressful, especially for first-time online learners.

Finnish Bookstore: Case Study

In 2006, the Finnish Bookstore wanted an experiential training program for its sales staff, so the company created a simulation that allows its employees to practice sales and service skills in a context similar to its bookshops (Slotte and Herbert 2007). The simulation presents the trainee with a difficult virtual customer. Two separate dialogues occur with the customer: During the first dialogue, the salesperson gathers information about the customer's needs and talks about the product. In the second conversation, the salesperson overcomes objections, takes orders, and closes the sale. Because the course is delivered online, it is delivered in a cost-effective manner that eliminates travel to a central location for training. Instead, the training takes place in the individual bookstores on store computers.

In-house subject matter experts (SMEs) assisted with the development of the salesperson dialogues in order to make them realistic. There is a blended-learning element: the store manager coaches the salesperson during the lesson. The after-course data are collected using a web-based survey with Likert-type scoring.

The results of the first offering indicated that a majority of the respondents (86 percent) strongly agreed or agreed that the sales training simulation was useful. Sixty percent of the respondents rated the course effective, and 20 percent said it was extremely effective. By any standard, these are impressive results!

Web-Based Workplace Learning

Corporations have been slower than educational institutions to explore online learning. Nevertheless, since the percentage of employees with access to a computer in their workplace (not to mention at home) increases every year, organizations are capitalizing on the networked corporate computers by delivering training over the Internet. Interestingly, most corporate e-learning is asynchronous (Welsh, Wanberg, Brown, and Simmering 2003).

Many professional societies (particularly those in technical fields such as engineering or telecommunications) have been fairly quick to post their publications and conference proceedings on the web. To the extent that a significant amount of continuing education takes place through these organizations, we can say that the professional sector is taking advantage of the web for personal learning activities. In addition, many adults are involved in taking courses from post-secondary institutions, which are using the web extensively. While the web may not be in formal use by many training departments at present, a large percentage of working individuals may already be engaged in web-based learning.

e-Learning's Impact on the Learning Process

Web-based learning offers an exciting and powerful resource. It provides a way to find information for course assignments and projects without the need to physically visit a library or buy books. It also allows learners to post their own work (articles, poetry, art, music, and video) in a public location and save it to a portfolio that anyone in the world can access. The Internet provides access to thousands of online magazines (e-journals), newsletters, discussion groups, and entertainment sites that can broaden intellectual horizons. Further, the Internet goes a long way toward breaking down geographical, socioeconomic, cultural, and gender- and age-related barriers to accessing information and interacting with others.

As mentioned above, e-learning may be synchronous or asynchronous. Synchronous e-learning tends to be less complex to develop. Asynchronous e-learning typically requires more development time because the content must be proofed. Further, asynchronous e-learning should be graphic-intensive (meaning lots of visuals) and interactive. Typically, a team of designers, graphic artists, programmers, and others create the asynchronous program (Piskurich 2004).

E-learning may be hosted on a website, or it may be offered through a course management system or learning content management system (CMS/LCMS). Both are effective approaches. Having looked at e-learning in general, let's examine the learning management system (LMS) and learning content management system (LCMS) to see how they impact the design of instruction.

LMS and LCMS Comparison

The learning management system (LMS) is the earlier version of a learning content management system (Robbins 2002). Both still exist and serve different functions, although more current systems attempt to combine the two.

What is an LMS? A *learning management system (LMS)* automates the administration of training events and records data on learner progress (Dobbs 2006). An LMS can help launch e-learning courses. Through use of the LMS, Human Resource (HR) professionals or supervisors can observe patterns in courseware enrollment and usage. They can track learner completion of required courseware or select electives. The LMS can include classroom management, competency management, knowledge management, certification or compliance training, personalization and mentoring, and chat and/or discussion boards. With the advent of learning management systems, many of the previously tedious logistics of course management can be handled online, as a self-service function.

More recently, the *learning content management system (LCMS)* was developed. It does not replace an LMS but rather may interface with an LMS or enterprise resource planning (ERP) system (a large management information system that uses a single database and handles both internal and external business functions on one platform—further described in chapter 7). The LCMS can be used to develop, maintain, use, and store instructional content. If designed properly, the LCMS can offer measurement and reporting of results. According to the researcher and author Rita Dobbs, there are more than seventy LCMSs on the market (Dobbs 2006, 508).

The LCMS offers very attractive features for the learner. They include the ability to design a customized learning approach, track progress, collaborate with others, create a personalized web page, and document training completion.

Typically, an LCMS is most appealing from an enterprise-wide training delivery viewpoint because of the separate set of functions for the instructor. The LCMS allows the instructor to author materials as well as import existing materials and develop, assemble, reuse, and repurpose content. These functions make the task of developing training much easier. Similarly, it allows for collaborating and reporting. Maintaining and updating the courseware is quite simple; there is no need to be able to program. And the instructor can deliver content in real time in multiple formats, even accommodating different languages (Perry 2009).

Some of the most widely used learning systems include Blackboard, CertPoint, CEGOS, LearnShare, Meridian, Mzinga, OutStart, Saba, and SumTotal.

However, many organizations develop their own LMS or LCMS in-house, because proprietary systems may be more cost effective than leasing one of the larger-scale systems. Some systems combine the course management and learning content management functions. Furthermore, a good LCMS should be able to interface with an LMS or other enterprise resource planning (ERP) system.

Not all LMSs and LCMSs cost money. Moodle (*http://moodle.org*) is an open-source learning system: anyone can use and customize it. The advantage of Moodle is that you can experience an LMS without making a major investment.

Tips and Tools for Learning Management Systems

* Large-scale training programs for course design software typically rely upon a combination of a learning content management system and a learning (or course) management system or ERP to manage instruction.

* Moodle is an open-source learning system and, as such, allows you to experience an LMS without purchasing or building one. Moodle can be accessed at www .moodle.org.

Learning Objects

Learning objects (LOs) are digitized units of learning that are offered over the web; they are also known as "reusable chunks of instructional media" (Wiley 2002, 116). Learning objects can be repurposed in a variety of ways, and many believe that LOs are fast becoming the norm in e-learning delivery.

A learning object may be a module or a lesson or an entire course. It may include a combination of PowerPoint, hyperlinks, digital audio, digital video, PDF files, and word documents. The appeal of the LO is that it is exportable as a digital unit and saved to a special database (Wiley 2002). It is subsequently importable to a variety of courseware. While you may need a special database to house the learning objects, and not all learning objects are compatible, the power of the learning object and the advantage of not having to re-create the object with each new course makes learning objects an attractive option. Many off-the-shelf learning management systems allow the designer to create lessons and save them as learning objects to be shared. So, for instance, if you had a module on leadership ethics that you wanted to embed in all of your leadership course offerings, you could create it as a learning object. Learning objects may include audio, video, graphics, and text. You could then import that module into each leadership course.

California State University sponsors an *open-source* (free for use and modification) learning object database called MERLOT (Multimedia Educational Resource for Learning and Online Teaching). This repository is usable by anyone with Internet access. It is also possible to contribute educational materials to the MERLOT database. You may submit a learning object or you may simply access and use the ones that are in the existing database. Learning objects are powerful and save costs, and the capacity to create them is built into most learning content management systems.

Regulatory and Legal Information

Over the years, as web-based instruction has matured, legal standards and best practices for the design and distribution of web-based instruction have emerged. We will talk more about design best practices in chapter 4. However, we will introduce some regulatory and legal e-learning standards here.

Most off-the-shelf learning management systems developed in the United States comply with scalable content object reference model (SCORM) standards. Referred to as SCORM, these standards for interoperability—promoted by the Advanced Distributive Learning Initiative of the U.S. Department of Defense—specify rules regarding content learning objects (learning objects). Even if your organization is not U.S.-based, these standards are important.

SCORM contains simple programmer-level ground rules for creating shareable content. It does not specify size or type of learning object but rather sets standards for sharing across a learning platform. The goal is interoperability and interchangeability. Most U.S.-developed LMSs and LCMSs are SCORM compliant. SCORM learning objects are organized in a package similar to a hierarchical tree structure, such as a course structure, or according to a hierarchy of content. SCORM does not specify a particular depth of the structure and description, and it does not define any particular nomenclature for the levels of the hierarchy, such as "course, lesson, topic" or "unit, module, lesson." You are free to use whatever labeling scheme you like. You can mix and match learning objects at all levels of technical compatibility within the same organization. The goal of SCORM is to make the content reusable. SCORM compliance avoids duplication of effort. For more information about SCORM, visit the following website: *www.adlnet.gov/Pages/Default.aspx.*

It is very easy to incorporate articles, documents, and scanned textbook pages into an e-learning or multimedia product. It is therefore also quite easy to break U.S. copyright law. Important copyright principles and laws affecting e-learning for U.S. organizations include the fair use doctrine and the TEACH Act.

The important point to take away is that no one should profit from the unique published works of another author without obtaining that author's permission to use those ideas. Most relevant to e-learning are the requirements for posting copyrighted materials online. The fair use doctrine permits limited use of copyrighted materials without the permission of the copyright holder under certain circumstances; the user is typically required to obtain permissions for copyrighted materials if the materials are used for profit. You do not need permission to use works in the public domain, because these are works not protected by copyright.

According to the American Library Association's website, the Technology, Education, and Copyright Harmonization (TEACH) Act states that a user must:

- Limit access to copyrighted works to students currently enrolled in the class.
- Limit access only for the time needed to complete the class session or course.
- Inform instructors, students, and staff of copyright laws and policies.
- Prevent further copying or redistribution of copyrighted works.
- Not interfere with copy protection mechanisms.

Again, this is a U.S. law that applies to organizations that are headquartered in the United States and/or that distribute learning materials to a U.S. audience. Remember, the guidelines specify that you only post in your online courseware those documents for which you have obtained usage permission.

Rights of publicity and privacy are also important. For instance, do not use a photo or picture of a person if you do not have his permission. These rights hold true for use of a misappropriated name, face, image, or voice. To avoid damaging lawsuits, get permissions in writing.

Rules and Regulations for e-Learning Content—SCORM, Fair Use, TEACH Act

Fair use and the TEACH Act are U.S. legal doctrine and law for U.S.-based organizations. They govern the posting of copyrighted works. Brief overviews of the law appear on this site:

www.ala.org/ala/issuesadvocacy/copyright/teachact/teachactbest.cfm

Guidelines for the fair use doctrine appear on this site:

www.copyright.gov/fls/fl102.html

A checklist for compliance with the TEACH Act appears on this site:

www.library.appstate.edu/services/reserve/teach_act_checklist.html

For details about SCORM, visit the following website:

www.adlnet.gov/Pages/Default.aspx

Simulations

E-learning can be designed as simulations—representations of analogous situations or behavior—which can vary in size and complexity depending on factors such as the breadth and depth of instructional content, desired learning architecture, simulation format, and technological platform, among others. Some common formats include device simulations, branching stories, interactive case studies, allocation games, or a combination of these. Technological platforms can range from static screens of html content to web-delivered animation and video to rich game-based learning.

Before deciding on a format and platform, you first need to gather requirements for the simulation from the department or partner who is sponsoring or requesting the development of the simulation. Then, determine the formats and platforms that are appropriate for the learning architecture and ultimate goals of the project. Next, determine if your organization has the technology to support delivery of the simulation. In an ideal world, requirements are gathered by an analyst with specialized skills in defining the requirements of an application that will meet the needs of the end user. Simulations can be included in and offered over a learning management system or hosted on a server. Simulations can provide powerful, interactive learning events.

OHIC Insurance Risk Management Simulation: Case Study

Christopher Keesey

Many organizations use simulations to create realistic, effective training. OHIC Insurance, headquartered in Columbus, OH, has been creating medical liability insurance that meets the needs of the healthcare community for twenty-five years. For the past ten years they have partnered with Ohio University Without Boundaries (OUWB) to provide a unique certification program for healthcare risk management professionals.

Although OHIC has extensive expertise in providing high-quality education to healthcare risk managers, their educational efforts were limited to face-to-face seminars. In an effort to break down the boundaries of time and space and make education available using "anytime, anyplace" access, the company implemented an e-learning simulation for risk management training.

OUWB, in partnership with OHIC, developed an animated, interactive, online simulation called "Blue Mountain Medical Center." This courseware is designed to help individuals learn more about risk management and develop the understanding and skills necessary for the practice of healthcare risk management. The Blue Mountain Medical Center Simulation is based on a constructivist approach to learning, in which learners construct new knowledge from their experiences; as such, the simulation is built around a number of learning projects. Each project places the learner in the role of a risk manager at Blue Mountain Medical Center and poses a real-world problem or challenge. The simulation then asks the learner to use all of the resources available and make a decision about the proper course of action.

End-of-unit tests indicated improved performance when compared with previous training that addressed the same material as a single team project. Additionally, participant reactions were very positive, indicating that the participants felt more highly involved and enjoyed the learning experience.

Christopher Keesey is the design and technology manager for LexisNexis Performance Development. For the past ten years, Christopher has managed, designed, and implemented training simulations, games, and a variety of other interactive technologies that successfully add value to learning experiences.

Virtual Worlds

Virtual worlds provide another e-learning venue. The virtual world known as Second Life has been tapped for instructional purposes by educational institutions such as Harvard in the CyberOne: Law in the Court of Public Opinion (Lamont 2007). Many other organizations in a variety of industries have a presence in the virtual realm.

Virtual worlds require participation using an *avatar*, which is a two-or three-dimensional graphic representation of a being. The avatar can talk, walk, dance, swim, run, fly, and make a variety of gestures initiated by the owner using keyboard codes or a mouse. The avatar's owner logs in to what appears to be a three-dimensional world where the natural laws of the real world do not exist. Once in that virtual world, the owner controls the avatar and may communicate through the avatar by speaking into the microphone on the computer (using Voice over Internet Protocol) or a text-based chat feature. Avatars may also leave notes for those who are not "present" in the virtual world to read when they log in.

Virtual worlds provide an attractive, fun learning environment. They present boundless opportunities for creative applications, including:

- Simulating situations
- Marketing a product or service
- Conducting "office hour" discussions (e.g., professor)
- Gaming, used as a learning activity
- Testing a hypothesis in another world
- Creating three-dimensional design projects
- Offering facilitated distance learning that directs the user to online learning assets and short form games or simulations on relevant topics (usually in Flash) (Weinstein 2010).
- Practicing skills in a safe environment (Mansfield 2008; Mason 2007).

There are some caveats, however, regarding use of virtual worlds for business and educational purposes. Obstacles to using virtual worlds such as Second Life include technical and interactive issues. The system requirements on users' computers are quite sophisticated; they must have a high-end graphics card and broadband Internet access in order to participate in most virtual worlds. Some virtual-world participants—called *griefers*—display antisocial behavior and the possibility of encountering griefers makes the environment less than ideal for learning. To protect participants from those who would ruin the learning environment, organizations have established their own islands and limited access to those enrolled in the training. Organizations investing in virtual worlds must be aware of the risks. Owners of most virtual worlds retain at least some right to the objects created "in-world" (deBurgh 2008). Those attempting to have proprietary conversations can be overheard. Even within private areas, all information contained within a virtual world is available to the world's administrators and owners (16). Unlicensed use of copyright and trademarked items is rife in virtual worlds. Possible areas of vulnerability for organizations using virtual worlds include potential breach of privacy, loss of intellectual property, or release of proprietary information (Andriole 2010). So keep in mind that organizations must enter virtual worlds with their proverbial eyes open!

There are, however, organizations that are using the virtual world effectively. IBM Canada conducts what they call "speed mentoring" sessions on IBM-owned pods in Second Life (SL). Protégés are placed in groups that meet with mentors (executives, managers, and seasoned IBMers) who conduct question/answer sessions for fifteen minutes at a time. Then the protégé group moves to the next mentor in a separate pod and works with that person for fifteen minutes before progressing to the next. This interaction maximizes the time contributed by the mentors, saves travel costs, and allows real-time interactions with higher-level management within the organization (Dobson 2009).

Northrop Grumman—a leader in global security—relies upon Second Life when training soldiers and police officers to operate the Northrop Grumman Corporation's Cutlass bomb disposal robot. Learners from across the U.S. can attend training on how to use the robot at the secure SL Space Park installation. They log in to Second Life from their workplace and attend realistic training in a three-dimensional world without having to travel (Morrison 2009).

Johnson & Johnson, Inc. (J & J), a large pharmaceutical corporation, now has their 3-D University, which is offered in a virtual world. J & J uses a variety of training methodologies in this virtual environment, including improvisational (short form) games and simulations on relevant topics (Weinstein 2010).

These organizations maximize the attributes of virtual worlds by offering real-time learning that is cost effective and experiential. They have surmounted the obstacles, realizing that this format requires adaptation and, as such, that there is a learning curve. Once participants create their avatars, they receive assistance to learn how to communicate and move about. Brief training and job aids are also provided.

Tips and Tools for Making the Most of e-Learning Products

Free or shareware (available as a demo for use before purchase) examples of each of the approaches described are offered online. Visit these websites to get complimentary versions. Try them out, and see what you think. You will also see examples of the technology when no free version exists.

- Learning management system—Moodle: *http://demo.moodle.net*
- Learning object database—MERLOT: *www.merlot.org/merlot/index.htm*
- Free audio editing and recording—Audacity: *http://audacity.sourceforge.net*
- Free PowerPoint conversion to Flash for website—iSpring: *www.ispringfree.com*
- Video making—Windows Movie Maker: *http://explore.live.com/windows-live-movie-maker*
- Computer simulation screen recorder with audio—Camtasia (shareware trial package is free):
  www.techsmith.com/camtasia.asp?CMP=KgoogleCStmhome
- Simulations:
  Avatar creation—Oddcast: *www.oddcast.com/home/demos/tts/tts_example.php*
  Virtual worlds—Second Life: *www.secondlife.com*

Key Points about e-Learning

This chapter has given you an overview of some of the e-learning terminology and tools. We examined the benefits and drawbacks of e-learning and investigated regulations that apply to e-learning. The Tips and Tools focused on free software that you may use to examine the features and functions of different e-learning elements. We also examined the cost benefits and presented some legal considerations.

What follows are some of the key points about e-learning:

- Research shows that technology-based training can be as effective as classroom instruction and usually results in savings of both time and cost.
- Many forms of technology, such as simulation, have been shown to be more effective than conventional forms of training.
- Learning via technology-mediated venues and learning through classroom instruction highlight different learning styles even when they involve the same content; combining technology-based learning and face-to-face instruction is the most powerful approach.
- Performing a cost-benefit analysis of training technology provides valuable information that informs the decision-making process.
- The two cost categories that technology usually reduces are travel and facilities; equipment (and possibly development) costs often increase.
- The greatest value of technology is often in terms of increased job performance (i.e., lost opportunity costs and transfer of learning).

We have only scratched the surface with this overview of e-learning—its benefits and drawbacks, the variety of synchronous and asynchronous delivery methods, and its cost effectiveness. The "Digging Deeper" section presents some additional detailed e-learning references. Those will be useful as you develop your library of e-learning-related books and prepare to invest in e-learning technology.

E-learning is particularly important to HR professionals because of its flexibility, the positive impact it can have on learning transfer, and its many uses for employee development. In addition, e-learning provides a cost-effective delivery mode that can supplement or, in many cases, replace face-to-face delivery. E-learning does not have to be boring. Through the use of multimedia, video, podcasting, simulations, and even virtual worlds, the courseware designer can create meaningful, effective interactive learning events.

Conclusion

In this chapter we demonstrated how e-learning allows for rapid content production, distribution, and updating of interactive instruction as a cost-effective alternative to face-to-face training. We provided case study examples and offered some cautions regarding the legal and regulatory considerations.

e-Learning Technology Selection, Design, and Implementation: What Makes Sense

e-Learning Technology Selection Approach

Several considerations must influence the selection of technology for an e-learning course. The choice of adult learning theory for course design, the technology's strengths and weaknesses, the organizational and general culture, the existing infrastructure, and organizational readiness all impact technology selection.

Theories of adult learning can be categorized into five schools or orientations, and each school has its own advocates and instructional design implications. There are times that one theory is more appropriate than another because of the content being taught and the characteristics of the target audience.

Adult Learning Theories

There are many adult learning theories; in this book we will rely upon the following five schools or orientations (Merriam and Caffarella 1999; Swanson and Holton 2001):

1. Cognitivist
2. Behaviorist/objectivist
3. Humanist
4. Social learning/collaborative
5. Constructivist

Each of these adult learning orientations or schools has proponents who define the principles of instructional design for that theory and identify forms of evaluation (assessment of whether learning has occurred). What follows is a brief description of each school (also called an orientation) and some of the well-known authors representing that theory:

- *Cognitivist*—Cognitivists focus on how humans learn using internal processes of acquiring, understanding, and retaining knowledge. Cognitivists believe that learning occurs when humans reorganize experiences, making sense of input from the environment. Instructional methods include providing learning guidance using patterns, acrostics, mnemonics, etc., to stimulate the direction of thought and keep the learner on track. Assessing performance is in two forms, checking for reliability and validity to be sure that learner performance is consistent under a variety of circumstances (Anglin 2005). Robert Gagne (1965) is a well-known advocate of the cognitivist learning theory.
- *Behaviorist/objectivist*—Behaviorists concentrate on learning through control of the external environment. Their emphasis is on changing behavior through processes such as operant conditioning and positive reinforcement. Behaviorists believe that learning is built on three assumptions: (1) changed behavior indicates learning; (2) learning is determined by elements in the environment; (3) repetition and reinforcement of learning behaviors assist in the learning process (Merriam and Caffarella 1991). Assessment of learning should be directly tied to the objectives. Probably the best known theorist in this field is B. F. Skinner, however, from an instructional viewpoint, Robert Mager (1988) and Walter Dick and Lou Carey (1996) represent well-known behaviorist instructional design theorists.
- *Humanist*—Humanists believe that learning must be geared to the development of the whole person; they place emphasis on learner motivation, attitudes, perceptions, and values. This orientation views individuals as seeking self-actualization through learning and being capable of determining their own learning. Members of this school embrace self-directed learning. Instructional methods include self-directed learning and instructional approaches that reinforce learning principles of *andragogy* (adult learning). Assessment of this type of learning occurs in observing changed attitudes and behaviors aligned with potential. Malcolm Knowles (1970) proposed principles of adult learning instructional design for this approach and therefore serves as its main theorist for our purposes.

- *Social learning/collaborative*—Social learning theory focuses on the social context in which people learn, focusing on how they learn through interacting with and observing other people. Because people can learn from imitating others, role models and mentoring are important to this school of learning. Methods for social learning include mentoring and the instructor as guide. The standard 360-degree performance review can provide assessment feedback indicating if learning has occurred. Albert Bandura (1986) addresses the social learning theory from an instructional design viewpoint.

- *Constructivist*—Constructivism stresses that the learner rather than the teacher develops knowledge and asserts that creating opportunities for knowledge construction by the learner eclipses any direct instruction provided by a teacher. Constructivism is best suited to content that is fluid and flexible, with no "right" answer. The impact on design can be seen in opportunities for learners to draw their own conclusions based upon the information provided. Problem-based and project-based learning approaches are both constructivist. Evidence of learning can appear in self-reporting or, in the case of problem-based learning, solutions that align with best practice. Two instructional designers who articulate this viewpoint are Thomas Duffy and David Jonassen (1992).

Each of these major theories of adult learning has its own design implications, and it's important to take these into consideration when planning online instruction. The theoretical base should at the very least impact the tools you select for delivery of instruction, the expected learning outcomes, the specific activities assigned, and the method of evaluation.

Technology and Adult Learning Theory

Gary Anglin (1995) was one of the first to demonstrate the relationship between late-twentieth-century instructional technologies and adult learning theory. He defines the following role for instructional designers: "Designers use their knowledge of learning theory and the varieties of human capabilities to make media selection decisions, as well as their knowledge of the extensive research on media" (139). The chart that follows, which is based on the work of a number of authors who address the topic, summarizes the relationship between adult learning theory and media for the twenty-first century. It highlights the technology used for instructional methods and the adult learning theory that best supports that method. The following chart is updated to include the technologies of the twenty-first century.

CHART 4-1 Twenty-First-Century Instructional Technologies and Adult Learning Theories

Technology	Objectivist/ Behaviorist	Social Learning/ Collaborative	Cognitivist	Humanist/ Sociocultural	Constructivist
Instructor and student networked computers	X				X
Computer-assisted Learning (e.g., CBT)	X		X		
PowerPoint as training, audio, video (delivered over the Internet)	X				
Key response pads in a face-to-face classroom	X		X		
Threaded discussion		X	X	X	X
Learning Content Management systems (LCMS)	X	X	X	X	X
Electronic Performance Support System (EPSS)/ Artificial Intelligence (AI)			X		X
Simulation					X
Virtual reality		X			X
Synchronous communication (e.g., chat, texting)		X	X	X	
Groupware		X	X	X	
Social networks		X	X	X	X
Asynchronous communication (e-mail)		X	X	X	
Mobile technology (cell phone, palm-held devices)	X	X	X	X	X
DVD/CD-ROMs	X		X		
Audio (podcast) or video files	X		X		

A closer analysis reveals that the theory of learning is impacted by who controls the learning environment, a need for realism in the learning environment, the view of knowledge and the view of the learning. Dorothy Leidner and Sirkka Jarvenpaa (1995) wrote an important analysis of the relationship between technology and the schools of adult learning. Linking a particular technology or instructional method with the theory that provides an underpinning can help you create an effective and cohesive training program. For example, if there is a learning topic that is best explored through peer group learning or social learning, then position the learning in a social context and follow the design principles for social learning. If the student must create her own understanding and knowledge of a topic, design the course using a cognitivist approach. When knowledge is abstract, take an objectivist approach. When the context must be real and the problem is not well-defined, use a constructivist design.

Once you have determined which theory of learning you should use, you are ready to select the technology. Leidner and Jarvenpaa (1995) also emphasize the importance of allowing the theoretical approach to drive technology selection.

The process of technology selection begins with a clear understanding and intentional choice of adult learning theory. Identify the topic and choose the best theory under which to design the content, then match the technology to your design. Leidner and Jarvenpaa, when writing for *Management of Information Systems* journal, press the point that technology should not pull the cart; rather, theory pulls the instructional cart and technology follows. Why is this important? Because without examining the content and making an intentional design choice, technology takes on a life of its own that may or may not support the desired course learning outcomes. What follows is an example of intentional technology selection based on the course content and desired learning outcomes.

Harvard's Media Selection Process for Internal Training: Case Study

Patricia Goodman and Bill Ganzenmuller

Workplace training programs can be overwhelming, especially for decentralized institutions such as Harvard University, which employs approximately 15,000 staff across fifteen colleges. Harvard's Office of Human Resources (OHR) is a centralized department governing upper-level personnel policies and procedures across all of the colleges. When the Massachusetts State Legislature required annual training for workers who have access to high-risk confidential information (HRCI), OHR sought a training plan for compliance. PeopleSoft, Harvard's integrated human resource management system, was the most efficient means to identify the associated staff and deliver the training. The "ideal" compliance training program needed to be available for all identified staff with little additional cost and minimal interruption to their work environment. Since there were specific standards of learning and testing involved, it suited an objectivist design with quizzes to ensure comprehension.

An interdisciplinary team with representatives from the Security, Technology, and Human Resources Departments gathered to explore the options for the HRCI training program. They reviewed the positives and negatives related to four training delivery alternatives: instructor-led, webinar, an off-the-shelf product, or Eureka. The first and second alternatives (instructor-led and webinar) were attractive because they allow learner control over the content and provide opportunities for students to ask questions and have them answered in real time. However, both approaches had drawbacks: Assessing knowledge and tracking the enrollment data would require increased staff time. Moreover, the instructor-led delivery would generate logistical problems, such as finding the classroom space and coordinating the presenters and resources. The third alternative, an off-the-shelf product, offered online training modules including confidentiality compliance. However, the content is generic, has a user fee, and does not interface with PeopleSoft to track course completion, etc. A fourth delivery alternative was the Eureka Learning Management System. Eureka is a custom online learning management system developed by Harvard's Education Systems and Technology Office. It integrates with PeopleSoft and has reporting capabilities to track accountability. The courseware offered over Eureka could be customized for the Harvard audience, with quizzes to assess knowledge, and offered easy updating capabilities.

The team decided to use Eureka. The training manager developed the course content based on the state's policy and the implication of HRCI within Harvard. The HRCI course content is interactive and offers a visually intriguing learning experience. The graphics department assisted, using graphic "signposts" to separate the units, topics, quizzes, and final assessment. The training manager tested and edited the pages as they were produced. After final testing of the courseware, the identified staff received e-mails from OHR with directions on how to register into the Eureka system to complete the compliance training.

In order to obtain the university's final signoff on the course, the final assessment required each learner to obtain a minimum score of 70 percent. It was decided that both the course content and the quizzes would be made available for the learner to review. Upon the learner's completion of the assessment, the data were automatically captured within PeopleSoft for reporting purposes. Approximately 3,900 staff registered for the course, and 90 percent of those who took the course satisfactorily completed it. Clearly, the HRCI course delivered over the Eureka LMS provided an effective learning experience that met the university's objectives.

As training is required annually, the development team has recommendations to enhance the Eureka training. The next iteration will enable bookmarks, add the ability to submit questions and receive answers, and create individual quizzes by randomly drawing from a pool of questions. In an effort to diversify user satisfaction of the Eureka course, an online end-of-course survey will be administered for feedback and future enhancements.

Patricia Goodman, Ed.D., earned her doctorate from George Washington University. She is the financial administrator at Harvard University Graduate School of Education, Professional Education.

Bill Ganzenmuller has worked in the e-learning industry for the past ten years. In his current position at Harvard University, he designed and collaborated in the development of the Eureka Learning Management System, which is used to educate staff employees about the university's compliance policies and business applications.

Strengths and Weaknesses of Different Technologies

Adult learning theory and the context of the culture in which the training takes place are not the only two variables to consider when choosing a learning technology. Each technology has strengths and weaknesses that should impact media selection.

Technology Strengths and Weaknesses

	Strengths	Weaknesses
e-learning (online learning)	Inexpensive	Passive
	Reliable	Not designed with adult learners in mind
Threaded discussion	Worldwide distribution	Delay loses energy of discussion
Posting assignments	Accessible anytime	Software incompatibility
Video	Dynamic	No interaction
	Reaches large audiences	Development time/costs
Audio podcasting	Global distribution	No interaction
	Inexpensive	Favors technology savvy
Web-conferencing	Audience participation	Complexity (some types)
	Immediacy (real-time)	
Multimedia	Interactivity	Development time/costs
	Highly appealing	Maximum bandwidth necessary
Social networking	Interactivity	Expertise required to develop
	Updating	

	Strengths	Weaknesses
Performance	High job relevance	Development time/costs
Support systems	Uses existing systems	Expertise required
Simulations and virtual worlds	Authentic learning	Development time/costs
	Higher skill levels	Expertise required
		Maximum bandwidth necessary
New media	Immediate learning	Depends upon reliable connectivity
Communication (Twitter, chat, wikis, blogs)	Collaborative	Not all information may be accurate
Mobile learning or mLearner (Available on mobile devices)	Collaborative	Use of text limited
	Widespread access	Small screen size

Keep in mind that no single technology can do everything. For this reason, well designed training programs normally involve a number of different media, each of which is used for a different purpose. This also reduces the pressure to select the "perfect" medium and mitigates the consequences if a single technology doesn't work out. Of course, using multiple media makes the logistics of media preparation more complicated and raises the issue of how to integrate/coordinate different technologies in a single training program. If the program is well designed by experienced instructional technologists, this should not be a significant problem.

Blended Learning Using Communities of Learning (CoLs) to Facilitate Global Collaboration: Case Study

Martin Rehm

In partnership with a large international organization operating in the field of development assistance, Maastricht Graduate School of Governance (MGSoG) developed a blended learning program for more than five hundred of the organization's middle- and top-management staff. The ultimate objective of the program was to secure and enhance the impact of the international organization in its daily practice by strengthening key staff members' ability to continue playing an active role in development assistance, as well as engaging in discussions and negotiations with other major players in the field. In order to achieve this goal, the design of the learning program was based on the theories of social constructivism and situated cognition, where participants engaged in updating their knowledge and skills by collaboratively discussing real-life tasks and cases. These items were directly linked to participants' everyday working environments and identified in cooperation with a team of the international organization's senior staff members.

With participants from nearly one hundred offices worldwide, the program employed a blended learning approach, consisting of an online course as well as a face-to-face workshop. The inclusion of the online course was of great importance, as it provided a very cost-effective means to provide training without staff having to physically travel to training venues for prolonged periods of time, leaving their workstations and thereby causing the organization to accrue considerable direct and indirect costs.

The duration of the online course was fourteen weeks and included no scheduled real-time meetings. The overall workload amounted to an average of five hours per week. The learning materials, including lectures, manuals, and readings, were all accessible via a dedicated virtual learning environment (VLE), powered by Blackboard©. The lectures were provided in different formats, namely as high- and low-resolution video files, as well as audio podcasts. Moreover, taking into account that Internet connectivity varied considerably between individual participants, all course materials were also distributed via DVDs. In addition to its role as an easily accessible content storage system, the VLE also hosted a set of elements for self-study, as well as collaborative learning activities.

In terms of self-study, participants were required to prepare a range of empirical readings relevant to the participants' work. Moreover, these readings were complemented by a lecture by a renowned topic expert and a "Context Note" from a senior academic staff member introducing the topic and linking it to the overall goal of the program. Both elements were recorded via a capture station that combined the video-input with applicable PowerPoint files into a single output file. Additionally, participants could complete voluntary formative assessments in the form of online multiple-choice quizzes.

The collaborative learning activities constituted the backbone of the entire online course and were subdivided into a voluntary public discussion forum and a number of private discussion forums, where participation was obligatory. The public forum, which was accessible at course level, facilitated the general exchange of knowledge across all participants. The private forums were at the heart of separate communities of learning (CoL), organized by role-based organizations within the VLE, where ten to fifteen randomly assigned participants discussed the content of the course. In both instances, two types of forums were available. One type of forum focused on group-building processes. The other type was content driven, providing a platform to collaboratively work on the practical, real-life tasks and cases. The discussion forums were based on technology developed at Maastricht University, specifically designed to foster collaborative knowledge exchange. To facilitate the discussions, a team of two academic staff members was assigned to each CoL.

After the completion of the online course, participants clearly stated that they considered the course to be a valuable learning experience and that it provided them with a better understanding of the new concepts and methods to assess their everyday, work-related challenges. Furthermore, participants appreciated the fact they could collaborate with each other via the CoLs, irrespective of time and place. All participants indicated that the course had increased their capacity to face the challenges of their everyday work and to actively contribute to the discussions with other partners in the field. As one learner stated, "I found this training an enriching opportunity as a professional in the field. [...]

I feel that now I am prepared and skilled to fully interpret [my working environment]. Thanks for this opportunity. It was a valuable experience!"

Martin Rehm works for the Maastricht Graduate School of Governance as program manager, e-learning, and research fellow. As program manager, he is responsible for international projects, such as the Russian Senior Public Sector Training Program (Russian Ministry of Economic Development). As research fellow, he focuses on communities of learning for working professionals.

e-Learning Courseware Design Basics and the Role of HR

As the e-learning field matures, some design fundamentals have emerged. It is your role to ensure that the design basics are enforced. These points pertain primarily to e-learning offered through an LMS. Of course, there will be variations depending upon the course content, but keep these basics in mind.

- Limit groups within a larger class to twenty or fewer students to avoid unmanageable discussion threads.
- Prepare for and enable the instructor's role change from sage-on-the-stage to guide-by-the-side.
- Use graphics, metaphors, pictures, and other visuals to enliven the courseware.
- Employ multimedia when possible.
- Create an online learning community through the use of threaded discussions and group work.
- Provide easy access to key aspects of the course; do not involve multiple screens to accomplish a single task.
- Place navigation, function, and content buttons, as well as instructions and graphics, in predictable places; keep them there throughout the course and across courses in the same program.
- Set behavioral norms early, or have learners do so, and be sure that they are clear and agreed upon.
- Provide clear, prompt feedback because there are no other cues from which learners can receive the message.

Culture and Courseware Design

Technology-based courseware needs to be adjusted for cross-cultural interactions when the audience is multicultural. Jack Yang's (2006) article "The

Discussion of Media Selection and Accessible Equity in Distance Education"
provides insight into some critical design considerations.

Jack Yang (2006) encourages an examination of the culture before making design decisions (see chapter 2 for cultural characteristics). Variables that
impact design include:

- Learner-centered or teacher-centered: Societies with a small power distance tend to be more learner-centered, while those who accept a large
  power distance are more teacher-centered. The media should highlight
  the approach espoused by your audience.

- Comfortable with narratives: *High context indirect* is a communication
  style in which the context has ultimate importance. High context indirect
  communication uses nonverbal elements such as voice tone, facial expressions, gestures, and eye movements to convey a message. One talks around
  the point and embellishes it. Communication is seen as an art form, a way
  of engaging someone. For cultures where this type of communication is the
  norm, narratives, stories, and examples fit well. Just be sure that the story
  is one to which your audience can relate. For example, soccer is a familiar
  sport worldwide, whereas baseball is not.

- Jargon: Formal or informal approaches offer another differentiator. Formal
  societies are ritualized and predicated upon honoring hierarchies. In such
  a cultural context, jargon appears disrespectful and does not lend itself to
  translation.

- Acronyms: Acronyms create confusion. They assume a predominant language and culture. What is easily pronounced or understood in English, for
  instance, may be unfathomable in another language. Avoid acronyms.

- Humor: Humor is potentially dangerous because it can leave the learner
  wondering what the point is or, worse, feeling insulted. It is also difficult
  to translate. Avoid the use of humor in a cross-cultural course.

Tips and Tools for Designing Online Learning for a Variety of Cultures

When designing online learning for an audience of mixed cultures or for a culture different from your own:

- Design, develop, deliver, evaluate, and administer training differently based upon
  the target audience's culture and the way they prefer to be trained.

- Consider the underlying adult learning theory impacting the design of instruction
  and assess whether or not it works within the culture of the target audience.

- Remember that methodologies that are effective in one culture may be totally
  ineffective in another.

- Analyze technologies for aspects that may imply values (such as cooperation, open communication, control, equity, hierarchy, individualism, and so on) in order to select a technology that supports the dominant cultural norms.

Culture and Media Selection

In areas that require human interaction, culture will always have an impact. Activities taking place in another culture, in multiple cultures, or globally will overlap with strongly held national norms or values. Each culture has different ways of valuing and implementing work, learning, management, customer service, teamwork, etc.

e-Learners' General Needs

E-learners differ from traditional classroom learners in many ways. Their needs include the following:

- Increased structure
- Technology support
- Effective orientation programs
- Specific prompts to draw out "*lurkers*," those who do not participate
- A forum to be heard so that one person doesn't monopolize online discussion
- A means to communicate with other classmates

When these elements are present, the learning will eclipse any distractions from the medium. In fact, the venue will become transparent, and that is the goal.

Cultural Preferences and Training

When adapting training for specific cultural groups, avoid using materials that represent one culture as superior to another. Use illustrations as much as possible and tailor exercises to the target culture, using local names, titles, and situations but avoiding politics and religion. Modify the situations, alter the case studies, and rewrite applications to make the course more meaningful for your audience. The more technical the topic, the less change is needed. Training on soft skills, like communication or supervisory skills, are likely to require the most modification.

Translate materials for other cultures. If the training was developed in French but your audience is primarily Malaysian, have the materials translated into the predominant language. Note that translation is much more than a word-for-word conversion of text. Rather it requires adapting the language effectively, with appropriate cultural meanings, and aligning it with the learning objectives. Some words are not directly translatable, so keep that in mind. Be sure to write to the language skill level of the learners.

Michael Marquardt and Greg Kearsley, in their text *Technology-Based Learning* (1999), provide specific guidelines for designing or redesigning instruction for other cultures:

- Avoid culturally inappropriate or offensive pictures or scenarios.
- Use graphics, visuals, and demonstrations if the trainees are learning in a second language.
- Provide handouts and instructional materials whenever possible; these provide a takeaway that is valuable not only during the class, but in the future.
- Avoid corporate ethnocentrism, in which it is assumed that the company will be presented exactly the same worldwide.
- Make sure that the training materials are well organized and unambiguous, especially when adapting for Asian cultures that prefer clear and specific instructions.
- Provide written examples for all worksheets so the learners know exactly what is required.
- Provide complete and accurate summaries of all lectures.

Not all aspects of technology, however, are affected by culture or globalization. Many manufacturers of technology have already made adjustments to adapt to cultural and language differences. Nevertheless, material developers should assume cultural differences rather than similarities. They should treat each environment as unique and design (or redesign) culturally appropriate learning materials.

The following steps are recommended when creating training materials to use in another culture:

1. Include local instructors and a translator to examine training materials.
2. Debrief after the observation with the translator, curriculum writer, and local instructors.
3. Pilot the structure and sequence of the course, ice breaker activities, and materials with a representative from the target audience.
4. Involve designers from the target audience to contribute stories, metaphors, experiences, and examples from this culture that might fit the new training program.

5. Include an educational designer and curriculum writer when making changes to the training materials.
6. Train local instructors to use and deliver the materials online.
7. Ensure that the designer, translator, and native-language trainers are satisfied before publishing or posting the materials.
8. Pilot the materials with a sample group.

Taking into account all of the factors mentioned can make the design and delivery process quite complicated. In practice, decision makers tend to emphasize cost considerations over design. Our point is that design is very important. The good news is that if the course is designed with an adult learning theory in mind, the delivery media is selected to align with the theory, and the material is developed following best practices, then the learning materials are more likely to succeed!

Facilitator Role

With regard to the impact of culture upon media selection for online training, the most marked difference is the role of the instructor. Because of the lack of control that the instructor can exert over the learning process, in online training the instructor's role usually changes from sage-on-the-stage (or the one with all of the answers) to guide-by-the-side (or one who facilitates the learning process). In some cultures, learners prefer that the teacher be an expert lecturer (or sage-on-the-stage); consequently, they may find an instructor's shift to a facilitating role unsettling. Adjustments in media selection can help learners be more comfortable in the online learning environment. For example, in cultures in which students prefer the instructor to be an expert lecturer, the use of audio or video files of lectures to introduce new subject matter can be very effective.

In a synchronous online environment, the instructor's responsibilities increase. Most challenging for the instructor is the multitasking aspect, which may include watching e-mail, leading web surfing, responding verbally to inquiries, and monitoring bulletin boards all at the same time! Online instruction requires a lot of preparatory work, maybe as much as 20 to 30 percent more preparation time than face-to-face instruction requires (Piskurich 2004, 26). Remember, what looks like flexibility in the face-to-face classroom appears chaotic in an online course, so structure and preparation are very important to effective online training delivery.

Instructors in a synchronous online environment should also ensure that there are small interactions to keep involvement high. Start class promptly. Have a plan to deal with technical problems, so they do not affect the entire class's learning experience. Instructors who teach online must compensate for the lack of body language cues by creating more interactions, asking more questions, even using roll call to elicit responses from everyone in order to get the audience involved. Communicate any changes in writing through a medium that you know will ensure that all receive the message.

Tips and Tools for Media Selection—What to Use and When

To select technology for a training event, keep in mind a couple of important points:

1. You should have an adult learning theory that supports your selection and design of e-learning.
2. The adult learning theory that underpins the courseware should match the choice of technology approach, methodology, and evaluation approach.
3. For cross-cultural learning programs, include members of the target audience as reviewers, designers, and facilitators in order to avoid cultural mistakes.

Vendor Selection and Evaluation

When an organization does not have the expertise in-house to develop online courseware, it is possible to use a vendor. However, there are a number of questions to ask when selecting a vendor: Is it possible to use an off-the-shelf product or does the courseware need to be customized? Will the vendor do the design and development and relinquish course delivery to the organization? Be sure that you have identified the role that the vendor will play before inviting vendors to compete. The vendor should propose a plan outlining the approach, schedule, roles, and costs so that there are no surprises.

The available pool of vendors will differ based upon your location; the vendor list in Belgium or Brazil will differ from that in Kenya or Canada. An important way to approach vendor selection is to rely upon your connections within the industry. If there is a local community of practice or association of HR and/or training professionals, those members will have experience with vendors that you may interview.

Assemble a team. Depending upon the components of your e-learning project and the topic, you will need to bring together team members from various departments within your organization. Be sure that you include on your team a subject matter expert (SME) for the course topic. You may need members from the information technology department, finance representatives, marketing and sales people, graphic artists, etc. The team configuration will vary based upon the content to be delivered and the technology under consideration. The bottom line is that you should never design complex, tech-enabled courseware on your own. Technology decisions impact a variety of departments and ripple through the organization. It would be a waste of time and money to choose a technology that is incompatible with your existing infrastructure. Remember, it is not a sign of weakness to include other departments—rather it is collaborative. You will save yourself time and money by using these best practices.

Involve the team in preparing the request for proposal (RFP). Many RFPs are poorly assembled and prepared. Once you have a list of two or three vendors whom you are seriously considering, meet with them. Share ideas and ask them for opinions about how to structure your program. This will also be a good way to test your RFP to make sure you are asking the right questions.

Agree within your team on the evaluation criteria. Your vendor, once selected, will be a strategic partner. The vendor should be one with whom you can work well, and who will help you identify trends in your industry in the e-learning realm (Woodward 2008, 57–61).

Answer questions about installation beforehand. This may not seem relevant, as many organizational policies allow for software to be installed on computers involved in various projects. However, these are questions to consider when working with a vendor to select software infrastructure:

- For software systems that are server based, is an externally hosted software system allowed/encouraged/discouraged?
- For server-based systems, what processes are required to host the software internally?
- What technologies are necessary when an end-user is taking an e-learning course? Flash? JavaScript? Other? Does the content run on all of the company's operating systems?
- Does the authoring software either include its own media database or integrate into existing content management systems?
- Does your organization use rights-managed imagery and photography? This means that there is some form of per-use fee associated with the imagery. Are you able to track this usage to ensure you are not breaching licensing agreements?
- Is there a company standard design template for e-learning?
- Are you able to create a repository of all approved media, including learning objects, for any given project in your software infrastructure? (Unneberg 2007, 201–207)

Be sure that you know what you want the training to accomplish and how you want to achieve those objectives. Make your media selection before you begin development. As with other sophisticated technology efforts, you should have identified the functionality necessary to achieve the objectives. If the message is intended simply to communicate a change in procedure, you may be able to post on the company website a PowerPoint presentation outlining the new policy. However, if the organization is instituting a new program that affects a variety of your courseware, then you may need to consider leasing space on a *learning management system* or building one in-house to accommodate the program-wide learning.

Know your budget parameters before entering the vendor selection phase. Left to their own devices, vendors will usually encourage the most expensive option. By outlining your budget for potential vendors early in your discussions, you will not waste anyone's time—most importantly your own!

Do your vendor research. E-learning providers are abundant, although for the most part they deal with large organizations, and quality varies among them. How can you choose one that is right for you? Here are some steps to assist you in the process:

- Find a provider that deals with other organizations the size of your company.
- Ask providers for a case study of how they handled a customer of similar size and with needs similar to yours.
- Ask them for references.
- Identify vendors that have the library of content and expertise that you need.
- Look for a company that has an authoring capability so that you can take your company's specialized product information or new-employee orientation online.
- Look for an authoring tool that is easy to use and has a quick publishing turnaround.
- Thoroughly test courses from several providers by taking a demo course from that vendor and simulating the learner's experience.
- Examine the ease of navigation (or not), how fast the courseware loaded, and whether there was good documentation.
- Examine the vendor website to see what message they send about reliability, maintenance, past projects, etc.
- Test the technical support, which should be available twenty-four hours a day, seven days a week. (Tyler 2001, 87–90)

Tips and Tools for Selecting a Vendor

- Assemble a team.
- Involve the team in preparing the request for proposal.
- Agree within your team on the evaluation criteria.
- Answer questions about user system requirements, installation, maintenance, ownership of imagery, etc., beforehand.
- Establish the adult learning theory in general and training objectives in particular.
- Do your vendor research.
- Know your budget parameters.

Managing the e-Learning Multimedia Project— A Modified ADDIE Approach

If the e-learning will incorporate multimedia, audio, or video, then project management is critically important. The standard project management approach to training development uses the analysis, design, development, implementation, and evaluation approach (ADDIE), which is very straightforward. This protocol takes the guesswork out of what to do when.

However, when you are dealing with multimedia, audio, or video development efforts, project management is a bit more complex. Figure 4-1: Modified ADDIE Approach demonstrates the extra provisions needed to ensure a quality final product.

Important changes in the standard ADDIE process occur around the development phase. If there are programming, sound, or video components, start them at the development stage. They should be tested separately and validated by a third-party unbiased examiner who ensures that all aspects of the technology work as intended and that the message aligns with course objectives. Then, if modifications to the product are necessary, they will take place during the development phase, at the same time the course development is taking place. Always include a pilot of the entire training event before going live with the training. The pilot phase should include members of the target audience. Feedback during the pilot may require returning to the development phase for modifications. So the multimedia "loop" of design, development, and piloting occur concurrently with the development phase until the final product is ready for implementation.

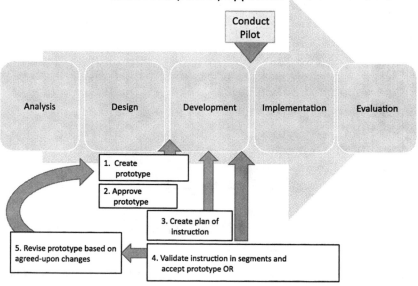

Modified Analysis, Design, Development, Implementation, and Evaluation (ADDIE) Approach (Adapted from Dobbs 2006)

Conduct Pilot

Analysis   Design   Development   Implementation   Evaluation

1. Create prototype
2. Approve prototype
3. Create plan of instruction
5. Revise prototype based on agreed-upon changes
4. Validate instruction in segments and accept prototype OR

FIGURE 4-1   Modified ADDIE Approach

Evaluating e-Learning Projects

Considerable attention has been paid to the issue of quality in organizations, due largely to the influence of W. Edwards Deming and the total quality management (TQM) movement. The emergence of the Malcolm Baldridge National Quality Award and ISO 9000 standards further defined the criteria for quality in the United States and around the globe. Most organizations have some form of internal quality assessment, a process in which HRD usually plays a critical role. While quality assessment is not the same as performance improvement, there is a lot of overlap between the two approaches, including use of the same methodologies (such as needs assessment).

The project management process is impacted by the quality movement. In particular, the following tips help ensure an e-learning project goes smoothly:

1. Define the quality assurance, review, and approval process before beginning the project.
2. Ensure that subject matter experts are available and able to dedicate time to the project.

3. Get commitment from the various stakeholders on the project.
4. Define the business outcome so that you can determine whether it was achieved.

Keep in mind that the business outcome must be measurable. For instance, if the training is intended to educate employees about a new computer system, identify the computer tasks the learner should be able to perform and then test the learners upon their completion of the program to ensure that they can actually perform the required tasks.

Conclusion

In this chapter we examined the many facets of media selection and then addressed the cultural issues that impact media selection for a multicultural training audience. Finally, we discussed the process of managing a multimedia project. Next, in chapter 5, we will examine options for learners who do not have access to e-learning delivered over the Internet.

CHAPTER 5

Leaders and Mobile Learning

T he journal *Learning in Action* carried an article describing a paradigm shift in the field of leadership. In it the authors described leaders of the twentieth century as being focused primarily on people and structure, both of which thrive in a world that is rational and filled with logical people. Unfortunately, as the authors went on to explain, the twenty-first-century organization is "intrinsically wild, messy, and unpredictable" (Bolman and Deal 2009, 14), rendering the old twentieth-century approach outdated. Leaders must be flexible and adjust.

The Changing Impact of Human Resource Development Leaders

Those with human resource development (HRD) responsibilities have a new role in the twenty-first century. Many of the benefits, personnel, training, and change management responsibilities of the previous century have been eliminated, outsourced, shifted to online self-service, or managed through Internet-enabled *human resource information systems* (HRIS). Consequently, Human Resource professionals—who are in the people-care business—have less contact than ever with the employees they serve. The Internet enables distribution of functions previously firmly entrenched in the domain of HRD.

The good news is that the human resource development function is vital to organizations' overall success and profitability. Responsibilities of HR leaders today go well beyond the twentieth-century roles. The new trends in HRD include a focus on:

Globalization: An emphasis on, and responsibility for promoting, global perspectives rather than parochial or regional viewpoints (Marquardt and Berger 2003).

Strategic planning: Strategic rather than minimal preparation (Garavan 2007).

Leadership development: Growth of programs to promote the skill development of new and existing leaders (Trehan 2007), with an emphasis on decision-making expertise (Chermack 2003).

Management training and education: An emphasis on the need for systemic and systematic training (Swanson and Dobbs 2006) rather than generalist training.

Each of these trends is supported by technology (Roberts 2008). In fact, technology is what enables the shift from the twentieth-century HR role to the twenty-first century HR paradigm.

Not surprisingly, modes of learning have also changed. Executives, small business owners, and those with HR responsibilities find themselves needing to find new ways to enable learning and develop leaders. The impact on HR is that Human Resource leaders must use theories of learning and instruction to promote adult learning—and do so cost-effectively! HR leaders in the twenty-first century will need to fight to extend equitable benefits to all the employees in their global organizations. They will need to think in ingenious, even risky, ways to find innovative, ethical solutions. These are the challenges of the twenty-first century. To meet them, the HR professional must use imagination and creativity.

We start this chapter with the changing role of HR, because it requires familiarity with nonstandard learning solutions for a global society. Unfortunately, twenty-first-century Internet technology does not yet reach every corner of the globe. In fact, even within the same country some may have Internet access while others only miles away may not. In a global organization, the varying levels of connectivity, infrastructure, and hardware cause great disparities and challenges to individual, team, and organizational learning.

In the 1990s, a quiet technological shift began with the introduction of digital (not analog) transmission technologies. Digital wireless—mobile phone technology—transmits both data and voice. This breakthrough allows mobile devices to possess sufficient bandwidth for the average user to send e-mail, surf the web, and play audio and video files. The technology is dependent upon satellite linkages that create an "Internet-in-the-sky" (Shotsberger and Vetter 2002). The result of this capability is that we can tap this surge in wireless technology to surmount inequities in training access and to provide equal opportunity and learning for all. Employees located in places with unstable Internet access should not be—and do not need to be—left behind. Although the tools may not be alike, the net outcomes can be equivalent. Mobile technology can be used to level the playing field, supporting ongoing learning and development for all.

Human Resource professionals can use their power and influence to help others see the possibilities and think outside the box. The first step is to examine the technology options that provide alternatives to PC-bound technologies, including the following: mobile wireless devices such as cell phones, portable media such as DVDs, digital readers, and MP3 players such as iPods. The mobile technologies extend learning to everyone within the organization, rather than confining it to a limited group.

This chapter explores options for those who do not have either reliable, consistent computer access to the Internet or broadband Internet for video and audio training products. In such cases, technologies exist that enable those learners to leapfrog over the prohibitive aspects of the personal computer technology. We will include case studies describing successful implementation of each innovative, alternative technology. We will examine your role in the media selection process. Throughout the chapter, we will highlight situations in which these tools would provide an effective alternative to web-based training delivery.

Virtual Learning Environments

Mobile devices offer an alternative virtual learning environment. There are about five billion cell phones in operation around the world (Whitney 2010), which makes it logical to explore cell phones and other mobile technologies as viable training delivery media. In fact, new options have been explored since the late twentieth century.

Mobile learning is now coming of age, although we are still exploring the possibilities. Learning that relies upon mobile devices like cell phones, palm-held, pocket, and tablet PCs is called m-learning. *M-learning* delivers digitized instructional content directly to wireless devices. Many developing nations, whose citizens may not have access to Internet-connected computers, do have access to cell phones, iPods, palm or pocket PCs, and smartphones. The m-learner approach extends learning to an audience that previously was marginalized or ignored because of a lack of broadband Internet access.

Benefits of m-learning include the fact that mobile learning:

- Is more widely available and accessible
- Offers a natural extension of e-learning
- Occurs just-in-time at the precise place and time on the job that you need it

- Provides learning on-the-go
- Is relatively inexpensive
- Promotes the development of information literacy
- Offers the possibility of collaborative learning
- Prepares the student for independent learning
- Delivers audio so you can listen and talk with a real person
- Provides a mix of both audio and text
- Overcomes the issues of limited bandwidth (Brown 2005)

The m-learning approach can deliver quality instruction. Pavel Rosman, in an article that appeared in *Ekonomie a Management* (2008), states, "The highly personalized nature of digital mobile devices provides an excellent platform for the development of personalized, learner-centric educational experiences" (119). Others agree. Clearly, digital mobile devices offer a feasible alternative to e-learning delivered to a computer via the broadband Internet

Mobile Devices

The handheld cell phone presents an inexpensive and portable medium that is available to most people throughout the world (PR Newswire 2007). Additionally, other mobile devices such as digital audio players and even digital cameras can accommodate mobile learning.

Using mobile devices, we can offer customized, personalized training to those who may be unlikely learners. The successful development of Bluetooth, Wireless Application Protocol (WAP), General Packet Radio System (GPRS), and Universal Mobile Telecommunications System (UMTS) enable wireless telephone and wireless computing (Rosman 2008). Coupled with software, such as Opera Mini, to reduce text to fit the screen, mobile devices are a viable training technology.

Mobile learning supports a broad range of media and the list continues to expand:

- On-device videos—MP4, M4V, WMV, 3GP, SWF
- On-web videos—FLV
- Audio podcasts—MP3, WMA, WAV
- Voice-based cellcasts—WAV, GSM
- Animated slide presentations—PPT, PPTX
- Mobile web pages/courses—HTML, TXT
- Adobe files—PDF

- Mobile assessments—XML, HTML
- Messaging/notifications—SMS, e-mail

Target Audience

Mobile devices allow the user to, in effect, surpasss the computer-based networked community to achieve similar functionality. Learners using mobile devices can receive documents, instructions, audio files, and video. The text messaging feature can also be used as a powerful, collaborative device, not to mention the phone features for teleconferencing.

M-learning is not the solution for everyone. Appropriate audiences for this tool include:

- Learners at risk or who have dropped out of school but who have mobile phones with Internet access (Naran 2010).
- Professionals who do not have reliable PC-Internet access but who do have mobile phone access to the Internet (Brown 2005).
- Medical professionals in remote locations who have mobile phone Internet access (Cornelius and St. Lawrence 2009).

The applications for m-learners can extend to other audiences as well. Those with HR responsibilities will know the "at risk" audience and whether or not mobile technology is a good fit. The purpose of using a mobile device for learning is not to replace the personal computer, but rather to broaden access to online training for an audience that does not have computers with reliable broadband Internet access.

Instructional Activities

Mobile devices enable a variety of educational activities such as note taking, simulations, and accessing digital textbooks. They can support language lessons, display animations for medical or other purposes, or serve as polling, data collection, or testing devices. Accessing educational materials on handheld computers is easy, and their strong search capabilities provide support for effective learning. Remarkably, many of the learning tasks made common by the computer can be accomplished using mobile devices.

The hardware for m-learning includes portable, handheld technology. The portability allows students to learn anytime, anywhere; in fact, the newest buzz phrase, replacing just-in-time learning, is "just-for-you" learning, in which the content is customized for the participant. Rather than emulating the computer, mobile learning tools serve as collaborative devices, allowing for new forms of interaction between students and teachers. For flexible services, m-learning may rely upon the pocket PC, mobile phone, and portable keyboard.

Impact on the Design of Instruction

Pedagogically, constructivism is the predominant school of learning aligned with the use of mobile devices (Billings 2005). However, mobile learning also lends itself to social learning where rich communication and interaction provide a wonderful context in which communities of practice can thrive (for descriptions of these theories, see chapter 4). When you combine both constructivism and social learning, you have a social constructivist design that capitalizes on all of the attributes of m-learning (Brown 2005).

In both the constructivist and social learning theories, the shift is toward a learner-centered method. Ultimately, though, the burden of developing a useful course is on the instructional designer—often the instructor—who predictably will spend a great deal of time preparing for and designing the course, as well as delivering it and following up with individual students.

The instructional design approach for m-learning varies slightly from that of standard e-learning. Keyboard-enabled mobile phones can use e-mail, listservs, threaded discussions, and text-based chats. However, in some cases text use may be more difficult because of the small screen and keyboard. Where text use is difficult, audio input can be substituted; both audio and video files can be played on these handheld devices. Instructional design must accommodate the smaller screen and keyboard of mobile devices.

Handheld mobile devices can be used to take notes, to conduct ad hoc collaboration between students and teachers, and to retrieve information such as documents or videos. The approach to instructional design for the mobile environment differs from offerings over the Internet. With m-learning, the learning becomes pervasive and is not relegated to a specific time or place. While the trend is toward blended learning in the mobile learning model (similar to the e-learning model), the best design for m-learning is to provide a rich set of learning resources. The training must be compressed and accelerated. Additionally, modules should be "unbundled" from the larger curriculum and offered as smaller modules with less text.

The instructor and student interact in a unique way when using m-learning. Because the goal is for instruction to be on-demand, the instructor must help students evaluate and synthesize information. The instructor can use short quizzes offered over the mobile device to identify at the beginning of the lesson where the knowledge gaps are and then tutor the students in those areas.

Students must be taught to use the handheld devices to do things such as obtaining, verifying, and uploading data. They can request assistance using microphones or instant messaging. Students can also use the cell phone to create logs (Billings 2005).

Burnwood Secondary School, KwaZulu Natal, South Africa: Case Study

Vanesh Gokal

Vanesh Gokal is the principal of Burnwood Secondary School in KwaZulu Natal, South Africa. Surrounding his school are approximately 100,000 people living in shacks in extreme poverty. Many families are headed by a child. The challenges are numerous. Consequently, a good education is not the top priority for most; finding food is more important than solving equations. This scenario is repeated all over South Africa.

Teachers are instrumental in convincing children that education is important. One of the ways they do so is by entering the world of the teenagers who understand digital devices, embracing the idea that teenagers are teenagers, irrespective of where they live.

Teenagers have an amazing ability to engage successfully with digital technology. This new breed of learners constantly uses mobile technology like cell phones. There is wide mobile coverage across South Africa, and it is spreading daily. So the school administration, under Gokal's leadership, decided to develop school content that would appeal to these teens. Popular Internet search engines produce information overload on any topic, making it very difficult for students to filter for appropriate content and grasp new concepts. Also, most math and science content on the Internet seems to compete to be the most advanced. There is a need for web content that is student-focused, with simple language that helps overcome language and learning barriers.

Having observed the students at Burnwood Secondary School, Gokal understood that the school had to take math and science into the students' world, and not the other way around. Almost all the children have cell phones that are Internet enabled, and they know how to use them. While the cost of airtime is a concern, Gokal decided to develop a mobile-friendly math and science site composed of very small files. The challenge was to make the web pages look great and still load quickly.

Gokal created the mobile website *www.smartlearner.mobi*, which has become very popular. It provides quick downloads on cell phones, composed of hand-coded HTML, rather than linking to a content management system. With reliance upon cascading style sheets (CSS), this approach has proven very successful. Gokal further developed new systems to create tiny images, small video files, and very small MP3 audio files. The software offers a chat site that allows for superscripts and subscripts and a testing section that gives immediate feedback. The free mobile browser, Operamini, works on inexpensive cell phones. Thus, SmartLearner does not require a smartphone to be useful.

Probably the most significant contribution of this delivery mode is that it engages the students. Although the use of cell phones for instruction is not widespread, and the regulations regarding protocols are very strict, government officials in the South Africa Education Department have taken notice. National radio stations and newspapers have written fantastic articles about SmartLearner. In a matter of weeks, there were well over 800,000 hits!

Gokal finances SmartLearner and writes the code himself, a time-consuming task. One funding consideration is the option of making it a subscription-only website. However, this would immediately exclude many of the students for whom SmartLearner was created. In order to make SmartLearner more accessible, Burnwood Secondary School invested in a big screen for the school. Together with Internet connectivity, a large sound system, and a data projector, SmartLearner leaped from the tiny screen onto the big screen. Lessons have become more exciting for students and teachers. The video solutions play like a movie, allowing teachers to walk among students and check on their work.

Gokal says it best: "Teaching is a place of work, but it should be a place of passion. Would it not be a great victory if students could experience their lessons at school on a big screen and then at home on their cell phone's tiny screens?" He is accomplishing just that!

Vanesh Gokal, principal of the Burnwood Secondary School, finances the mobile learning platform SmartLearner and writes code for the site himself.

Another impact of the cell phone has to do with gathering and distributing medical information as well as training. In 2009, a study was conducted regarding using text-messaging to disseminate an HIV-prevention curriculum to at risk groups of African American adolescents (Cornelius and St. Lawrence 2009). Because text messaging was a popular means of communication for the target audience, this method was used.

Communication on demand is highly attractive for most audiences, and text-messaging allows immediate communication. The advantage of the text-messaging approach is that it is convenient, inexpensive, confidential, and accessible to the target audience—adolescents. The text-message feature was used to send regular HIV-prevention messages to support a face-to-face curriculum. Also part of the program was the capacity for the recipients to respond. These exchanges between instructor and student require availability on the part of the instructor that extends far beyond standard work and student contact hours, another change to the instructor–student paradigm.

A resource for this technology is the European Consortium for e-Learning. This group has led the way in the adaptation and use of mobile technology. Many of the consortiums' work packages further inform studies of mobile technology uses. Clearly, mobile technology has only begun to impact and revolutionize e-learning!

Portable Media—DVDs and CD-ROMs

DVDs and CD-ROMs offer a format that is easily portable and can provide access to training for those who do not have Internet connections or who do not have broadband Internet but who do have DVD or CD players. While this technology is not new, it is viable as a media to deliver instruction in a variety of situations. *DVD* stands for digital video disc and can be used for video and data storage. *Compact Disc-Read Only Memory (CD-ROM)* is an earlier version of a similar technology. Both CD-ROMs and DVDs can be used to deliver multimedia. Let's first compare the CD-ROM and DVD technologies and then explore interactive multimedia.

Comparison of CD-ROMs and DVDs

CD-ROMs and DVDs are slight variations of the same concept. Both are used for data storage; DVD is basically a higher-tech version of CD-ROM. CD-ROMs hold about 650 to 700 MB of data, while DVDs can hold multiple gigabytes of data. The DVD reader mechanism is finer and more precise than the CD reader, which is the main reason that DVD drives cost more. DVD drives can also read regular CD-ROM discs with no problem. So the difference between the two discs is storage space, as well as the potential need for a different driver (CD-ROM drives will not be able to read a DVD while DVD drives can read both formats).

Depending on what you want to display in DVD format, you may need additional capabilities: If you want the DVD drive in your computer to play movies on DVD, you will need MPEG decoding capability. If you are using the DVD drive only for data, you won't need a decoder to process the audio and video data.

Interactive Multimedia

Multimedia refers to a combination of text, audio, pictures, animation, and video. Interactive multimedia is multimedia that uses digital computer-based systems to respond to the user's actions. Content is presented using a combination of text, graphics, animation, video, audio, etc.

The benefits of multimedia are that because of enriched sensory involvement, there is increased motivation on the part of the learner. Interactive multimedia programs capture even more attention and create greater engagement on the learner's part. Additionally, the use of multiple modalities accommodates a broader array of learning preferences for a wider range of learners. Also, multimedia is more realistic: the use of photographs, audio, and video make the content concrete. When case studies and simulations are included, the training situations become even more realistic. Text and captions can be used for multilingual materials. Multimedia may be used individually, in groups, or in pairs with the net effect being that multimedia usage improves the learners' digital literacy.

To appeal to diverse audiences, it is also possible to create multimedia video segments with speakers of different nationalities explaining or presenting information from a unique cultural perspective. Additionally, digital storytelling, which includes video—or pictures and audio—can be used to present a case, memories, or examples of surmounting problems (and their solutions) for training purposes. Digital storytelling provides a wonderful opportunity for reflection and deeper thinking (see *www.reflect2.org* for more on digital storytelling). It is culturally relevant for many societies that prefer high-context indirect communication emphasizing stories about traditions or history (see chapter 2 for cultural explanations). But all of these benefits require instructional designers and developers who have the skill and the knowledge to design an engaging and instructionally sound multimedia program.

Both CD-ROMs and DVDs can store multimedia, We include mention of CD-ROMs because some potential learners may have older computers that have not been updated for DVD use. Of course, the system requirements and equipment of the target audience must be examined in the design phase before implementing any multimedia program in order to select the appropriate delivery solution.

Interactive Multimedia Design and Development

While our focus is not on the design and development effort, it is important to have a general understanding of how multimedia programs are created. As with any instructional design effort, there is an extensive amount of analysis needed to specify the purpose and goals of the program, expected learning outcomes, the audience characteristics, the best delivery technology, and necessary system requirements for the target audience. Everything, except for the system requirements, are standard to the instructional design process.

As mentioned earlier, there are a number of technology issues to examine, and the agreed-upon solutions to those challenges impact the design and development of multimedia products. It may be necessary to develop multiple versions of the program that run on different types of system configurations. Once the program has been defined, the design work begins. Two features of multimedia must be considered:

- The user interface
- Specific multimedia features

Some of a multimedia product's level of interactivity has to do with the skills and multimedia knowledge of the designer. Nevertheless, the bulk of the design for interactivity should draw from the learning theory, strategies, objectives, and content.

Also for consideration is user friendliness. This refers to the interface between the learner and the system. User interface issues include:

- Navigation
- Error-handling
- Screen layout
- Response time

Guidelines exist for most of these. There are also design choices having to do with the multimedia features, including:

- Graphics
- Audio
- Video
- Animation

Design of multimedia features depends upon the content as well as the creativity and sophistication of the designers, the system constraints, and the proposed multimedia elements. Choose your designers well, because they will determine the interactivity and quality of the final product.

Upon completion of design, the development begins. We discussed the unique project management approach that occurs during the development phase for multimedia in chapter 4. In general, the steps during development include writing text, creating graphics, obtaining images, shooting video or recording audio segments, digitizing all components, and programming any interactive sequences (such as input and feedback messages).

The programming of multimedia materials requires authoring tools and possibly other software. For instance, for computer software training, Camtasia is a software that records keystrokes and mouse actions while displaying the computer's full screen, window, or region. Additionally, with Camtasia the developer can add audio such as verbal instructions, music tracks, plus picture-in-picture with a video camera to supplement the visual instructions. The final product can be saved as an MPEG2 or MPEG4 file and run as a standalone product or imported to a PowerPoint. The saved version allows learners to see the onscreen movements to perform a task using a computer system while the instructor's explanation is audible. Camtasia files can be integrated into multimedia.

Multimedia development costs will vary based upon the complexity of the training and whether feedback/correction is included. The cost effectiveness of computer-based DVD training makes it a viable training delivery option when the Internet is not reliable.

As of 2011, a variety of products are available to create a usable DVD, including:

- Sonic Scenarist
- Apple DVD Studio Pro (Mac)
- Sonic DVDit Pro (formerly DVD Producer)
- Sonic DVD Creator
- Adobe Encore CS5
- Mediachance DVD-lab PRO

Tips and Tools for Creating a Multimedia Environment

Before making a technology decision:

- Consider the location, infrastructure, and maintenance available to the target audience before selecting the delivery media.
- Examine the content of the course or program to be delivered.
- Consider the learning theory that best supports that content.
- Select the media based upon the audience capabilities, the content, the adult learning theory, and the technology fit.
- Think outside the box by examining all of the possible technology solutions, not just the familiar solutions.

Video on DVD provides another effective training application. This approach features an expert who models appropriate behavior and answers anticipated questions. While not interactive, it is still a powerful tool. Video instruction has been used for many years, based upon the premise that the power of authority and example can inspire learners to change their behavior.

A DVD that uses video training effectively is "Speaking Up: Presenting to Executives" (Love 2004). It is a training and career development program hosted by Rick Gilbert, president of Frederick Gilbert Associates. This DVD is designed to help managers learn new ways to promote their careers by teaching them to deal effectively with top-level management. The training program features discussions with seventeen senior-level executives, who share their knowledge and expertise on how to make successful presentations and conduct effective meetings. Over the course of this ninety-minute program, the executives offer pointers on how to prepare for meetings and cope effectively with the unexpected.

Typing Instructor—Example of Training Offered on DVD

Training on keyboard use, for those who have not used a computer, can be challenging at any age. One approach to learning to type is an off-the-shelf DVD called "Typing Instructor." Used for developing typing skills, the DVD prompts the learner through simple exercises to familiarize himself with the keyboard. *Scaffolded learning* (which includes related resources, a compelling task, templates/guides, and guidance on the development of cognitive and social skills) provides support to the learner which is gradually removed as the student becomes more proficient. The software adapts the level of difficulty with each level mastered by the student. The educational design uses entertaining themes and games as motivating features. When the student masters the content, he will be able to type with proficiency using a computer keyboard and the proper fingering for that keyboard. Students are presented with a variety of practice situations for refresher training as well.

CD-ROMs

Like DVDs, CD-ROMs have great storage capacity, and they can also be used for multimedia as a cost-effective delivery medium, with discs costing as little as a few cents each to produce. Because of its low cost, this format is superior to paper. It cannot be easily copied, and it has the advantage of a universally accepted format that any computer with a CD-ROM drive can read.

The traditional teaching methods of academia are fundamentally objectivist/behaviorist in nature. They are based on the principles of leading the student to an answer that is predetermined. The CD-ROM/DVD is a suitable medium for behaviorist-style training, because this medium can store training that is designed to provide learning activities requiring repetition, positive and negative reinforcement, progressively sequenced tasks, and stimulus-response techniques.

Tips and Tools for Multimedia Development Using DVDs or CD-ROMs

- Interactive multimedia brings together all forms of information presentation, including text, graphics, audio, video, and animation for delivery via a computer.

- CD-ROMs and DVDs provide a cost-effective delivery medium for multimedia programs.

- Learning benefits of multimedia include increased motivation, appeal to a broader range of learning styles, more realistic material, and facilitation of multilingual participation.

- Computer system requirements must be considered before development, because there is a wide variation in memory, speed, and graphic and audio capabilities.

- Since specific and varied skills and knowledge are needed to develop multimedia programs, a team approach to development is recommended.

- Limit costs of multimedia programs by being selective about the features and capabilities used.

Podcasts/Vodcasts

Podcasts/vodcasts refer to audio and video files that are distributed via the Internet to a computer or handheld device. Podcasts are easily created using open-source software. The recorded product can be exported in a format that is compatible with the device on which the podcast will be run. So, for instance, sound files offered over the telephone will have a different extension (WAV or other) than those run on Apple-compatible devices (typically an MP3 extension).

The following are strengths and weaknesses of podcasts/vodcasts. It is very easy to publish audio and video files. Free audio recording tools such as Audacity Sourceforge (*http://audacity.sourceforge.net*) allow the producer to create a variety of audio files that are compatible with any hardware. Further, it is not necessary to have an Internet connection in order to listen to a podcast. A computer, MP3 player, or cell phone will suffice to play an audio file. One caveat: When audio is provided, it should be accompanied by text in order to provide an alternative for the hearing impaired. The transcription process is a costly endeavor. Similarly, videocasts are easily produced as long as they are saved to the appropriate extension.

Digital Readers

E-book readers are a popular handheld digital technology for learning. With the cost of publishing rising, electronic books can certainly save money. On average, e-books are about one-third of the cost of a print book. (Note: For those who prefer the texture, smell, and look of printed books, please reserve judgment.) Several digital readers are on the market, including, but not limited to:

- KindleDigital Reader 1000
- Nook
- Samsung Tablet
- Onyx
- Cruz

Digital readers use a software and hardware platform for displaying electronic books (called e-books) and other digital media. The Kindle hardware devices use a special brand of "e-ink" and electronic paper display that features shades of gray. New digital readers use international wireless access in order to download e-books. The network used depends upon your digital reader, so look for versions that are accessible to your (international) audience. For instance, Kindle's Whispernet is an international Internet connection that is available in many developed countries and can be used without a computer. The digital reader does not require a wireless subscription. Digital readers provide a solution that saves on the space and costs associated with distributing training information and texts.

Tablet Computers

The *iPad* is a tablet computer designed and developed by Apple. It is specifically marketed as a platform for audio and visual media such as books, periodicals, movies, music, and games, as well as web content. It is more sophisticated than an e-book reader but can serve the same purpose. Its size and weight is somewhere between that of a smartphone and a laptop computer. It was released in April 2010 and Apple sold three million iPads in eighty days.

The iPad runs on the same operating system as the earlier iPod Touch and iPhone. Without modification, the iPad only runs programs approved by Apple. Other tablet computers on the market include the Hewlett-Packard Tablet, Lenovo Tablet (nicknamed the "Happy Pad"), Sony Tablet, Dell Tablet, Panasonic Tablet, and Microsoft's Slate Tablet. Because of tablets' popularity, *PC World* labeled 2010 the "Year of the Tablet PC." Each of these tablets is competing for a share of the iPad market. Relevant to this discussion is the fact that, at the time of this writing, tablet sales are poised for "spectacular" growth (Halliday 2011). Keep your eyes on this market!

Make, Buy, or Customize?

Once the method and mode of training delivery are determined, you must make a decision whether to hire a vendor to assist in the training development process. There are several options: You can use a vendor, select an off-the-shelf product, customize an off-the-shelf product, or develop the learning product entirely in-house. Budget, in-house capabilities, course subject matter and objectives, and whether in-house experts are available all impact the make, buy, or customize decision. Is the offering a standard course, such as government-mandated training? In that case, there may be a good off-the-shelf product that could be modified or used as-is. If, on the other hand, the training is highly specific to the organization, you will want to modify an off-the-shelf product or create one in-house. In any case, you may use a vendor to do the development. The vendor selection process and project management approach are described in detail in chapter 4.

HR-Intersect with Development of CD-ROMs or DVDs

The design and development of multimedia CD-ROMs or DVDs requires a variety of professionals with differing skills. Typically, multimedia, podcasts, and digital versions of instructional materials suit the team approach. The HR professional may provide the subject expertise or instructional design skills, but the other features require different skills. For instance, a multimedia team project may include a photographer, graphic designer, video team, programmer, instructional designer, and subject matter expert. There may be a vendor in that mix of professionals, as well as in-house experts. HR professionals must be prepared to collaborate with a wide variety of specialists.

Mobile Learning and the Role of the HR Professional

HR professionals should play a major role in the buy/make/customize decisions, the selection of the distribution method, and the design of multimedia and mobile training. They know the target audience best, and, therefore, they should know what serves the employees' working style, workspace, and habits. HR professionals are involved in the care of the organization's workforce and should represent the employees as stakeholders in technology-related decisions.

Conclusion

CR-ROM, multimedia, and DVDs are not new, but they are an option for areas without sstable Internet connection. Mobile learning, on the other hand, may be the way of the future, replacing PC-based e-learning as the deliverer of training. Because the reach of mobile devices has surpassed that of computers, mobile learning provides a viable alternative to PC-based e-learning programs. Only the future can tell if wireless mobile devices will replace the personal computer for training delivery.

Technologies for Managing Human Resources

The Human Resource (HR) Portal

Portals are powerful tools that serve as entryways to organizations; they're visible to customers and potential clients and offer points of access for employees. Providing a first impression of an organization, the portal is crucial to an organization's image. Its design must be intentional, incorporating a variety of features that showcase the organization's capabilities, provide information, and offer practical services. Not only are there portals with an external focus, but Human Resource portals are on the rise; they are used by those within the organization. What should the HR professional know about the functions, design, and maintenance of an HR portal? These are some of the issues we will address in this chapter.

What Is a Portal?

A *web portal* is a site on the Internet that typically provides personalized capabilities to its visitors, providing a pathway to other content. It is both the entrance and the kiosk of capabilities for a large corporation. Because it is usually the first thing that the visitor sees, first impressions really count. Business portals are designed to foster collaboration in workplaces. The content should be able to work on multiple platforms, including personal computers and handheld mobile devices such as cell phones.

Organizations that use a portal effectively take advantage of its features. The power of the portal is in the variety of tools, services, information, and communication techniques it offers. Using it as a website only is like attaching a racehorse to a plow: a silly—not to mention expensive—way to get the job done. Portals, like racehorses, have potential for high performance. So why not use all of the portal's capacity if you have decided to invest in one?

To achieve the optimal use of your portal, design is all-important. Portals are only as good as the content and services they offer. If the information isn't valuable to the visitors, the portal will fail.

Portal Elements

Portals can offer a number of different functions, and they can service both the organization's internal and external audiences. Internal portals are becoming more popular, as they bring a wide variety of information sources to the desktop. A portal can provide a workspace that offers shared access to information content, communications, and collaboration, but the design must be purposeful.

There are many design features that, when implemented, can increase the value of the portal to its users. Consider, when designing a portal, the following ideas: using RSS feeds, providing a single point of access for useful information, making navigation simple, incorporating new communication media, providing subscriptions, demonstrating clear content organization for ease of use, personalizing the portal, providing online decision support, and offering powerful search features. Let's examine each.

Really Simple Syndication (RSS) Feeds

One feature that many portals incorporate is the *Really Simple Syndication (RSS) feed*. RSS is a family of web feed formats used to publish frequently updated digital content. Really Simple Syndication feeds allow users to be notified of new content without having to actively check for it. The information presented to users is typically in much simpler form than that of most websites. This spares users the mental effort of navigating complex web pages, each with its own layout. Media files can be automatically downloaded without user intervention.

The advantage of an RSS feed for portals is that it can be used behind firewalls. So an internal portal for use within the organization by the organization's employees can provide access to information that may not make it past the firewall protecting the organization's network. It provides information such as news updates, stock prices, weather, and commodities. You can also receive podcasts. The RSS feeds can be customized to your business. RSS feeds are described in more detail in chapter 14, where we discuss social media.

Single Point of Access

The greatest power offered by organizational portals includes the ability to provide knowledge to workers with a single entryway, so to speak. From the single point of access users should be able to launch a variety of applications, access information databases, enact processes, and access enterprise-wide functions. This vision of the portal makes it a gateway or, as mentioned before, an entry-way that displays a wide spectrum of information, from corporate data to HR resources, travel arrangements, expense filing, internal purchasing, researching, and myriad other tools and information. The single point of access allows for employee self-service if systems are already in place.

Navigation, Graphics, and Social Communication

Portals must enable easy navigation while maintaining a consistent message and image. The look and feel must remain cohesive. The user should never get lost, but the portal should allow the user to move with ease from one feature to another.

The more the site engages users (sites that keep visitors interested are called "sticky"), the more likely the target audience will use the portal. One draw is to use video clips and graphics instead of text to convey a point. Podcasting (audio files broadcasted using an RSS feed) is another option that increases a portal's stickiness, maintaining the visitor's attention.

Many attractive and user-friendly portals now incorporate new media. Tools such as social networking allow employees to form internal communities of practice. Blogging by the CEO or a corporate-wide wiki can increase the reach and power of the portal, both internally and externally. Consider including social media to enhance the site and attract users. For more information on social media, see chapter 14.

Subscription

A portal that is built for subscriptions encourages visitors to sign up for special information available only with an agreement to pay. This type of portal must hook the viewer to ensure that she wants to return and purchase a subscription. The information must be clearly valuable. If you build it, they will come, but only if it is attractive and useful!

Subscriptions may be for content and/or may include communities. Portals with specific target audiences often create subscriptions for online content that is distributed to specific groups or communities of users. Subscription portals usually provide elite access to expert information and contact with specialists in the industry.

Portal Organization

The design of the portal sends a message to visitors. The portal must reflect clear arrangement according to a predetermined taxonomy, so the information should be categorized into content groups. One content group for an external portal might be products and/or services; other content groups could be awards or distinctions, staff members, or directions to the company headquarters. The content must be easy to find and read, so the writing must be clear and uncomplicated with a simple labeling scheme. The portal should include clearly planned navigation and directory structure. Failure to organize your portal well can spell disaster for information-rich portal sites.

Be sure to focus on business processes. Dan Sullivan, author of *The Proven Portal* (2004), emphasizes that portals should be designed to solve a problem. The problem should relate to an important business operation such as customer service or managing human resource functions. Be sure the portal provides access to multiple systems; it should not be the front end of one system, in which case the portal is underused. For an HR portal, if there are business processes that the portal can enable, that is a good use for the portal. The search feature that searches across multiple databases provides power to the portal. Keep these elements in mind as you create a Human Resources, knowledge management, or learning portal.

Ease of Use

The portal must be easy to use. If it is unnecessarily complicated, you will drive away users. Be sure that you focus on the user's perspective. Allow the user to personalize the services offered. Single sign-on services provide an attractive technique that makes the portal easier to use. A single sign-on environment reduces the number of passwords that users have to remember, because users sign on using one login and password and then have access to a variety of services.

Personalization

As Dave Zielinski writes in *HRMagazine*, "Personalization has become a hallmark of many next-generation HR portals. Dynamic portals cater to users who have little patience for slogging through benefits or policy information that doesn't apply directly to them" (2010, 107). Portals allow users to personalize their settings. Personalization can include anything from a custom start-up page, a custom directory, or automatic notification of new content. This is especially important for portals that are visited frequently by the user. Workplace portals used to access HR functions, for example, can be customized so that the functions used most often are the ones highlighted by and visible in the portal.

Online Decision Support

Decision support offers tools designed to help employees compare benefits plan features, examine insurance coverage, calculate approximate medical costs, and enroll in benefits. Some say that online decision support is equivalent to having a personal consultant because it guides you through the process of making a choice. For HR professionals, these decision support features in an HR portal significantly reduce time spent on routine tasks (like answering the same question multiple times), allowing the HR professional more time to spend on strategic initiatives (Lemmergaard 2008).

Search Feature

A powerful search feature in the portal will increase its attractiveness. Search tools should work across multiple systems. Further, through the practice known as *enterprise search*, search vendors now can create tools that index documents and other texts from intranets, document management systems, e-mail folders, and database applications. As the portal's search capabilities increase, so does the likelihood that the portal will be used.

Tips and Tools for Standard Portal Design Elements

The following features appear in well-designed portals:

- RSS feeds
- Single point of access
- Navigational ease
- Social media
- Subscriptions
- Content organization
- Personalization
- Powerful search tools

How to Create a Portal

Portals have catapulted to the forefront of business interests. To be useful, both the internal employee-focused portal and the external customer-facing portal require planning and design with an objective. When you create a portal, keep both the internal and external users in mind. For the customer portal, in particular, the designer must be aware of the customer interests so that the portal reflects those interests in the content and services provided. The point is not just to expose clients to the information but to improve the interest and action level for visitors. For internal HR portals, the customer/user is the employee. So portals should combine customer profiling and intelligent content technology to encourage return visits. Externally focused portals may also offer self-service links to external business partners in the enterprise supply chain.

Steps that need to be taken before investing in a portal include:

- Surveying the organization's target audience, using a web-based analysis tool
- Interviewing a series of potential users
- Mapping the information, people, and process resources required to prototype a corporate portal
- Soliciting feedback on the initial portal prototype
- Evaluating the proposed portal using a cost-benefit analysis tool

A University Portal

Examining a specific portal can help demonstrate the functionality of a well-designed portal. Figure 6-1 shows a screen capture for The George Washington University instructor's portal. Some of the features of this instructor's portal, which is customizable, include:

- Services—E-mail, Blackboard Learning Management System, Gelman Library, Course Administration and Grading, Personal Services
- Polling features
- Chat/Meebo—The ability to communicate with a live person using the chat feature; in this case the chat is with a librarian
- Messages—Current events and other critical messages
- Feeds—Daily events, campus notifications

Portal Examples

Some examples of well-designed portals representing government, services, business, and nonprofit organizations follow:

- Government portal example—India Government
  http://india.gov.in/
- Service portal example—American Express
  https://home.americanexpress.com

* Business portal example—Siemens
  www.siemens.com

* Nonprofit organization's portal example—National Wildlife Federation
  www.nwf.org

Calculating Return on Investment (ROI)

The cost of developing and maintaining a portal varies significantly. This leads some organizations to develop the portal in-house. Others turn to vendors' hosted services. In this case, the vendor handles the hardware and software for the newer dynamic features and functions. Subscription fees range from $40,000 to more than $100,000 (Zielinski 2010). If you do not have the in-house capabilities to develop a portal, then a vendor can fill those gaps.

Dan Sullivan, in his book *The Proven Portal*, provides us with valuable information regarding how to calculate profit from an investment of this nature.

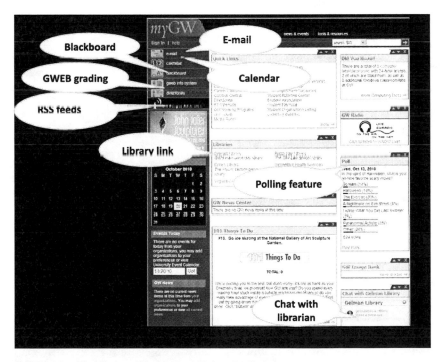

FIGURE 6-1   The George Washington University Portal
(Used with permission of The George Washington University)

He states that while no single measure is accepted as the best way to calculate the value of an expenditure on a portal, perhaps the best-known calculation is return on investment (ROI). This is the present value of future savings and increased income divided by the initial costs.

To calculate ROI, the benefit (return) of an investment (savings and increased revenue) is divided by the cost of the investment; the result is expressed as a percentage or ratio. However, it would be more accurate to use an ROI calculator. There are many such tools available online, one of which can be found at http://www.docsolid.com/roi-benefits/roi-calculator.

So for an external portal, there are initial costs (portal server, networking equipment, licenses, consulting, internal deployment costs, and training), but the recurring costs are minimal (administration), and the savings come in the form of decreased printing and distribution costs and reduced time searching for information. Revenue increases result from improved branding, more manager time on task, improved sales, and more effective advertising.

For an internal portal, it is very difficult to estimate savings and increased revenues. You can measure it in the business users' hours per week saved by using a portal-provided search engine. However, there are many other variables that impact cost, and there are hidden costs. Sullivan emphasizes instead the ways in which portals can lead to savings. These build the case for a portal from a practical viewpoint:

- Reduced printing and distribution costs
- Reduced telecommunications costs (e.g., long distance and fax costs)
- Decreased search time for information
- Decreased time spent finding operational information that facilitates decision making
- Improved forecasting based on better information
- Reduced training costs with single access point
- Reduced IT support costs through self-service
- Reduced duplication of data
- Reduced travel expenses
- Reduced call center and other support costs

The HR Professional and the HR Portal

An HR portal (one that offers access to in-house systems that handle HR functions) can be the first step in providing valuable information to employees. A well-designed HR portal can eliminate much of the administrivia, the small routine but essential details, handled day to day by HR personnel. Information about benefits, healthcare, and courseware for personal development can be offered to the internal audience by way of the portal. Knowing the core businesses within the organization enables the HR professional to target specific bodies of information that are valuable to the employee and that could impact job performance. For instance, if legislation exists that relates to the organization's goals and mission, the HR department could assist the developers to make that information available, along with other legal resources. Further, regular courseware or certification courseware can be advertised on the internal portal. Important communiqués relevant to the employees can be distributed through the portal. Thus, through input at the strategic level regarding the HR portal design, the HR professional can have a significant, positive impact.

HR-Intersect for Portal Design

Portal design and redesign offer opportunities for collaboration. HR managers will find themselves working alongside those in the Information Technology Department; that is a given. However, other key players may include members of Finance (for budget and costing), Marketing, Graphics, as well as executives. The HR manager can provide insight into the most valuable in-house, HR-based functions and how they can be offered through the portal. Further, HR can offer learning opportunities and information about communities of practice as elements of the portal.

Vanguard's Learning Portal: Case Study

Michael Smith and Catherine Lombardozzi

Vanguard is one of the world's largest investment management companies. Its mission is to help clients reach their financial goals by being the highest-value provider of investment products and services anywhere. Vanguard University is committed to accelerating learning so that the crew (employees) are well prepared to achieve business results. Envisioning the future of learning at the company, Vanguard University's management team in late 2008 adopted an "anyplace, anytime, any method, any pace" mantra as a goal for learning. The phrase captured the excitement of making "just enough" learning available at the point of need. That kind of access is, of course, made possible by technology, and a learning portal project was a critical enabler of the new vision.

At the time, Vanguard University was investing substantial technology dollars in improving the crew experience related to searching for and enrolling in formal courseware. On internal services surveys, crew consistently gave the university only 45 percent favorable ratings on questions related to the ease of use of the learning management system. Plus, as the university management team contemplated supporting learning more broadly with informal learning assets and shorter, targeted, electronically delivered material, it was clear that the LMS would not be up to the task.

The vision for the learning portal was to create an intuitive one-stop shop for all learning at Vanguard that would eliminate the crews' frustrations with the current system. To achieve this ideal future state, Vanguard University targeted the development of key functionality for learners, which included a less cumbersome enrollment process, greater access to both formal and informal learning, the ability to personalize their learning experience, recommended course notifications, and increased visibility for learning-related items.

The previous LMS provided search capabilities that were, frankly, clumsy. Feedback from crew consistently showed frustration with finding courseware, as well as with the multiple step enrollment process. The new portal enables crew members to tap into the existing corporate intranet search function to find learning assets, providing a seamless search experience that yields more accurate results. The enrollment process was streamlined to a simple click of the mouse. While the search and enrollment process was improved, Vanguard also included a learning category for informal learning. Informal learning enhances the crews' ability to be well-informed, well-skilled, and well-supported at the point of need. In addition, as the university envisions a future of crew-generated content, the informal learning capability will allow all crew to create content and share it with peers across the company via the learning portal.

Another significant enhancement the learning portal brought was the capacity for crew to receive learning recommendations, via the *Recommended for You* functionality. Crew members no longer have to search e-mails to locate the name of a required or suggested course or a pre-work assignment. The system sends alerts containing important information. To further support learning through this functionality, crew members can set learning preferences that cue the system to push learning to them based on their development goals and career interests and content that is relevant to their current jobs. Furthermore, the *Recommended for You* functionality allows for peer-to-peer recommendations, supporting the crews' desire to access relevant learning to support them in their role or career path.

The learning portal exists on the corporate intranet as the My Learning page, which combines all of the functionality into a one-stop shop for learning at Vanguard. The My Learning page also displays all learning activities for which crew members are currently enrolled, have in progress, or need to take action. While the My Learning page serves as the hub to access all of these great resources, the university recognizes that crew may not visit this page regularly enough to take advantage of all of the capabilities. To provide greater visibility to the crew, a convenient portlet was created on the corporate intranet's homepage. This provides crew quick access to all of the latest learning recommendations and scheduled learning for the coming two weeks, so the crew can be well supported in their learning at Vanguard.

The learning portal launched to rave reviews in 2009. In the first week of launch, "planned learning" jumped from seventy-five additions per day to more than 240. Over the last year, we've seen ratings on ease of use climb at last into "green" territory, with an 80-percent favorable rating. Crew members have been performing thousands of searches per day within the learning portal and are frequently accessing informal learning through this channel. But among the most important outcomes of the project was positioning the organization to take advantage of the proliferation of SharePoint sites and the accompanying learner-generated material. The learning portal will be able to make the treasures of those many sites more readily accessible to crew through portal search.

With the launch and continued upgrading of the learning portal, Vanguard is indeed able to support learning anytime, anyplace, with any method, and at any pace.

Michael Smith is a workplace learning professional with more than ten years of experience in instructional design and e-learning development. Smith manages the Creative Learning Services team for the corporate university at Vanguard. This team is composed of editorial, multimedia, and e-learning consulting professionals.

Catherine Lombardozzi, Ed.D., is a career workplace learning professional with more than twenty-five years' experience in learning management and instructional design. She manages best practices for the corporate university at Vanguard and serves as adjunct faculty in instructional design and adult learning for Penn State Great Valley, Chestnut Hill College, and The George Washington University.

Conclusion

Portals can be used in a number of ways, as has been demonstrated throughout this chapter. Typically, the organizational portal is what is presented to the customer. It can be customized to serve the internal audience of employees and, furthermore, can serve a particular function such as an access venue for HR functions in general or, as is the case with Vanguard, as a learning portal to provide access to everything learning-related. Portals surpass websites in functionality because they are interactive, service-oriented, and resource-laden. For the HR professional, a portal is a beautiful thing.

CHAPTER **7**

HRIS Selection and Implementation Processes

What Is an HRIS?

A *human resources information system* or *HRIS* is a powerful tool that is used to handle a variety of the previously labor-intensive paperwork associated with people care. The times have changed, and many trends support the move toward an HRIS. Some of the social and economic trends include the alternating periods of expansion and downsizing as well as that restructuring and redeploying that takes place continually within organizations. Increased security that necessitates background checks is a time-consuming and paper-intensive process. And the shift to view employees as "human capital," rather than assets, forces HR to position itself differently. Outsourcing HR, in part because it is not a direct profit center, has become increasingly more attractive to organizations. Everyone knows that even though outsourcing to another company may make the HR functions faster and cheaper, an outside organization does not understand the culture and the employee profile of an organization.

The good news is that systems from all of the well-established and longer-term vendors have now reached a mature state (Meade 2003). The look and feel has been standardized, so now is a good time to invest in an HRIS. But if you are not yet convinced, peruse the list of situations below that indicate when you need an HRIS.

You Know You Need a Human Resource Information System When...

This (partial) list can be used to determine whether your organization should invest in a human resources information system. You know you need an HRIS when:

- HR is overwhelmed with "administrivia," tedious but essential routine tasks. When HR professionals spend more time on paperwork than they spend actually developing, assisting, and training employees, or when HR spends more time on things than people, it is time to consider an HRIS.
- HR staff spends 60 to 70 percent of its time on employees' questions. If there is a communication and information-flow problem, then it is time for an HRIS.
- HR professionals need to concentrate on strategic work. If the HR Department is mired in detail and has no time to contribute on the strategic business level, it is time for an HRIS.
- the organizational strategy is for employees to take charge of their own HR management. If the management of some HR functions should be handled by those directly affected by the decisions, then it is time for an HRIS.
- HR seeks a leadership role in knowledge management. When HR realizes that it has the knowledge and information to assist in the knowledge management effort, it is a good time to invest in an HRIS.
- the business lacks competitive advantage. If the organization would be made leaner and stronger by reducing endless hours of HR administrivia, then it is time to invest in an HRIS.
- the organization is struggling to recruit. When the marketing and search agencies are not yielding the results that the organization requires and the organization is not drawing in quality employees, it is time to think about an HRIS.
- the goal is to transform HR and take leadership. If HR is taking a backseat to all of the other divisions and it is time to get into the driver's seat, then that is a good time to get an HRIS.
- legacy systems must be replaced with new millennium technology. This is especially true when the rest of the organization has updated its technology, but the Human Resources Department lags behind. It is time to get an HRIS.

HR-Intersect for HRIS Selection

As in most areas involving HR and technology, the HRIS selection process requires collaborative decision making. There are two separate kinds of linkages: external and internal. You may consider partnerships with outside vendors in order to obtain the most effective HRIS configuration that satisfies your organization's needs. In-house, you should collaborate with line management, the Information Technology (IT) division, the Finance division, and the Marketing division. The IT division can provide details regarding the organization's current systems and infrastructure. This critical information will have an impact on the solution. It is possible that you will need to use modules within an existing enterprise resource planning system, or this may be the first time your organization has made a foray into HRIS territory, in which case the infrastructure will play a major role in your selection process.

Line management will have varying degrees of involvement depending upon how much of the HR role has been pushed to managers. For instance, if performance reviews such as the 360-degree reviews are distributed, collected, and handled by individual managers, then they should have input on the requirements for that feature. The IT department is a critical partner in these decisions and *must* be involved. Finance will have budgetary information and should participate in the cost-benefit analysis as well as in the requirements gathering phase. Marketing may be using a customer (or client) relationship management (CRM) system that collects valuable client information necessary for that division. It may be that HR functions will share the same database as the CRM. In any case, collaboration is the rule of the game!

The Ideal HRIS

The human resource information system (HRIS) evolved over the past thirty years. It began with a focus on data, storage, process, and flows that resulted in summative-level reports for management. It moved toward a management information system (MIS) that had an information focus, this time with an inquiry and report generation feature. Next it migrated to a decision support system that had flexibility and adaptability and quick response, allowing for user-initiated and controlled support for personal decision making (Thite and Kavanagh 2009).

Recent Developments in the Evolution of HRIS

The most recent phase in HRIS evolution is what some identify as a human resources management decision system (HRMDS). The HRMDS has report formation and generation capabilities that aid in managerial decision making, can categorize reports by management level, generates reports at a frequency and timing based on use, and provides historical information so that results of previous decisions are documented. The HRMDS ideally combines all of the best features of the earlier verision HRIS. It provides critical information for decision making, and in so doing, it goes well beyond the standard system.

The HRIS configuration will vary based on the organization. While there are standard functions basic to the human resource practice, the organization's mission, vision, policies, and procedures should impact the features included in the HRIS.

Standard components of an HRIS include:

- Performance management
- Compensation
- Benefits
- Payroll

Other features offered as part of an HRIS may be:

- Recruitment and selection
- Training and development

Employee self-service (ESS) can provide direct access to the employee so that he may make decisions and register those decisions directly into the system without the intervention of a middle-person or HR representative. These can be enabled by an HR portal such as those described in chapter 6. The cost benefits of this approach are obvious.

Enterprise Resource Planning

Made possible by relational databases, *enterprise resource planning* (ERP) business applications handle a wide variety of organizational functions such as human resource–related functions, the general ledger, accounts payable, accounts receivable, order management, inventory control, and customer relationship management. In short, ERPs integrate all processes within and around the organization. ERPs are reliable, well-structured backbones of large organizations. They use technologies that are proven to execute process flows in a secure environment. ERPs have front-end software for customer-relations management, call centers, e-mail, project planning, mobile maintenance, and other features (Hofmann 2008). The typical ERP system runs multiple databases and applications on back-end servers. The user interface runs on desktop PCs or laptops. ERPs are, however, complex and expensive. A more recent version of the ERP is "agile ERP," enabled by cloud computing (Pincher 2010).

Databases and the HRIS or ERP

The HRIS relies upon a database. A *database* is a permanent, self-descriptive store of interrelated data items that can be processed by one or more business applications and serves as a central repository for electronic data (Marler and Floyd 2009). The early file-based data structures functioned much like storage in paper filing cabinets with a drawer for each type of business document. This type of organization resulted in redundant data, poor data control, inadequate data manipulation, and excessive programming. These databases were good at handling transactions, but not as good at handling queries. The file-based databases were typical in the mid-1960s and early 1970s (Kavanagh and Thite 2009, 30).

In 1970, E. F. Codd introduced the concepts for a relational database. Most databases today are relational databases or object-oriented relational databases. Why do you care about these differences? First, as a central repository of data, a database is a valuable organizational asset and, therefore, needs to be managed appropriately. Second, the differences impact cost and the ability to query the system for specific information. Additionally, because data are the lifeblood of an organization, database production and maintenance are critical to the operation of the organization (Marler and Floyd 2009).

Hierarchy of Knowledge

Databases have, at their core, assumptions about the hierarchy of knowledge, about what's important and what isn't. Data represent the facts. Information is the interpretation of the data. Knowledge is information that has meaning. Data, information, and knowledge are all important to capture and store, tasks that can be done using a database. We will expand on this hierarchy in chapter 16, but for now we will deal with the first three levels: data, information, and knowledge.

The Database Management System

A *database management system (DBMS)* electronically manages stored data (Kavanagh and Thite 2010). A DBMS is a set of software applications that are used with their associated databases to allow organizations to manage data. The main functions of a DBMS are to create the database, insert, read, update, and delete database data, maintain data integrity and security, and prevent data from being lost by providing backup and recovery capabilities. Through the DBMS, organizations identify data to store, store the data, preserve its quality, query, retrieve the data, create reports, and determine who has access to those data.

Relational Databases and Relational Database Management System

A relational database differs particularly in the way that data are stored. In *relational databases*, data are stored in tables. Each table represents an entity and all

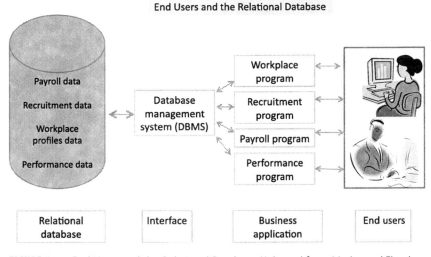

FIGURE 7-1   End Users and the Relational Database (Adapted from Marler and Floyd 2009)

of the related information about that entity (Marler and Floyd 2009). The value of this form of categorization is that it eliminates redundant data and allows sharing of information between functional units and management levels and across geographically dispersed locations. This easy exchange of information makes possible large-scale integrated applications like an enterprise resource planning (ERP) business application. For a visual representation of how the end users access the relational database, see Figure 7-1.

The relational database structure allows for flexible linkages and thus more powerful queries. ERPs and HRISs are dependent upon relational databases. Common fields in an HR database would include information like the employee ID, first name, last name, gender, veteran status, skill code, training/certification, job code, department, division/location, benefits, etc. The database management system serves as the interface with the database. The HR professional uses the application software (such as the HRIS), which links to the DBMS for access to the database.

Microsoft Access Database

Another option for smaller organizations (because it is less expensive) is the Microsoft (MS) Access database. It differs from other commercial databases in that it integrates the database application and DBMS into one relational DBMS.

Because MS Access is a relatively small database, it should be used only for smaller organizations. It requires limited knowledge of database programming. The functions provided in MS Access allow you to:

- Create databases containing tables and table relationships
- Add new records, change table values in existing records, and delete records
- Use built-in query language by which you can obtain immediate answers to questions you ask about data
- Generate reports using a built-in Report Wizard, with which you can produce professional-looking, formatted reports from your data

Protect the information stored in the database through security, control, and recovery facilities (Kavanagh and Thite 2009). The data in the MS Access table can be exported to other database applications or to spreadsheet programs. This allows further analysis. MS Access handles more data than spreadsheet software programs. As mentioned before, smaller companies—of 1,000 or less employees—can use an HRIS such as HRVantage or HRSource, which are based on MS Access (37–38).

Queries

Now we get to an important aspect of databases: the queries. Once you have chosen the database and entered the data into it, you can create different types of questions—queries—that form the basis for the wide variety of reports available from a database. Queries result in valuable management-level decision-making information.

The conditions that drive the selection of a database include budget and the size of the organization. The complexity of the database needed will increase with the size of the organization, and, not surprisingly, the complexity will also impact cost.

The option of using open-source HRIS is in its infancy but is becoming more viable (Roberts 2009). *Open-source* software "is available under a no-fee license that permits users to download, change, and improve the software, and to redistribute it in modified form," according to the Open Source Initiative (see *http://opensource.org*). Open-source HRIS is currently not yet viable, but it will mature (Roberts 2009). Available open-source HRISs do not offer the level of privacy and security necessary for most organizations, but when the technology comes of age it will offer significant cost benefits.

Build, Customize, or Buy

Three basic choices are involved in the physical design of the HRIS: build your own organization-specific HRIS, customize an off-the-shelf (COTS) system, or buy, meaning outsource development to an external vendor. All three choices impact costs to varying degrees. Kavanagh and Thite (2009) detail these strategies and the appropriate situation for use.

Build

When the business need is unique and the in-house skills exist both at the functional and technical level, then there is a good case for building the system in-house. Additionally, there must be an in-house, skilled project manager. The development timeframe can be flexible if using in-house developers. The advantages include customization and control over all aspects of the development. The software will meet 100 percent of the business requirements. And there will be increased flexibility and innovative solutions for business process accommodation.

Customize

A *customized off-the-shelf (COTS)* system is appropriate when the business need is considered standard. COTS is a prepackaged commercial product that has been tested and is stable. It can be purchased and implemented in a short timeframe. The bad news is that there will, no doubt, need to be modifications made to customize the system, because most purchased systems will meet, at most, 70 percent of the organization's need (Kavanagh and Thite 2009). In that case, the organization will have to work with the vendor to customize the system or do the customization in-house. The potential risk is that the software may be incompatible with the organization's business processes. This increases the costs. And if the vendor has an upgrade, the customization must be redone.

Outsource

Outsourcing, or buying, the development through an *Application Service Provider (ASP)* is the third option. Outsourcing has its advantages. For one thing, the external developer has more resources to bring to bear. Further, the Application Service Provider (ASP) has experience and technical skills specific to the HRIS design process. The downside, however, is that the ASP must be permitted access to proprietary information, which can easily be misused. Also, it can be a costly process, regardless of the resources.

TABLE 7-1 Strategies for Software Acquisition

Development Strategies	Business Need	In-House Skills	Project Management Skills	Timeframe
In-House	Unique	Functional and technical expertise in-house	Project has skilled and experienced project manager	Flexible
COTS	Standard	Functional expertise exists	Project manager in-house with experience to coordinate and manage vendor relationship	Short
Outsourcing	Noncore function	Functional and technical expertise not in-house	Project has manager with experience to manage an outsourcing relationship	Flexible or short

Table 7-1: Strategies for Software Acquisition is adapted from Kavanagh and Thite (2009). It demonstrates the pros and cons of each strategy.

In the three approaches of in-house development, customizing an off-the-shelf product, and outsourcing, four different elements should influence the final decision: the business need, in-house skills, project management skills, and timeframe all have an impact on that acquisition strategy.

HRIS Selection Approach for Small to Mid-Size Organizations

According to Gueutal and Stone (2005), some of the questions that should be considered when selecting an HRIS include:

- What is the cost?
- Does it offer a centralized database?
- How easy is the updating process?
- What technical support is offered?
- What is the implementation timetable?
- How will it integrate with other HR systems?
- What are the demands on internal Information Technology (IT) resources?

These questions are a starting point in the process, the answers to which offer baseline information necessary for HRIS selection. There is, however, a well-defined due diligence process. HRIS selection requires rigorous research, which must take place before vendors can be invited to show their wares and certainly before the company makes an important selection.

James Meade (2003) clearly delineates the HRIS selection process in his text entitled *The Human Resources Software Handbook: Evaluating Technology Solutions for Your Organization*. Meade emphasizes the following steps: gather requirements, write a demonstration script, create a vendor selection checklist of requirements, identify qualified vendors, invite three or four vendors to present capabilities according to the script, and generate a vendor comparison report before making the selection. Each of these steps will be described in greater detail.

Gather Requirements

Requirements gathering is a skill in and of itself. The purpose of the requirements gathering phase is to detail all of the HR functions and their associated system requirements for the HRIS. This information is collected through survey, interviews, and process analysis; it is the equivalent of a self-assessment and internal needs analysis (*HR Focus* 2009). The purpose is to identify what is in place that must be replicated or improved and what additional features are needed. Once those requirements are collected, they should be ranked based on the organization's mission, vision, and values. Weigh which features will bring fast and dramatic bottom-line impact, such as lowering costs, improving processes, or increasing revenue or cash flow. Identify solutions and vendors who may be part of that solution.

Write a Demonstration Script

Put all of the requirement information into a chart or spreadsheet (Meade 2003; Kavanagh and Thite 2010). Create categories and sort the information by category in the order of importance. You may even add a point value to weight each factor. Then create a list of scenarios for the most important features, basing the scenarios on real-life examples. For instance, ask how the application would handle documentation for maternity leave or how it accommodates the Family and Medical Leave Act.

Create a Vendor Selection Checklist of Requirements

Before inviting vendors to present their products, create a vendor assessment and selection checklist from the requirements list. Place the system requirements down the side of the chart and a column for each vendor, with enough room to record the vendor's ability to meet each system requirement (Meade 2003). The request for proposal is also a possible venue to find vendors, albeit more complicated and time-consuming (*HR Focus* 2009). During the vendor demonstration you will use the checklist to evaluate how well the vendor met the system requirements and to assess each vendor's capabilities. Ensure that critical items in the list are weighted (*HR Focus* 2009). Invite other HR professionals within the organization, as well as other involved individuals, to observe the demos. Use the checklist as a guide, but don't just stick with the script, because the vendors may have useful capabilities that were not previously identified.

Identify Qualified Vendors

How do you find appropriate vendors? Research possible software solutions; use Internet searches and analyst reports. Refer to trade publications, attend tradeshows, and discuss your organization's HRIS needs with members of your community of practice or other associations to find potential software vendors. Contact the vendors with which the organization currently has a contract to research integration information. Create a list of vendors resulting from your research. Then reduce the list of vendors of interest to three or four.

Invite Vendors to Present Their Capabilities

Once you have a short list of vendors, invite them to come in to demonstrate their system. Generally the vendors should come at separate times, not all at once. Provide them with the script beforehand so they are prepared to show that their software addresses each of the identified requirements. You should also request sample reports having to do with the roles identified.

Schedule a block of time—at least two hours—for the demonstration. Vendors should follow the script. Observe how the software application performs in response. Be sure that you have also assembled a group of qualified evaluators who know how to use the vendor assessment checklist and who can be relied upon to help with the assessment process.

Generate a Vendor Comparison Report

After conducting the vendor demonstration sessions, examine and assess the data. Create a vendor comparison report. Take into consideration any reactions of the evaluators to the presenters and their presentations, and weigh those responses into the mix. Sometimes body language and the interplay that takes place during a demo between the vendor and the panel provides good qualitative information that may indicate how well the vendor will work with your organization.

Make the Selection

Finally, make the selection based upon the vendor who best met the requirements criteria. Then build a business case in support of the choice. If possible, calculate the estimated return on investment. Examine the licensing agreement, term, and work needed to implement the system, and identify the impact on work processes, and calculate the project cost. These are standard components of a business case. Be sure to follow up with the vendors that you have not chosen as a courtesy.

ERP Government Adaptation of PeopleSoft: Case Study

Richard Ray

For purposes of this case study, names and locations have been altered to protect identities.

In the late 1990s, Congress mandated that government agencies collaborate across government to look for ways to reduce cost, increase the use of technology in managing human capital, and develop "lines of business" designed to offer government agencies shared services. Human Capital Information System (HCIS) was developed by leaders at a 150,000-employee agency to meet this congressional mandate. It was anticipated that a budget of $50 million over a seven-year period (by 2002) would lead to 800,000 federal employees being able to access their personal and payroll information in a shared services format. This would potentially save the taxpayers $80 million a year in total human resources management. It was further decided that this budget would be expended through the use of contractor labor with a minimal-supervision staff of federal employees. A competitive bid was held, and Contractor America (CA) agreed to perform the work in four years for $40 million. Additionally, it was determined that a commercial off-the-shelf-software (COTS) would be used to save costs in development, to learn lessons from other private sector organizations, and to speed implementation to an agency-wide system.

By 2002, more than $150 million had been "invested" by federal agencies, mostly through purchasing services from CA and more services from CA and affiliated consulting groups. The program office created for HCIS continued to seek funding, engage CA, and sell their services to other agencies. By 2004, approximately $212 million had been expended, but only 144,000 employees had signed in to the system (not 800,000), with only 17,000 (not 800,000) using it on a "regular basis." The leadership of the HCIS program office was a continually revolving door. The only thing consistent in the operation was the utilization of CA consultants and programmers to develop and "help administer" the system.

There was often debate about the real mission of HRIC among its leadership team. The strategic nature of creating an engaging and user-friendly system gave way to the day-to-day management of how many rows of code had been programmed and which legacy system had to stay live.

The technology selected was a standard COTS. PeopleSoft was selected because of its comprehensive platform and offerings. It could manage the payroll interface, time and wage tracking, benefits administration, etc. While a very vague statement of work was signed between HCIS and CA, continual contract review and negation occurred. A great amount of renegotiation and modification occurred, which resulted in expensive overruns. System "reworks," the addition of new PeopleSoft experts, and poor leadership contributed to the overruns as well. Not only was the leadership unstable (three leaders in five years), "special projects" and promising/selling the system often pulled resources and staff in directions inconsistent with senior leadership and the congressional mandate.

The technology was supposed to facilitate employees' and supervisors' learning and administrative independence over their own personnel data. If deployed as intended, users would be able to use the modified PeopleSoft functionality to manage their competency development, performance management, and training/knowledge acquisition.

Currently, the implementation has resulted in 200,000 (not 800,000) employees signing on to the system, with approximately 50,000 (again, not 800,000) determined as regular users. Almost $270 million has been spent to this point, and the agency has launched an audit to investigate how the taxpayer investment has been spent and whether the original objectives of the program are being met.

An unplanned cost (other than the nearly $220 million overrun) is that HR leaders, operations leaders and employees have lost confidence in the HCIS program leadership. Stakeholders have also become weary of the promises that the HCIS will solve their human capital problems.

There are many lessons that can be learned from this implementation.

1. Before investing in a human resources information technology such as a knowledge management or a payroll performance management system, it is important to make sure that the leadership strategy is clear and can be communicated to all stakeholders.
2. Create an audit process that ensures that the HR leadership is in charge of the project—*not* the consultants. Often, when leadership is unsure, consultants stop becoming advisors and become de facto directors.
3. Identify clear phase checkpoints to make sure that deliverables are met on time and that an independent audit process is created to evaluate the changes.
4. Project leadership should participate in leadership team training, which might include action learning, communication skills, decision-making skills, conflict management skills, and general team project management.

Richard Ray, Ed.D., is a managing partner at Workforce Systems Design.

Tips and Tools for Selecting HRIS Software

1. Identify and gather requirements
2. Create requirements script, including role-based scenarios
3. Write vendor selection checklist with weighted requirements
4. Identify Qualified Vendors
5. Invite vendors to demonstrate software, provide reports, and submit proposals
6. Generate a vendor comparison report
7. Make your selection and write a business case supporting your decision

The vendor software selection process follows a clearly defined approach. At its core is the need to find the software best suited to the organization's needs. The process should not be taken lightly. Once made, the decision will impact the purpose, workflow, and job descriptions of the HR department and most of the positions within the organization.

Conclusion

Human resource information systems vary in size, sophistication, and functionality. An HRIS may be part of a larger ERP, or it may be a stand-alone system. While there are a variety of features that are offered by an HRIS, selection of an HRIS should be based on what the organization needs the HRIS to do. Collaboration is the key in the HRIS selection process. Although the system primarily handles HR functions, many departments will be impacted by the HRIS, so representatives from other functional areas should participate in the selection and implementation of an HRIS.

CHAPTER 8

e-Recruiting

In the twenty-first century, a new breed of online recruiting organizations has seized the recruiting niche of corporate job site hosting (Brooks 2001). Instead of handling the complex hiring process as a face-to-face endeavor, organizations turn to Internet-enabled solutions to streamline the recruitment process. E-recruiting allows users to handle the recruitment process from a desktop computer.

E-recruiting is not new, but it is gaining in popularity, and there are several new developments. How does e-recruiting in this century differ from the last? What kinds of candidates are attracted to e-recruiting? Why use e-recruiting? And how does e-recruiting implementation impact business processes? This chapter addresses these questions and more. Both the positives and negatives of e-recruiting are investigated, and options for e-recruiting are examined. Additionally, the corporate and IT governance issues for implementing large-scale e-recruiting systems will be discussed.

How Twenty-First-Century e-Recruiting Differs from e-Recruiting of the Past

In the twenty-first century, e-recruiting allows the host organization to perform all of the computer-based actions related to recruitment. From the comfort of their computers, users can create a library of job requisitions, establish those requisitions, post to more than 1,000 job boards, and use a centralized database of candidates for searches and management of applicant information. The most significant departure from twentieth-century recruiting is the Internet-enabled aspect, which makes the recruiting process better, faster, (potentially) cheaper, and more strategic. The strategic aspect made possible by e-recruiting results from HR's participation in the recruitment with a purpose.

An enduring business shift has occurred in the twenty-first century. Compared with the previous century, when "assets" typically referred to the cash and physical property a company owned, the early twenty-first century is an era in which a significant portion of organizational assets are composed not of physical property, but rather of intellectual property and human capital (Reynolds and Weiner 2009). This raises recruitment to a higher level of importance in an organization's success. Strategic impact occurs when HR joins with other senior executives to answer questions such as:

- How many and what sort of worker do we need to succeed and move forward?
- What challenges present themselves as we compete for this talent?
- How will we address potential shortages of people and skills in the available talent pool?
- How will we preserve and enhance the culture and values of the organization?
- What measures can we take to identify and retain effective strategic leaders for the future?

Answers to these questions frame the pursuit of an e-recruiting strategy.

e-Recruiting Positives and Negatives

Like any other process, e-recruiting has both positives and negatives.

The positive aspects of e-recruiting attract organizations. E-recruiting can produce significant cost savings: companies have reported savings of 95 percent when changing from traditional to online recruiting sources (Pfieffelmann, Wagner, and Libkuman 2010). E-recruiting can also provide higher applicant yields (Cober, Brown, Blumental, Doverspike, and Levy 2000). Software can be used to screen out unqualified applicants. Applicant data are easily imported into the database, and searches for résumés can be done using keywords, job histories, etc. And the recruitment cycle can be shorted by the efficiencies offered by online recruiting (Gueutal and Stone 2005).

On the flip side, there are negative aspects to e-recruiting. Poor website design can harm recruitment outcomes. If the navigation and user interface are poorly conceived, job seekers may not be attracted to the site. Poor design also reflects negatively on the organization, thereby potentially diminishing the power to attract high-caliber applicants. Further, if the website does not accurately represent the organization, an applicant's disappointment may impact her satisfaction, performance, commitment, job involvement, and tenure once she is hired (Pfieffelmann, Wagner, and Libkuman 2010). E-recruiting *does not always* draw higher-quality candidates. However, it consistently attracts those with higher levels of education (Chapman and Webster 2003). E-recruiting may have a perceived invasion of privacy, which could deter some from applying. E-recruiting systems may be subject to unauthorized access to data through a breach of the system's security (Harris, Van Hoye, and Lievens 2003); if this should happen, it would negatively impact the entire organization, not just the HR department.

How e-Recruiting Relates to Recruitment Objectives

Undeniably, e-recruiting has both negatives and positives, but the important issue for any organization is whether e-recruitment aligns with the organization's objectives. That is the touchstone for whether e-recruiting is right for the organization.

Standard recruitment objectives typically include cost, speed of filling job vacancies, psychological contract fulfillment, satisfaction and retention rates, quality and quantity of applicants, and diversity of applicants (Lukaszewski, Dickter, Lyons, and Kehoe 2009). If e-recruiting satisfies all of these objectives, why even continue reading?

There is some controversy over whether e-recruiting satisfies these standard recruitment objectives. For instance, cost savings can be realized through e-recruiting; but wait just a minute before you place that call. Failure to examine and map out the entire recruitment process, including how to process résumés, screen out unsuccessful candidates, etc., can result in more paperwork rather than less. So the labor hours to process résumés could actually increase rather than decrease. Such a scenario, should it occur, would mitigate the potential cost benefits.

Additionally, the e-recruiting system must be evaluated to see if the target number of yield ratios and placements align with the organizational goals. The number of applicants generated through an e-recruiting tool can place an increased processing burden on the organization. Or the tool may not attract the people needed for the jobs. The economies of scale can be undermined by these issues.

With regard to filling job vacancies, research shows that online recruitment can decrease cycle time and increase efficiencies. This is a good thing. However, what about the quality of those hired? Although the process to placement time may decrease, how can the organization be assured that the best candidate was chosen?

Employee satisfaction and retention rates also inform decision making about whether to invest in e-recruiting. The information applicants obtain and the perceptions they form during the recruitment process can impact retention rates. Although e-recruiting may shorten the cycle time from application to hiring, the missing human touch can adversely impact the process. Some cultures find this omission particularly troublesome. Further, if those who are hired do not get their questions answered before starting or if they do not receive the attention they need, they may not be properly invested in the company, and this may negatively impact retention. If the message applicants receive during recruitment differs from the reality of the workplace in significant negative ways, the new employee may become disgruntled. For example, if the candidate wants to telecommute, and the organization disallows telecommuting but does not make that clear through the e-recruiting process, the employee may find that the time and expense of traveling becomes a disadvantage of the job and may choose to leave the job. So the recruitment website must clearly portray the organization's message and not create unrealistic expectations.

The brand that is portrayed on the company website must align with the true culture of the organization. Clear identification of the organization's mission, values, and culture on the e-recruiting website removes the guessing game for the applicants. It is more likely that the organization will attract individuals who will work well within the organization if the applicants know what to expect.

Similarly, the recruitment message must be realistic. The job for which the organization is hiring must be accurately described. Realistic job and culture previews hosted on the organization's recruiting website can provide a balanced view of the organization and the job opportunity.

Legal Ramifications

The United States has very clear regulations regarding handling of applicant information. U.S. laws dictate that employers maintain detailed information about applicants. The quantity and quality of applicants is heavily dependent upon the screening that occurs during the e-recruiting process. The U.S. Office of Federal Contract Compliance Programs (OFCCP) establishes four criteria by which a true applicant is identified:

1. The individual must submit an expression of interest in the job through the Internet.
2. The company considers the individual for employment for a specific job.

3. The individual's expression of interest also indicates that the individual is qualified for the position.
4. The individual at no point prior to receipt of the offer of employment removes himself or herself from consideration.

Online selection processes should be mapped to these criteria in order to be compliant with U.S. federal law. Although many seekers may approach the job website, only the truly qualified should become applicants. In order to avoid diluting the pool of true applicants with those who are unqualified, follow the preceding guidelines.

Candidates for e-Recruiting

E-recruiting is not for everyone; nor is it a panacea to all hiring needs. One consideration to keep in mind is how the applicant pool is affected by the online environment. Another cause for deliberation is the literature on the types of candidates who are attracted to e-recruiting websites.

Age, gender, and ethnic differences come into play in the online recruiting environment. Research indicates that young, computer-literate, and well-educated individuals are attracted to online recruitment (Galanaki 2002). Age may be negatively related to the perceived ease of using the Internet to apply for a job. Employed men are more likely to search for jobs on the Internet. Research also indicates that, while the differential use rates between men and women no longer exist in the United States and Canada, sex differences in level of e-recruiting usage remain in most other countries (International Telecommunication Union 2002).

Because online recruiting requires individuals to have a computer, those who do not have computers are less likely to apply using that medium, even if public access through library computers or other sources is available. Additionally, the individuals who prefer e-recruiting tend to be looking for high-level jobs. Ethnic minorities are less likely to use online recruiting, although African American candidates may be more likely to use e-recruiting than personal recruitment sources. An explanation of the attraction of e-recruiting for African Americans is the assumption that discrimination is less likely to occur in an online environment (McManus and Ferguson 2003).

Educational background and personality characteristics may also come into play with regard to whether a candidate finds e-recruiting attractive. McManus and Ferguson (2003) state that the Internet tends to attract those with four-year or graduate degrees. Conversely, those with high levels of computer anxiety or low levels of confidence using computers are unlikely to use an e-recruiting tool (Van Rooy, Alonso, and Fairchild 2003).

Finally, McManus and Ferguson (2003) state that those who research jobs using online recruitment may have a less-attractive background (meaning perhaps they have something to hide) than those recruited by face-to-face methods. They may also stay on the job for a shorter period of time.

Social Networking and e-Recruiting

A recent trend in e-recruiting has been the use of social networking sites as an approach to screening candidates. We address social networking in detail in chapter 12, although here we'd like to note that social networks are online groupings of individuals who are like-minded and want to exchange ideas and interests. Social networking can be used for personal, interest-based, or professional reasons. In recent years, applicants for jobs have been asked to submit the social network sites they use for review by the hiring organization. Hiring managers examine the sites as a kind of background check, in order to determine the potential new hire's sense of propriety and ability to separate their work life and behavior from their personal life (Brandenburg 2008, 601). While this practice is under legal review, it is being done on a regular basis (Society for Human Resource Management 2010, 102).

Recruiting Cross-Cultural Candidates Online

Using an online recruitment approach to attract qualified candidates can have its challenges. They are not insurmountable, but they certainly must be considered. The most obvious barrier is language. Online recruitment systems must be able to adjust to a variety of languages. This is especially necessary with global industries that may find talent in any number of places worldwide.

Adjustments must be made to the assessment process for bilingual and native-language candidates. Otherwise, a pool of talented candidates could be unwittingly eliminated. Translation of major portions of the recruitment and selection process with a language proficiency test in the core language is one way to ensure adequate fluency. Another possible scenario for dealing with multicultural, multilingual barriers is to develop a separate recruitment program for each targeted location of a business operation. Alternatively, the global program can have a bilingual and native assessment in multiple markets (Reynolds and Weiner 2009).

When considering implementing an online recruitment system for a multi-cultural, dispersed audience, the organization must be sure to accommodate the candidates. What adaptations must be made to enable assessment of applicants in a multicultural, multilingual e-recruiting audience? The kinds of considerations can be grouped into the following categories: administrative considerations, measurement quality, professionalism, and technology (Reynolds and Weiner 2009).

Administrative considerations include language requirements and adaptations, gauging language proficiency in the business language of the region, and implementing complicated assessment practices. It is important to make the policies clear and to establish processes for identifying candidates' primary language and proficiency. When providing candidates with an option to be assessed in another language, it is crucial that those instructions also be clear.

To ensure measurement quality for cross-cultural assessments, the assessment instrument must be adapted for the culture. Adaptation includes providing clear guidelines; converting content so that it features relevant, culturally appropriate examples, terms, and graphics; having an expert translator review the assessment tool; piloting the tool before it goes live; ensuring that the measurement tools are equivalent across cultures; and adapting the tool to the educational level of the applicants. Finally, select an assessment instrument that is culturally appropriate.

The International Testing Commission publishes comprehensive guidelines for adapting tests to a cross-cultural audience. Adhere to these standards. They can be found at the following website: *www.intestcom.org/itc_projects.htm.*

Technology has its challenges, and they are perhaps even greater when a multicultural audience is involved. Basic design considerations—such as the user interface and ease of navigation through the assessment tool—become even more important. How to print, submit information, identify progress, and so on, must all be clearly delineated. The system designer must incorporate different language packages and find a simple way to portray the language choice to the user. There may be a need for a helpline or call center to support the users if there should be any technical difficulties.

When implementing e-recruiting on an interregional or global scale, many issues arise that are not considerations for a single-culture target audience. Think about these issues *before* deployment, and find solutions that fit your intended audience. If the online recruiting may attract qualified candidates from other cultures, preparations must be made to accommodate them.

The Technology of e-Recruiting

Recruiting technologies have changed in this century. Problems that emerged from using a combination of large-scale systems and customized software add-ons can be solved more easily now. A variety of innovations allow systems to talk with each other and share information.

In the past, for example, an organization may have implemented an HRIS or enterprise resource planning system (ERP) and then determined there was a need to automate the tests as part of the selection process. If the selection system was not part of the larger HRIS or ERP, it was difficult to move information from one system to another. However, new integration facilitators such as integrating software systems and *Simple Object Access Protocol (SOAP)* enable easy access. SOAP operates as a set of instructions using a standard language, XML, which allows information to be transferred between systems (Reynolds and Weiner 2009). Test scores, for example, can be obtained from the testing system by transferring that information to the HRIS.

Service-Oriented Architecture (SOA)—The New Paradigm

The new paradigm for integration moves beyond reliance on programming languages to a tool called *service-oriented architecture*. A service-oriented architecture (SOA) is the underlying structure supporting communications between computer services. SOA defines how two computing entities, such as programs, interact in a way that enables one entity to perform a unit of work on behalf of another entity. Each interaction is self-contained and loosely coupled.

Sandy Carter (2007) explains SOA in her book *The New Language of Business SOA and Web 2.0*, that SOA obtains its power from the fact that it can connect systems that typically cannot talk to each other. Another way to look at it is by using an analogy: The key word to understanding SOA, Carter points out, is the word "architecture," and she likens the SOA process to that of building a house. The approach to SOA is similar to homebuilding in that you create design blueprints, set your foundation, and build from the inside out, making sure that, all the while, you can move freely from one room to another without being hindered by walls or doors—"walls" and "doors" being proprietary applications (xiv).

Whether you realize it or not, you've probably relied upon SOA, perhaps when you made a purchase online. You look at a company's catalog and choose a number of items. You specify your order through one service, which communicates with an inventory service to find out if the items you've requested are available. Your order and shipping details are submitted to another service, which calculates your total, tells you when your order should arrive, and furnishes a tracking number that, through another service, allows you to keep track of your order's status and location en route to your door. The entire process, from the initial order to its delivery, is managed by communications between the web services—programs talking to other programs, all made possible through SOA (*www.techtarget.com*).

What relevance does SOA have to e-recruiting? It has a lot. The need to connect different parts of the organization can be enabled through SOA. Stand-alone e-recruiting systems must be integrated with existing HRIS and enterprise resource planning systems (ERPs). Sandy Carter (2007) relates that "the average Fortune 500 company has more than forty-eight different financial systems and three enterprise resource planning systems" (103). Success requires that the organization leverage what currently exists. SOA can do that by loosely coupling the systems together. SOA is, however, an expensive endeavor that will likely not be a feasible solution for small to mid-sized organizations.

Cloud Computing (SaaS, PaaS, and IaaS)

White papers and articles abound on the topic of cloud computing. It is not a fad but rather a solution that is quite attractive. What is *cloud computing*? Stated simply, cloud computing is web-based processing in which shared resources, software, and information are provided to computers and other devices on demand. A cloud service has three distinct characteristics that differentiate it from traditional hosting. It is sold on demand, typically by the minute or the hour; it is elastic—a user can have as much or as little of a service as they want at any given time; and the service is fully managed by the provider. The consumer needs nothing but a personal computer and Internet access (*www. techtarget.com*). Miller and Veiga (2009), cloud computing experts working for Noblis, Inc., describe the taxonomy of cloud computing in their article "Cloud Computing: Will Commodity Services Benefit Users Long Term?" They explain that there are three layers to cloud computing: the top layer is the software-as-a-service (SaaS) model, in which applications are delivered on demand; the next tier, or middleware, called platform-as-a-service (PaaS), provides application services or a platform for offering services; the final tier is the flexible infrastructure-as-a-service (IaaS) offering distributed data center services. All three services rely upon the Internet for delivery of services (57). Typically, a single user will access the cloud through a service provider like Salesforce, Amazon, or Google.

Dave Zielinski (2009) writes in *HRMagazine* that software-as-a-service (SaaS) has made life easier for HR managers in a variety of ways. An organization establishes a contract with a cloud computing vendor, and under that contract, information technology maintenance is handled by the vendor's staff, upgrades are made easier, and self-service and automated reporting features offload some of the more mundane features of the HR job. Most attractive are the cost benefits because, rather than buying the software or hardware, you pay only for the software that you use. Think of cloud computing as a pay-as-you-go plan. An analogy might be getting milk delivered to your home rather than buying a cow in order to get some milk!

Enthusiasm for SaaS is shared by many, including Robert Desisto of the Gartner Group's research team. He states in his article "Four Steps to Get in Front of the SaaS Curve" that SaaS enables companies with limited IT resources to use software capabilities that they otherwise could not afford (2010). However, the article warns that preparation for implementing SaaS should include determining the value of the software-as-a-service, developing a governance policy, creating a SaaS vendor evaluation framework, and developing an integration strategy. Without these steps, implementation may fail.

Before getting totally enthralled with SaaS, however, it is important to know the drawbacks, and there are some. Lingering concerns about cloud computing include privacy issues, liability concerns (if the system should get hacked), data security (because you have ceded control of personal information to third parties), and billing complications. Seizing on the billing issue, Dave Zielinski (2009) warns that there are hidden costs that can emerge in case of security breaches or lawsuits tied to noncompliance with state employment laws or privacy restrictions.

Software-as-a-Service (SaaS) versus ASP Delivery Models

Douglas Reynolds and John Weiner (2009), in their book about online recruiting and selection, compare SaaS and application service providers as they relate to e-recruiting. The *application service provider (ASP)* hosts and maintains the software on its own servers. Two variations may occur: either the client gets a copy of the software, so the client has a unique instance of the tool, or clients are pooled together on the same system, but they cannot see one another's data. The advantage is that the ASP handles all maintenance and upgrades because the vendor is running the system.

The SaaS approach differs in the following way. SaaS requires only that the user have a web browser; no portion of the SaaS software resides on the user's computer. Client organizations pay for a subscription to use the software. There is no licensing, and the client does not own the software. In fact, the SaaS vendor pools all organizations using the software on the software platform so that the client organizations share the software code, but client information cannot be seen by other organizations sharing the code. SaaS is one type of *cloud computing*. It offers a cost-effective way to obtain e-recruiting services.

Outsourcing

Outsourcing is always an option and may be a good approach to e-recruiting for certain organizations. Those features that can be standardized, automated, or moved outside large businesses are often outsourced. *Outsourcing*, also called subservicing, is the practice of contracting an organization's noncore business services to a third-party vendor. Outsourcing HR functions occurs frequently, because HR functions are strictly overhead. As a result of a growing trend to outsource various aspects of a company's operations, start-up companies have emerged to specialize in those services. According to Douglas Reynolds and John Weiner, "Benefits services, retirement programs, time tracking and payroll, outplacement services, and recruiting are just some of the frequently outsourced HR services in many large organizations" (2009, 8).

Outsourcing is attractive, especially for larger organizations, and there are positive side effects to outsourcing. Among the benefits are the required standardizing and automating of tasks in order to interface with the e-recruitment partner. This analysis results in internal process changes that allow organizations to better support e-recruiting tasks; clearly defining tasks also strengthens the internal functions of the organization. Outsourcers must also standardize and automate processes to align with those of their clients; in so doing, they realize efficiencies of scale and can pass those along to their clients, making outsourcing a cost-effective alternative.

Odyssey One Source, Inc.—e-Recruiting: Case Study

Christina Stovall

Odyssey One Source, Inc. (Odyssey), is a human resources outsourcing firm, headquartered in Texas, that provides its clients with a full range of human resource services such as payroll and taxes, risk management, training and development, benefits programs and administration, employee relations, and strategic HR consulting. Essentially, Odyssey is a one-stop shop designed to meet all of its clients' HR needs under one roof, thus allowing clients to focus on their core businesses. Odyssey has had the privilege of being ranked the number one Professional Employer Organization (PEO)/Administrative Service Organization (ASO) in the United States for three consecutive years by *The Black Book of Outsourcing*, published by Brown-Wilson, an independent firm considered the foremost authority on outsourcing.

Increasingly, companies understand the importance of hiring the best and brightest candidates available in order to propel their businesses forward. Two-thirds of the employee life cycle (Attract, Recruit, Select, Hire, Retain, and Transition) is related to hiring. Odyssey's clients look to the company as a partner in HR, to assist with employment challenges, including hiring, and to use the necessary tools and resources to streamline the process and ensure they have the best candidates.

Among the services offered by Odyssey is its Applicant Tracking System (ATS). Odyssey's ATS enables clients to leverage the software, tools, and resources of a larger organization without spending money and time researching, implementing, and maintaining sophisticated systems. In addition, the ATS interfaces with other systems, such as Odyssey's human resource information system (HRIS), the background check company's systems, and the skills testing and assessment vendor's database. This means that instead of requiring separate log-ins and having candidate and employee records in many different locations, the information is merged into one record available through Odyssey's HRIS. The ATS also allows for easy storage, better management and uploading, or even integration with hiring tax credits and EEO information for Affirmative Action Plans. The ATS program automatically complies with current regulatory and legal mandates.

Odyssey's ATS offers easy-to-use features, streamlined technology, and other efficiencies that enable hiring managers and recruiters to manage their candidate pools. Further, a candidate can go online and enter her profile, which is then housed in the ATS. The hiring manager or recruiter can easily move candidates through the process of selection, narrowing the pool, submitting final candidates to the background check vendor, or submitting them for skills testing, all within a few clicks. Upon hire, the client manager can push the information to Odyssey's HRIS for payroll processing, benefits enrollment, and performance management.

Outsourcing the applicant tracking reduces the hiring cycle time, eliminates redundancy, and reduces the errors that would otherwise occur if the process was dependent upon multiple systems and vendors. Ultimately, that time can be refocused on revenue- or capital-producing initiatives rather than nonproductive work. Managers, payroll and benefits representatives, HR generalists, and the like can better view and manage employee information through the Odyssey approach.

By utilizing the ATS technology, Odyssey's clients enjoy increased efficiencies. They may track employee records from candidacy to separation, and they have easy access to employees' profiles. Without an integrated system, HR processes are much more complicated, involving multiple steps to access separate systems in an effort to piece together a comprehensive picture of the employee.

The Odyssey One Source ATS creates greater efficiency and allows the HR Director to focus her time on strategic efforts, driving the company's human capital initiatives forward to meet the vision, goals, and objectives defined for the organization.

Christina Stovall is director of the Human Resource Service Center for Odyssey One Source, Inc., a human resources outsourcing firm. Ms. Stovall currently serves on the Texas State Council as the SHRM foundation state coordinator and is a member of the Society for Human Resource Management (SHRM).

Corporate Governance Process for Large-Scale e-Recruiting Implementation

For Fortune 500 organizations, corporate governance affects all major decisions. *Corporate governance* is the set of processes, customs, policies, laws, and institutions that influence the way an organization is administered. Corporate governance is multifaceted. The major theme of corporate governance is the accountability of individuals through mechanisms that reduce error and emphasize shareholder welfare.

The board of directors, management, and other personnel implement governance measures to provide reasonable assurance that the organization will achieve its objectives related to reliable financial reporting, operating efficiency, and compliance with laws and regulations. This may involve the use of internal auditors, who test the design and implementation of the entity's internal control procedures over its financial reporting.

Corporate governance standards emphasize that there must be a balance of power in decision-making processes. No single individual should hold more than one role; the president must be a different person from the treasurer, and so on. Separation of power is further developed in companies where separate divisions check and balance one another's actions. Corporate governance is especially important to deal with the internal complexities of large Fortune 500 corporations.

For an excellent summary of corporate governance issues, consult the article by Stephen Letza, James Kirkbride, Xiuping Sun, and Clive Smallman entitled "Corporate Governance Theorizing: Limits, Critics and Alternatives" (2008), which provides an overview and explains why it is difficult to craft a global corporate governance standard. The European Corporate Governance website (*www.ecgi.org*) also provides insight on the topic of corporate governance from a European perspective.

Information Technology (IT) Governance

In addition to corporate governance, Fortune 500 organizations must adhere to an IT governance approach when dealing with large-scale system implementations. IT governance sets the guidelines for oversight of large-scale system

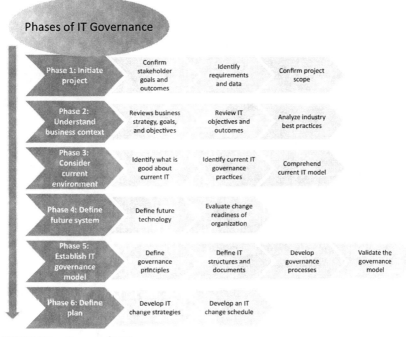

FIGURE 8-1   Phases of IT Governance

analysis, design, selection, and implementation. IT answers to its own rules of governance, which are separate from the corporate governance policies, though they should reflect the organization's mission, values, goals, and objectives. Figure 8-1 provides a graphic presentation of IT governance.

The phases of the IT governance process are similar to project management phases, with the addition of some extra checks and balances. Michael Kavanagh and Mohan Thite point out that some organizations have their own IT governance processes that they use as a standard approach for all internal system implementation efforts. This process of large-scale IT implementation (such as an HRIS or e-recruiting system) takes time, anywhere from six weeks to three years (2009, 60). There are a variety of ways to manage the process, but it is important to examine key issues and organizational goals.

A major premise of IT governance is to exercise due diligence in the planning phase for any large-scale IT project, including e-recruiting, enterprise resource planning (ERP), or human resource information system (HRIS) design. The planning stage is absolutely key. Michael Bedell, Michael Cannif, and Cheryl Wyrick (2009) in the chapter entitled "Systems Considerations in the Design of an HRIS" in the book *Human Resource Information Systems*, indicates that all of the following topics need to be discussed with the organization's mission, goals, and objectives in mind:

- Planning
- Project manager or project leader
- Steering committee/project charter
- Implementation team
- Project scope
- Management sponsorship
- Process mapping
- Software implementation
- Customization
- Change management
- "Going live"
- Project evaluation
- Potential pitfalls (45–68)

Typically these topics are addressed very specifically under the IT governance plan.

At a much more detailed level, the IT Governance Standards Commission (COBIT and ISACA) provides the standards for a large-scale IT implementation effort and maps out the process. For more than forty years, ISACA has been a pace-setting global organization for information technology governance, control, and security. For information on the entire IT governance approach, the ISACA website is very helpful (*www.isaca.org*).

The RACI (or RASCI) Tool

An area of significant contribution for the HR professional can be input on or oversight of the development of the Responsible, Accountable, Consulted, or Informed (RACI) and Supportive (RASCI) matrix. This tool can be developed using any spreadsheet software (including Excel or Microsoft Project). RACI basically addresses roles and responsibilities. Because defining and documenting responsibility is a fundamental principle of corporate and IT governance, this simple and powerful tool serves as a vehicle for communication. The RACI model is used during analysis and documentation efforts. See the subsequent sample RACI list. The letters of the acronym mean:

- R—Responsible for correct execution of process and activities, or the person responsible for getting the job done.

- A—Accountable means ownership of the quality and the result of the process. One, and no more than one, person must be accountable for each activity.
- C—Consulted refers to the person's involvement as a source of information and/or knowledge.
- I—Informed means receiving information about the process and quality.
- S—Supportive role means that this person can assist, thereby turning the RACI into a RASCI model.

General guidelines include:

- Only one "A" per task can be defined (ensures accountability; more than one "A" causes confusion).
- At least one "R" per task, with more than one being appropriate where there is shared responsibility.

This RACI (or RASCI) tool helps organize and establish roles and responsibilities for large-scale efforts involving change management, corporate governance, and IT governance.

The role of the HR manager or business manager in the governance process is to become familiar with corporate and IT governance practices, and to contribute at the strategic level in the selection and oversight of a large-scale HRIS project. Hiring a COBIT–certified IT governance expert can also help!

Conclusion

In this chapter, we discussed the pros and cons of online recruitment. We examined the types of candidates who are attracted and how to adjust for an international audience. We demonstrated the variety of options available for implementing e-recruiting in small, medium, and large organizations. Finally, we addressed the role that corporate and IT governance play for Fortune 500 organizations planning to implement large-scale IT solutions.

Handling HR Functions with an HRIS and/or Specialty Software

This chapter examines some of the specialty software, or add-on features, of an HRIS (human resources information system), including employee self-service, time tracking, e-enabled assessment, and performance management. These functions may be a part of a larger system, such as an ERP (enterprise resource planning) system, or they may be add-on features; they may also exist as stand-alone software. Regardless of design, HRIS systems must support the goals of the organization and improve organizational performance by capturing, maintaining, and utilizing key information assets.

Employee Self-Service

Typical *employee self-service (ESS)*, enabled by the HRIS, offers employees the opportunity to access information, make choices pertaining to benefits and personal development opportunities, and update personal data. ESS offers a wide variety of services through the Internet in categories including professional development, communications, benefits services, and personal data (Isenhour 2009, 220). Within those categories, some of the features include:

- Development
  - Enroll in training courses
  - View completed training
  - Access e-learning internal/external courses
  - View/apply for internal job vacancies
  - Complete employment tests for new jobs

- Communications
  - Review company communications
  - Access company policies or procedures
  - Access HR policy manuals and e-mail inquiry/help request
  - Complete employee surveys or 360-degree feedback data
  - View/respond to personal information requests from HR
- Benefits services
  - Research and view plan rules and requirements
  - Enroll in cafeteria-style programs (medical, dental, insurance)
  - Add and/or delete dependents
  - Model retirement and/or access 401K savings investment records
  - Model health plan alternatives' costs (e.g., HMO, PPO)
- Personal data
  - Correct errors in personal data (degree, graduation date)
  - Update emergency contact, address, telephone information
  - Change W-4 withholding forms
  - View previous/current pay and performance information
  - Enter time reports, vacation/sick days, and travel expense reports

Clearly, the employee self-service option gives a great deal of decision making and control to the employees. The organization benefits as well: an ESS can lower the cost of operations, increase productivity, and position HR as an organizational leader and strategic business partner (Weatherly 2005). Studies estimate with a wide range of variance—that between 50 percent and 100 percent of organizations currently use ESS applications (Gueutal and Stone 2005, 195). The trend is unquestionably toward greater use, with more organizations adopting an ESS approach.

The downside to the implementation of ESS, however, is that it may impact the HR department. Because the trend is toward consolidation of HR functions and toward moving many of these consolidated functions to an HRIS, there are questions about what will happen to HR staff. The answer is that resourceful HR specialists will be freed to focus on value-added functions that support the goals and objectives of the organization. Those individuals in HR who are dedicated solely to handling the functions that will in the future be administered by the HRIS must be ready and able to participate at a more strategic level.

Implementing an ESS requires reexamination and reengineering of existing HR processes. The process of setting up an ESS often leads HR managers to identify and weed out ineffective or time-intensive HR processes. The result is streamlined processes that eliminate or automate those tasks that add time or create delays for HR transactions.

Time-Tracking Technology

The task of time tracking—once tedious—has been revolutionized by time-tracking software. Each employee enters her own information into the time-tracking system. Easy access to the software on the job facilitates the process and makes it less of a chore. These packages also can be used to track accrued vacation and sick leave and allow reporting in a variety of ways such as actual hours worked, reported sick, taken as vacation time, etc., by individuals or groups or overall.

Most HRIS packages include some kind of tracking for attendance and time. There are, however, companies like Trakware Systems, Qqest Software Systems, TimeForce, Exaktime, and Presagia that have mastered the art and science of tracking employee time. Their products may be used as stand-alone systems or as add-on modules to HRISs. Time-tracking software, similar to the other add-ons mentioned in this chapter, can also be part of a larger enterprise resource planning (ERP) system. When the software package is designed specifically for time tracking, regulatory compliance features are often built into the software. In fact, the software can take the confusion out of a complex process.

Industries have varying levels of emphasis on time and attendance. Workers in manufacturing environments may check in and out with time clocks. The HRIS software vendors companies do not provide the hardware, such as time clocks, that feed information to the time-keeping software. In this case, time-keeping systems used by the organization will capture the hourly data inputted by the workers from various time clock readers throughout a site. That information has to be downloaded to the HRIS. The time-tracking systems are used to perform employee scheduling. It is also used to gather actual hours worked as well as sick time and vacation time, which is then reviewed before electronic submission to the HRIS payroll. Other industries, such as consulting or legal firms, track billed time and utilization levels, and time-tracker software can be customized to that work environment (Bedell, Cannif, and Wyrick 2009).

Biometrics is an interesting technology that can be used for time tracking, among other things. *Biometrics* relies upon devices, such as fingerprint scanners, that use either an optical reader or a computer chip to identify people. Fingerprint scanners of either type use finger geometry to confirm identity. Other biometric technologies include retina scanning, voice recognition, facial scanning, and signature recognition systems. While none of these systems are 100 percent accurate, they can reach very high levels of accuracy (Roberts 2003).

Biometrics eliminates losses for time and attendance associated with lost cards and buddy punching. The attendance information gathered from biometric check-in can be transferred to payroll software, assuring accurate time tracking. Used by organizations such as McDonald's, Hilton Hotels, and Dunkin' Donuts, as well as municipal governments, to keep track of staff hours and missed days, biometrics applications are growing (Wright 2009). Some emergency medical services (EMS) use biometrics to access patient records in urgent situations (Roberts 2010).

The legal ramifications of using biometrics are still being discussed. Concerns include the fact that scanning devices may be vulnerable to data theft or may be linked with personal information and misused to invade personal privacy. Additionally, there may be health risks associated with the technology (Agnvall 2007).

e-Enabled Assessment

Another responsibility typically assigned to HR is oversight of the employee assessment process; this function can also be handled through an HRIS. *E-enabled assessment* is the evaluation of internal or external applicants for job positions, conducted via the Internet or HRIS. It is tied to e-selection and provides valuable information about applicants. The users of e-enabled assessment systems are:

- People who will be assessed by the system, typically job candidates
- HR specialists who will be accountable for the functions performed by the system
- Managers who will use the system to make personnel decisions (Gueutal and Stone 2005, 65)

An e-enabled assessment system may stand alone as independent software for employment selection, or it may be integrated into another HR system. The assessment system may be narrowly defined and used; for example, the system might be used only for employment test administration. Or it can be more generalized, used not only to gather employment test and competency data, but also to gather data on development, compensation, job history and progress, training, background, and performance. Hal Gueutal and Dianna Stone (2005) clarify that this level of integration requires the host organization to specify legal criteria in the development phase. This includes provisions for confidentiality and privacy, data access, and data use—all standard requirements whether the system is e-enabled or not.

The challenges presented by e-assessment include access channels, user interface, data management, and some professional challenges. There are five major channels for presenting an e-assessment opportunity for e-selection. These include testing centers within the business location, third-party testing centers, interactive voice response, access via the web from any location, and semi-proctored environments.

Lloyds, Inc., is a large multinational company with a reputation for providing development for long-term career opportunities. In 2004, this provider of personal and corporate banking, mortgages, insurance, investments, and pensions received 3,800 applications and hired 102 management trainees for its two-year graduate program (Pollitt 2005). The bank uses an online application form that has an e-selection component of competency-based questions and a twenty-minute numerical-reasoning test that is completed by candidates online. The bank then vets applicants based upon their scores and follows up by interviewing the best-scoring candidates. Lloyds has assessment centers at its management-training centers that can accommodate twelve to twenty-four candidates at a time. At the centers, which are open on specific days for twenty-four hours, there are interviews, case-study presentations, group exercises, and roleplay exercises. Applicants also take a paper-based numerical reasoning test, which verifies the online test score. The paper-based test is used to assess the candidates' problem-solving and reasoning skills. This second test is scored on a computer, and the test results are also stored on computer. Test administrators are present during the online test. An advantage to this approach is that the test results are easier to analyze. The mixture of online and face-to-face testing offers a broad spectrum of information for use in the assessment process.

The user interface generally tends to have a businesslike, no-fuss approach. There is nothing glamorous about most online test sites. However, organizations have recently begun trying to engage applicants by using a more pleasing and motivating approach. To do so, sites employ multimedia, video-based approaches designed to convey a realistic preview of the job. These high-fidelity experiences are attractive to applicants even as they assess the prospects' fit for the open position.

Online assessments require substantial technical attention, which makes this approach to assessment more complex and one that requires a data management effort. Assessment setup is enabled through the use of relational databases, including several tables for complex work simulations. Designing for this e-enabled assessment environment adds time and cost to the assessment process. Quality assurance/control involves beta testing the software to ensure that the database and the code are interacting properly. This requires many dozens of tests to ensure that it works 100 percent of the time. The attraction to e-assessments is, in part, because of the complex and rich reporting function made possible by the relational database. Real-time reporting of scores can accelerate the decision-making process.

The most important aspect of e-assessment is ensuring that there is appropriate oversight, administration, and test security. You must be able to confirm the identity of each candidate. The fundamental principles for constructing online assessments are similar to those used for the face-to-face approach.

Performance Management

Performance management (PM) ensures that goals are consistently being met in an effective and efficient manner. According to Charles Fay and Ren Nardoni, during the 1990s, the performance management process replaced the outdated performance appraisal process. This is important, because the PM process now encompasses much more and relates directly to the overall organizational goals. The PM process has three parts: (1) performance planning; (2) observing performance and providing positive, corrective feedback; and (3) developing performance summaries fundamental to performance planning for the next period (2009, 341).

Grouped with talent management, performance management also impacts onboarding, developing employees, evaluating employees, and managing the workforce. It connects to other areas within HR such as recruiting, staffing, career management, 360-degree assessment, development management, retention management, and workforce planning. An HRIS function pertaining to performance management must also link to each of these features of the HRIS. In fact, companies increasingly are turning to employee performance management software to evaluate and manage performance on an individual basis (Robb 2004).

Performance management should be collaborative, a joint effort of the manager and the employee. For all job titles, there must be clearly defined and communicated performance dimensions, measures, and standards. Performance management formats, performance periods, and performance summaries differ by job description and employee level. Clerical, nonmanagement positions have a relatively standard set of criteria, whereas management positions may have a format featuring weighted competency components. Both sets of data are easily handled by a web-enabled employee performance management system.

Typical performance management data inputs include job and individual data and organizational-level data (such as unit and organizational goals, as well as strategies and business plans). The job-level data include key tasks, responsibilities, and outcomes. Most of the information is individual-level data.

Manager input includes the performance criteria developed by the manager for the individual, measures to rate performance, and standards for each measure. The entire performance contract is entered into the performance management system. Usually, the system will allow supervisor and other rater observations, as well as performance incidents. Also, there is space for positive and corrective feedback, together with sections for recommended development activities. The real value of these data is the link to overall corporate goals; this is enabled by the performance management system.

From these data, the HRIS produces standardized reports. These reports will act as performance contracts for each employee, as well as the annual performance summary for each. The system also provides aggregate performance data for units and reports comparing one aggregated unit's performance to another's. Archived data are necessary in order to track long-term performance trends both at the individual and group levels.

The data can and should flow to other systems. For example, performance and compensation systems may be linked, as typically there is a connection between job performance and pay. Merit pay is based on a merit matrix. At the summary level, each employee's data are matched to the matrix and performance dimensions entered in the system. These metrics are used to make decisions about promotions, layoffs, training, and developmental assignments.

The performance management system should also support decision making. The data of importance to decision making include performance criteria, performance measures, performance standards, and performance documentation. These contribute to managers' decisions about whether intervention should occur. The system itself can be programmed to flag performance problems.

Selecting an Employee Performance Management System

There are a number of valuable features of the Performance Management (PM) system. Consider some of the following factors when selecting PM software.

- Flexibility to meet the needs of overall management as well as the individual business units
- Ease of use and an interface that is attractive and does not require training
- Features such as manager guides to improve employee performance
- Availability from a variety of in-house and remote locations
- Globalization that adapts to the languages of your employees, to meet local regulations about privacy, etc.

Dewberry, Inc.: Case Study

Leslie Keelty

Dewberry is an 1,800-person professional services firm operating nationally in the United States. With more than forty locations, Dewberry provides services in program management, planning, engineering, architecture, surveying, geographic information services, and the environmental sciences. Clients include government agencies, corporations, real estate developers, colleges and universities, school districts, and other commercial and institutional organizations.

As is typical in most companies, Dewberry has had numerous iterations of its performance development process (PDP). In 2004, the PDP form was shortened in an attempt to fine-tune the process for managers. In 2008–2009, managers asked to have the ability to complete the form electronically. What ensued was a partnership between HR and IT to explore how to automate this process, which resulted in creation of an interactive fifteen-step automated process for the PDP, which is now referred to as ePDP.

An existing automated process notified managers that an employee's PDP was due. This step was the first in the process and was driven through the organization's HRIS system. A new platform was required to engage and connect people to the other steps in the PDP process, so a web-based workflow application was integrated into the HRIS system. The HRIS system had already been utilized to program other HR processes, such as requests for new hires, terminations, employee profile changes, and so on. The system captured all employees and their assigned business unit managers, all of whom had grown accustomed to using these online tools. Moreover, the web can connect any employee who is part of the process—not just those located in the same office. The culture was moving more toward automated processes in general, as automation was seen to be more efficient and less time-consuming.

This technology facilitates learning by prompting an interactive process to occur during the performance development cycle. It enables new employees and their managers to sit down in the early stages of employment to establish performance goals and measurements. It is a highly participatory process that allows all employees to provide input by completing a self-evaluation, helping to set their goals for the coming year, and to communicate and be clear with their managers about their future career aspirations. It provides a mechanism for managers to get input from others about their employees' performance. The core competencies that are in place emphasize to employees and managers which behaviors and competencies are important for success at Dewberry. An agreed-upon plan for career development and strengthening of performance competencies is an integral part of this process.

Help icons are available on each screen as the employee, contributor, manager, or approver is completing the steps in the process. These online learning tools provide samples of performance goals, measurements, competency ratings, career development goals, contributor ratings, and so on for the most highly populated positions within the company. For example, samples are available for engineers, architects, project accountants, project managers, IT developers, surveyors, business unit managers, and administrative assistants. The enhanced career development section prompts a discussion of future career aspirations. Employees are now asked what their most likely/most desired position is and whether they would be willing to relocate to another office within the firm. Managers learn what motivates their employees. Employees recognize that relocation may be an important element of advancement, particularly in an organization with many long-term employees and many smaller offices with limited opportunity to advance into key positions. It also reinforces to managers the need to consistently develop and challenge their employees and make succession planning a priority.

Since implementing this technology in September 2009, there has been an increase in the number of employees with formally documented performance goals during their first month of employment. In the past, people would get to the end of the year and sit down for their first PDP without clear goals to evaluate their performance. With the advent of the ePDP tool:

- The number of employees completing a self-review has multiplied dramatically, as this part of the process in no longer dependent on whether an individual manager requests it.

- The number of managers seeking input from contributors about employees' performance has also increased.

- More attention is being given to the career development section. Managers report that questions regarding next desired job and willingness to relocate have generated meaningful discussions with employees about their personal and professional goals.

- The new system has stretched the organization's expectations of the PDP process. This has prompted managers to suggest ideas for ongoing improvement and enhancements.

- Once the goals are populated, they carry forward for the following year.

- The ePDP is archived for easy retrieval so that the employee and manager can view it at any time.

- A journaling tool is available for note taking during the year.

A database of core competencies and desired career roles, together with a list of people who are willing to relocate, now exists. This will aid the organization in making decisions about promotions and succession planning.

Leslie Keelty, Ed.D., SPHR, is currently the corporate director of training and development with Dewberry, an architectural/engineering firm headquartered in Fairfax, Virginia. She is responsible for the firm's corporate university, The Dewberry Learning Center, which provides a wide variety of leadership and professional development programs to employees.

HR-Intersect for Implementation of an HRIS

Already addressed in some depth in chapters 7 (small and mid-sized firms) and 8 (large organizations), HRIS implementation and its impact on business processes remain a concern among HR professionals and nontechnical managers. Collaboration is important to the success of any technology-related effort; typically, HR works with the Information Technology department. There is no need for one HR professional to perform the analysis, design, development, implementation, and evaluation of the HRIS. In fact, HRISs are selected, developed, maintained, and improved through collaboration among various departments, including HR, Corporate Communications, and Information Technology.

Business Process Reengineering

Usually, when a new computer system is implemented, there is an impact (sometimes a dramatic one) on business processes and how work gets done. Business process reengineering (BPR) is an approach for redesigning the way work is done to better support the organization's mission and reduce costs. Reengineering starts with the organization's mission, strategic goals, and customer needs. The HR professional asks questions such as, "Does our mission need to be redefined?," "Are our strategic goals aligned with our mission?," and "Who are our customers?" Reengineering often occurs with installation of an HRIS. Realigning positions and business processes requires a step back in order to examine these fundamental questions.

Within this assessment of mission and goals, reengineering concentrates on the organization's business processes, including:

- The steps and procedures that govern how resources are used to create products
- Services that meet the needs of particular customers or markets

As a structured ordering of work steps, a business process can be divided into specific activities then measured, modeled, and improved. A business process can also be completely redesigned or eliminated altogether. So the start of a business process reengineering effort should be the identification of the *as-is* processes. There is great value in defining the processes as-is. First, it highlights current processes and the way things operate. Second, it shows how employees currently do their work. Third, it helps identify areas of pain, where things are not working as well as they should.

The next step is to define the *to-be* processes, or the way things will operate in the future. This step is crucial as well. In this phase, you essentially develop requirements—what the business must have—for the new system. The benefits of defining what will be, including defining necessary processes, are that the to-be model creates your operational approach and drives the selection of a new HRIS. It helps to define gaps between the current way of doing business and the future, new way. It helps identify performance indicators and, finally, the to-be process indicates future report writing needs—it outlines the information you will want from the new system.

Reengineering identifies, analyzes, and redesigns an organization's core business processes, with the aim of achieving dramatic improvements in critical performance measures such as cost, quality, service, and speed. Reengineering often occurs when an HRIS or other IT project is implemented because the processes are impacted or replaced by the HRIS functions. Reengineering focuses on redesigning the whole process in order to maximize the benefits to the organization and its customers.

HRIS Legal and Regulatory Issues

As noted earlier, the country that hosts the HRIS has a major effect on its development and implementation (Beaman 2002). Labor laws in the home country dictate the context for business and provide the basis for employee protection. So as part of the first step in any HRIS implementation effort, you must identify the local laws and regulations. The most complex legal and regulatory issues occur in the United States, where federal laws may be complicated by further layers of state laws (Kavanagh and Thite 2009).

In a meta-analysis of European HR legal and regulatory issues, the authors Irene Nikandrou, Eleni Apospori, and Nancy Papalexandris (2005) examined eighteen European countries' HRM strategies and practices from a longitudinal perspective. A major conclusion of the study was that the countries are affected in varying degrees by the extent to which they adopted the European Union's policies and procedures. In the final analysis, the country and its general environment have a major impact on HRM and the adoption of an HRIS.

The United States, on the other hand, has detailed laws and regulations that impact every organization doing business within or headquartered in the country. Because labor laws provide the foundation of employee protection in the workplace, they are of utmost importance to understand. Of course, we cannot address all of the laws that affect human resources; however, we'll mention a few here. For more detailed information, see the "Digging Deeper" section for this chapter. Some of the laws and regulatory agencies that impact the practice of HR in the United States and affect selection of an HRIS include:

- Sarbanes-Oxley Act
- Health Insurance Portability and Accountability Act (HIPAA)
- Fair Labor Standards Act (FLSA)
- Family and Medical Leave Act (FMLA)
- U.S. Civil Rights Act of 1964, Title VII
- Equal Employment Opportunity Commission (EEOC)
- International Organization for Standardization (ISO)
- Occupational Safety and Health Administration (OSHA) [OSHA is the Occupational Safety and Health Administration, not Act]

In Table 9-1, each of these important laws and regulatory bodies is described briefly.

TABLE 9-1 U.S. Acts and Regulatory Bodies That Impact HR

Regulatory Acts and Regulating Bodies	Description
Sarbanes-Oxley Act	The Sarbanes-Oxley Act of 2002 (often shortened to **SOX**) is legislation enacted to protect shareholders and the general public from accounting errors and fraudulent practices in the enterprise. The act is administered by the Securities and Exchange Commission (SEC), which sets deadlines for compliance and publishes rules on requirements. It defines which records are to be stored and for how long (*Techtarget.com*).
Health Insurance Portability and Accountability Act (HIPAA)—Title I and Title II	HIPAA's Title I protects health insurance rights for individuals and their families if they change or lose jobs. Employers' plans must now give workers insurance credit for the amount of time that they had prior credible health coverage without a break of 63 days or more. Title I also limits the nature and number of restrictions that health-insurance companies can impose in regard to covering care for candidates' preexisting conditions. Title II includes four different rules that address different aspects of healthcare information security: privacy rule, transactions and code sets rule, security rule, and unique identifier rule (*HRworld.com* or *www.hhs.gov*).
Fair Labor Standards Act (FLSA)	The FLSA establishes minimum wage, overtime pay, recordkeeping, and youth employment standards affecting employees in the private sector and in federal, state, and local governments (*www.dol.gov*).
Family and Medical Leave Act (FMLA)	The Family and Medical Leave Act (FMLA) provides certain employees with up to twelve weeks of unpaid, job-protected leave per year. It also requires that their group health benefits be maintained during the leave (*www.dol.gov*).
U.S. Civil Rights Act of 1964, Title VII	Title VII prohibits employment discrimination based on race, color, religion, sex, and national origin. The Civil Rights Act of 1991 (Pub. L. 102-166) (CRA) and the Lilly Ledbetter Fair Pay Act of 2009 (Pub. L. 111-2) amend several sections of Title VII (*www.eeoc.gov*).

(Continued)

TABLE 9-1   U.S. Acts and Regulatory Bodies That Impact HR *(Continued)*

Regulatory Acts and Regulating Bodies	Description
Equal Employment Opportunity Commission (EEOC)	The U.S. Equal Employment Opportunity Commission (EEOC) is an independent federal law enforcement agency that enforces laws against workplace discrimination. The EEOC investigates discrimination complaints based on an individual's race, color, national origin, religion, sex, sexual orientation, age, disability, and retaliation for reporting and/or opposing a discriminatory practice (*www.eeoc.gov*).
International Organization for Standardization (ISO)	Issued by the International Organization for Standardization (ISO), the ISO 9000 family of standards represents an international consensus on good quality management practices. It consists of standards and guidelines relating to quality management systems and related supporting standards. ISO 9001: 2008 is the standard that provides a set of standardized requirements for a quality management system, regardless of what the user organization does, its size, or whether it is in the private or public sector. The other standards in the family cover specific aspects such as fundamentals and vocabulary, performance improvements, documentation, training, and financial and economic aspects (*www.iso.org*).
Occupational Safety and Health Administration (OSHA)	The Occupational Safety and Health Administration (OSHA) performs two regulatory functions: setting standards and conducting inspections to ensure that employers are providing safe and healthful workplaces (*www.dol.gov/compliance/guide/osha.htm*).

The good news is that many software and HRIS products have compliance standards built into the programs. Additionally, HR management systems can help with regulatory compliance by offering electronic access to data and information. Finally, compliance software systems created for the express purpose of dealing with complex compliance regulations exist and can be used as add-ons to HRISs.

One example of compliance software is Cigna Leave Solutions, developed by Cigna Group Insurance of Philadelphia. Cigna Leave Solutions can help companies stay current with the complicated leave regulations that originate from federal and state regulations. Since this challenge is increasingly complex, a system that can handle compliance issues really helps. Cigna Leave Solutions also enables employers to manage administration of FMLA, short-term disability, military duty, jury duty, and bereavement leave (McCormack 2004).

HRIS and Financial Data

The reputations of organizations can rise and fall based upon data and metrics. Eric Krell of *HRMagazine* indicates in his article "Notable by Its Absence" that HR data can be provided in annual reports, although they are currently missing from most. HR data are available, and in the future annual reports should include more sophisticated links between workforce investment and financial performance. These data can be mined and analyzed using an HRIS, because human capital management metrics can be correlated with financial performance. Human capital management information (some of which may be available through an HRIS) include:

- Training and tuition reimbursement costs
- Recruiting costs (the degree to which an organization is developing talent internally)
- Annual turnover rate, which illustrates the degree to which the company's investments in training, tuition reimbursement, and recruiting pay off
- Succession planning, to ensure that there are no gaps in coverage between those leaving and their replacements
- Customer service improvement efforts, as affected by processes such as Lean Six Sigma (a process that yields quantifiable data such as improved customer satisfaction)

Research from Mercer Human Resource Consulting indicates that 14 percent of Fortune 100 companies include at least one hard number related to workforce performance in shareholder letters (Krell 2006, 57). Some top-performing organizations, such as Hewlett-Packard (HP), far outperform other organizations and earn a spot in the top ten of the Fortune 500 with their sophisticated approach to workforce planning.

HP and the HR Optimization Model: Case Study

Shawn Williams

Hewlett-Packard (HP) is the world's largest information technology company, with revenue totaling $126 billion for fiscal 2010. It ranks number ten as a Fortune 500 firm and is nicknamed the "Grandfather of Silicon Valley." Guided by the principles of its founders, Bill Hewlett and Dave Packard, HP continues to pursue excellence for fully integrated information technology services and products, a goal it has maintained since its founding in 1939. HP's 300,000 plus employees serve more than one billion customers in 170 nations on six continents. As such, it is one of the biggest organizations on the planet. Enterprise Services (ES) is an HP business area.

The HR optimization model (HROM) is a workforce planning and strategy tool that was internally developed and used by the HP Human Resources organization. This workforce planning analytics system gathers employee, financial, and business data to connect them and analyze relevant patterns. HROM can be used to monitor the health of the organization, relying upon four key data elements: cost, quality, productivity, and engagement. The resulting information supports decision making, forecasting, and modeling future possibilities. Endorsed by the HP organization, HP offers levels of HROM certification for its employees to consult their businesses around the globe.

As mentioned earlier, the four quadrants of the tool are cost, quality, productivity, and engagement. This robust tool proved invaluable in the economic downturn of 2008 and 2009. The cost data were used for internal decision support that examined a variety of scenarios for reducing costs. Productivity data provided measurements that help to plan for recruitment, hiring, and staffing. Financials indicated revenue and profitability tied to everything from the business unit level down to the individual level. Engagement information revealed types of competencies needed, matching skills to existing, pending, or possible future projects. By taking an inventory of these projects, as well as those that may reach the end of the project life cycle, the tool indicated the people needed to meet the company-wide workforce demands.

This tool can be used to identify new markets within other countries. The regulations and legislations of each country are built into the tool in order to ensure compliance. New markets in Panama provide an example of the value of the HROM tool.

Before entering Panama for new business opportunities, HP used the HROM tool's analytics. HP examined the educated population, government stability, as well as transportation and technology infrastructure, calculated the risk, and designed risk mitigation techniques. The model identified the cap on number of employees for hire relative to the entire population. Because Panama was a new market, the tool also helped decision makers to apply social responsibility tenets, or the green approach, to Human Resources. HP monitored the employable population, infrastructure, and economic conditions and modeled the potential impact of HP's entrance on Panama's economy, security, and political stability. Using HROM to calculate ample skills sets, etc., HP had a top number of employees, or cap, in mind. Entering a new country requires examination of government regulations with regard to land lease/buy decisions, payroll infusion, and potential government subsidies for training, real estate, and tax breaks.

Hewlett-Packard in Panama is now filling to capacity with new hires who are able to meet necessary skill requirements for available jobs. Call centers, financial services, and Human Resources are now operating out of Panama. The HP employees there represent an enthusiastic, skilled, loyal employee base.

The HROM tool is so thorough in the country selection process that it sets standards for other companies, enabling other organizations to move into the country. Again, the tool assesses the impact of a possible talent war as others organizations gain entrance and compete for the same human resources. These estimates impact the HP implementation plan.

A tribute to HP executives' strategic planning empowered by the HROM tool is the following. In a down economy, HP surpassed its primary competitor to take first place as the largest technology company in the world. Year after year, HP continues to demonstrate revenue and market share growth. HP divisions are so diverse, covering the entire gamut of IT services and products—both commercial and personal—yet every division ranks number one or two in its market. Every business unit within HP is doing well and can stand on its own. Many attribute this success to the power of the HROM global workforce planning tool for decision support, forecasting, and modeling future possibilities.

Shawn Williams is the vice president of Human Resources for Hewlett-Packard—Enterprise Services. Williams's team has and continues to develop much of the workforce methodologies that have become the industry standard.

HRIS Trends

In today's 24-7, internet-driven society, organizations need access to data and information instantaneously. Thus the trends in HRIS include greater use of Web 2.0, software-as-a-service (SAAS), service-oriented architecture (SOA), and enterprise portals. Let's look at each one. We will mention the section within this book where you will find more information regarding these trends.

Web 2.0

In chapter 1 we addressed the imminent widespread distribution of Web 2.0. This is a faster Internet that enables transmission of multimedia, video, and other media that require bandwidth. Examples of Web 2.0 include social networking sites, wikis, blogs, podcasts, RSS personal websites, web services, and sharing files (Bughin 2009). Most HRIS and associated systems will rely—or already do rely—upon this faster, better Internet.

Software-as-a-Service (SaaS)

We examined the emergence of cloud computing as a viable alternative to purchasing, leasing, or outsourcing in chapter 8. You will remember that software-as-a-service allows organizations to have direct access to fully functional applications over the Internet rather than storing the software on the user's server or computer. One possibility that will become more attractive is the offering of HRIS software-as-a-service. Because of the significant potential savings, SaaS will extend the use of HRIS packages to small and medium-sized enterprises (Kavanagh and Thite 2009).

Service-Oriented Architecture (SOA)

Another IT solution that is gaining momentum is the use of service-oriented architecture (SOA). Also described in chapter 8, SOA is a business-driven IT approach (Carter 2007) that links existing systems to perform business functions. Its benefits include the fact that it simplifies interconnection to and use of existing legacy systems. The relationship to the future of HRIS is that the flexibility will allow HR to create a hybrid defined by the process and to select pieces from third parties or from internal or legacy systems. SOA can link them all together seamlessly (Roberts 2006). This offers tremendous cost savings by leveraging existing systems.

Enterprise Portals

We address portal technology in chapter 6. The enterprise portal, unlike other specialized portals, offers ubiquitous access to all of the work services, software, individuals, and so on, through the enterprise system. More sophisticated portals include marketing applications, collaborative tools, company and industry news, and a host of other features. The glory of the enterprise portal is that all the information gets delivered through a single web page that individual employees can customize to their own job and information needs (Zeidner 2005).

Conclusion

In this chapter we examined human resource information systems (HRISs) in general and other systems such as employee self-service, time tracking, e-enabled assessment, and performance management. We talked about the role of the enterprise resource planning (ERP) system. The legal issues and regulatory bodies relevant to the practice of HR in the U.S. were explained, and we emphasized the fact that HRIS must support the goals of the organization and improve organizational performance by capturing, maintaining, and utilizing key information assets.

CHAPTER 10

Electronic Performance Support Systems

When you talk about electronic performance support systems (EPSS), you must reference Gloria Gery. For more than two decades, Gery has advocated for electronic performance support systems (EPSS) through her various contributions on the topic. This includes extensive research, application, and experience. We'll begin this chapter with her definition of an EPSS. Next, we'll provide an overview of the attributes of an electronic performance support system. Proceeding from there, we will discuss the use and design of a EPSS and then address the impact of an EPSS on business processes, with a brief section on Lean Six Sigma. Finally, we will address the relationship between organizational learning and an EPSS.

What Is a Performance Support System?

The emergence of *electronic performance support systems (EPSS)* heralded major changes in learning and knowledge management. Gloria Gery (1991) defined an EPSS as a system that provides users with "individualized online access to the full range of ... systems to permit job performance" (21). Simply put, "performance support systems provide the right information to the right user at the right time" (Nguyen 2009, 95).

Performance support systems can:

- Provide access to discrete, specific information needed to perform a task
- Be used on the job, while engaged in the activity
- Be accessed by the user whenever the need arises (Bersin and O'Leonard 2005)

The goal of performance support systems are, in Gery's own words, to "fuse learning and doing to enable immediate performance with minimal external support" and "to institutionalize best practices on an ongoing basis, all of the time ... to enable people who don't know what they are doing to function as if they did" (Gery, quoted in O'Driscoll and Cross 2005, 6).

EPSS and Training

If performance support systems do what they are supposed to do, they diminish the need for training. Gloria Gery calls it reaching the "performance zone," the moment where the learner "gets it" (Gery, in O'Driscoll and Cross 2005, 6). Unfortunately, training may not help people "get it." Training courses often are separated from the point at which work is being done, so the user forgets what she learned in training before she can actually use it. Performance support systems, on the other hand, make "training" available at the point of need: in the workplace.

Because the primary objective of the performance support system is to help the learner complete a task as rapidly as possible, the EPSS provides tools that are easy to access, and the instruction is typically short and concise. The information can appear as text, audio, video, or simulations that assist the learner in completing the task.

Attributes of Electronic Performance Support Systems

Performance support systems can provide assistance in a variety of ways because the performance support system enables the worker to access the equivalent of training as he is doing the work. Typically, performance support helps the worker to do the job while he is on the job. There are many advantages to this approach. For instance, since a task and work process analysis is performed before instituting a new EPSS, the work processes are evaluated and often are redesigned, providing a more logical approach to the tasks. This analysis institutionalizes the best approach. Through purposeful design, the EPSS can contain embedded knowledge in the interface, support resources, and system logic, thereby making it a powerful, multifaceted tool. The EPSS reflects natural work situations, so the learner/worker learns on the job with feedback that occurs in the context of doing the job. Also, through a performance support system (PSS), the worker can access helpful information and tools without breaking the flow of the task. A well-designed PSS can provide layers of functionality to accommodate performer diversity and adapt for language, level of difficulty, and so on. Some of the tasks can be automated through the PSS. In fact, the PSS attributes offset and may totally replace the need for some training.

With this kind of power, it is a wonder that all training is not supplanted by performance support systems! But just hold on for a minute: There are some issues to consider, such as under which circumstance an EPSS is appropriate and under which it is inappropriate.

When to Use an EPSS

Allison Rossett and Lisa Schafer (2007) provide some examples of when and where to use performance support as a solution:

- When the performance is infrequent
- When the situation is complex, involves many steps, or has many attributes
- When the consequence of error is intolerable
- When performance depends on a large body of information
- When performance is dependent on knowledge, procedures, or approaches that change frequently
- When performance can be improved through employee self-assessment and correction with standards in mind
- When there is high turnover and the task is perceived to be simple
- When there is little time or few resources to devote to training (21–26)

All of these situations provide a suitable context for an EPSS.

When *Not* to Implement an EPSS

Conversely, as mentioned earlier, there are times when a performance support system is not the right solution. For instance, do not use performance support systems if it would cause the user's credibility to be damaged such as a trainer using a performance support tool when providing training; using a performance support system might indicate to the students that the trainer did not know how to perform the task. Do not use a performance support system if performance speed is critical. If there are unpredictable or novel work processes, do not use performance support. If the performance must be smooth and apparently second nature, do not use a performance support system. If the employee has trouble with reading, listening, or reference skills, or if the employee is generally without motivation, then a performance support system is inappropriate.

Components of an EPSS

There are different ways to describe the components and characteristics of EPSS. For example, one description views an EPSS as four different functional levels that should be brought together. The first level is the user interface shell (human computer interface) and database; the second level is composed of generic tools (help system, documentation, text retrieval system, intelligent agents, tutoring facility, simulation tools, and communication resources); the third level is application-specific support tools unique to the system with which the EPSS will work; the fourth level is the target application domain (schools, particular business settings, military, etc.).

Thomas Cavanaugh (2004) further explains the types of EPSS support in terms of a taxonomy or spectrum of offerings. At one end of the spectrum, with the least connection to the task is the *external* performance support. Examples of an external EPSS include job aids or manuals, demonstration videos, or call centers. These services reside outside, or external to, the system. They are separate from the task and require effort on the part of the learner to locate and use.

A bit more transparent is the next level of support, which is *extrinsic* and again provides a low level of support. Examples of extrinsic performance support include the help function embedded in a software application, an interactive kiosk, such as a map at a museum, or Internet bookmarking. Extrinsic support is outside the functions of the system.

Intrinsic performance support, on the other hand, is integrated into the context of the task. Examples of intrinsic performance support include a cellular phone's stored list of called numbers and software packages that have their own software wizards.

A level of transparency up from that is *intuitive* support, which is also integrated into the workflow but it is more seamless. In other words, you hardly notice the intervention—it seems transparent. An example of intuitive support would be an ongoing spell and grammar check feature in a word processing software package. It does not have to be invoked.

Finally, intelligent performance support is the highest level of integration. In this case, the task and the assistance are fully merged, and the user does not notice the intervention. Some examples include mechanical equipment that will not function unless properly held. The Wii™ gaming piece is an example of an intelligent support handheld wireless controller that can be used as a handheld pointing device and detects movement in three dimensions. The sytem will not function properly without the handheld device.

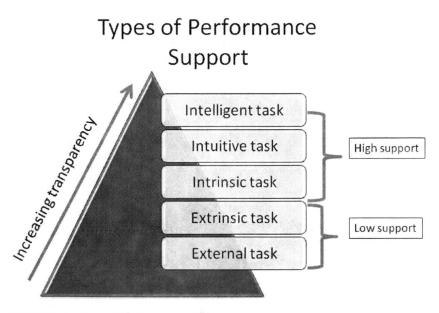

Types of Performance Support

FIGURE 10-1   Types of Performance Support

Designing and Developing an EPSS

While the computer technology used to deliver an EPSS tends to get most of the attention, the design process associated with the EPSS is what most determines its effectiveness (Nguyen and Hanzel 2007). The design will differ based upon the organization's preferred project management process. However, several components are required for best practice. We present a hybrid of approaches defined by Frank Nguyen and Craig Woll—experts in the design and development of EPSSs—and Ryan Watkins, professor at The George Washington University and author of several books on performance improvement. Although the process looks linear, it is in fact quite complex. Adjustments may be needed before implementation, and maintenance to the system is ongoing; both require returning to an earlier stage of the process. The approach described in subsquent sections is not intended to provide all of the details but rather general guidance.

Phase 1: Needs Assessment

In this first phase, you conduct a need assessment. The assessment will identify performance gaps, pinpoint relevant content for the intervention, and indicate the users' needs. It may include using interviews, focus groups, surveys, and observation to identify the skills and habits the users possess, their comfort level with the technology, the working environment, any performance gaps, where the performance support will reside, and the users' attitudes toward an electronic performance support system. Look for the performance problem, finding the disparity between required performance and actual performance.

Phase 2: EPSS Analysis

Review the needs assessment results. Complete a task and performance analysis by observing the task(s) from start to finish in the environment in which it is performed and ask questions about why things are done that particular way. Keep in mind these questions: What does the performer need to know, do, or possess when commencing his or her efforts? What is done? What are the special circumstances or considerations? What does the performer need to do upon completion of the task(s)?

Define the clients' (or potential users') roles relative to the EPSS development effort, as you will need initial and ongoing involvement of the target audience. The client should participate in the user and task analysis. They may also contribute suggested revisions and participate in the maintenance of the EPSS.

During this phase, the EPSS is examined as an appropriate solution. Be open to the fact that there may be a better performance improvement intervention. There has to be some "opt out" option implied, and at this point alternatives are explored. Of course, if the EPSS is not the agreed-upon solution, then this process of EPSS design and development stops.

Phase 3: EPSS Design

Define system specifications. Determine what style of EPSS this will be. Remember what Barry Raybould (2000) states in his article "Building Performance-Centered Web-Based Systems, Information Systems, and Knowledge Management Systems in the 21st Century": that "as support moves further from the tool and requires more time off the job, it becomes less powerful" (35).

Identify how you will assess the effectiveness of the system. What are the specific metrics that you can use as indicators? These considerations and provisions will add to the quality of the EPSS and save money in the long run as problems can be detected early on before the system goes live (Watkins 2007).

Identify and select performance support requirements. This involves developing the information to be provided by the PSS, such as help messages, database entries, and expert advice. This task may be easier than you think if the performance support system is tied to a learning object database containing training objects that can be repurposed for the PSS (Nguyen and Hanzel 2007). For more information about learning objects, see chapter 3.

Define the format, media, and software requirements. Choose the technology options for the EPSS. These have changed significantly in the twenty-first century. Rossett and Schafer (2007) provide the following taxonomy, updated to include all of the following technology options for an EPSS:

- The step format in sequence
- The tailored step format, which requires the user to provide input into the order of the steps
- The list format, such as product lists, employee directories, customers purchasing the same product
- The coach format, which prompts mindfulness to consider multiple factors
- The graphical format, which presents information visually including tables, charts, graphs, maps
- Quiz where a solution or conclusion is derived from a series of questions and user answers that guide to a solution
- Decision table formats that allow users to identify and compare potential solutions (e.g., when comparing health coverage under different plans)
- The navigation format, where the user provides information that guides him toward specific solutions (portals, menus, and dashboards use navigation formats)
- The search format (i.e., Google, Bing)
- Hybrid formats that combine several of the preceding formats

Note that the design may include combinations of approaches.

Phase 4: EPSS Development

Create a prototype of the support system. Do a pilot or beta test to examine the functionality and assess its performance. This process requires collaboration by a number of different departments to share detailed methodology over a relatively long period of time. Because the EPSS is typically under constant change, there is an ongoing need for piloting, revising, and collaborating on implementing agreed-upon changes.

In order to handle this complex process, be sure to create a performance support task force consisting of members from different groups, including the target audience. The task force needs support from upper management and representation that is inclusive of every group that will be using or impacted by the EPSS (Watkins 2007). Then review and revise the electronic performance support system as needed (Watkins 2007).

Phase 5: EPSS Implementation and Monitoring

Implement the EPSS. Monitor the performance of the users and the system to ensure that the objectives were met (Nguyen and Woll 2006, Watkins 2007). Examining the EPSS's performance is an ongoing process, so we do not mean to imply that this is the end of the project. The EPSS and its users must be monitored from point of implementation forward in order to make adjustments and improvements. Create and institute a maintenance plan. This is of utmost importance, because any change that is made by the systems group must be immediately reflected in the performance support. If you make changes to the performance support system, you will need to perform another job and user analysis and make adjustments so that the workflow matches the performance of the task.

HR-Intersect—Designing an EPSS

The design, implementation, and maintenance of a performance support system requires collaboration of different departments or groups within an organization. They include:

- Information technology that explains how the system works
- Systems engineering, which helps design the performance support architecture
- Training/technical publications groups—the training/publications groups must explain performance technology and can explain the intent of the PSS
- Performance technologist, from the systems group, for ongoing maintenance of the PSS

Performance Support and Return on Investment

Performance support systems have been shown to directly improve employee performance (Nguyen 2009). Not only does performance improve with a well-designed PSS, but performer attitudes improve. With all of this hype, the question arises, What about the costs?

We can examine the cost effectiveness of an EPSS from a return-on-investment analysis. Frank Nguyen and Craig Woll (2006) indicate the approach to calculating the ROI of a system includes (1) isolating your data from other variables, (2) limiting the number of key metrics to avoid overcounting, (3) converting the data into dollars, and (4) examining and calculating the outcomes for the same measures both before and after.

Specific metrics necessary for calculating ROI follow. The specific cost indicators have to do with the work hours saved over the life of the system. For the *new* employee, there is a "cost per employee/continuing worker hours saved" way to evaluate the cost savings offered by a PSS. Remember that the PSS is used on the job while the worker is performing a task, so there is no time off task dedicated to training. The points where the savings are realized include the reduced time to learn the system and reduced need for supervision, as well as less reliance on help from coworkers. The reduced number of calls to the helpline, reduced downtime, and fewer calls from the helpline to the supervisor (indicating overuse of the help service) also contribute to the return on investment.

Continuing savings occur over the life of the system in the form of:

- Reduced time for the worker to perform operations
- Reduced overtime
- Reduced supervision
- Reduced help from others
- Reduced calls to the helpline
- Reduced downtime
- Fewer mistakes
- Fewer employees needed to do the job

These very specific metrics provide important data regarding the ROI of an EPSS and could be used to evaluate an EPSS intervention.

Performance Support—Customer-Service Call Center: Case Study

Frank Nguyen

A Fortune 100 customer service organization had a virtual, phone-based, customer-service call center with approximately 25,000 call center personnel located in ten different sites globally. In 2002, the organization instituted a customized performance support system to assist the call center professionals. Having a widespread commitment to knowledge management, the processes and procedures included a global team of knowledge managers whose job it was to take information and enter it into the new, external performance support system. New hires received extensive training over a period of about five to six weeks, including use of the new performance support system. Because training courseware was difficult and cumbersome to update, the performance support system was relied on heavily to keep pace with constantly changing laws, compliance rules, business policies and procedures, and product information.

By 2010, the organization's performance support strategy was in serious need of an overhaul. In addition, performance support and content management technologies have advanced extensively, particularly since the introduction of Web 2.0 technologies, so the underlying technology was in dire need of refreshing. It became increasingly difficult for users to quickly locate the information they needed to support job performance amongst the vast base of information that had been collected over the course of almost a decade. Performers needed some way to link from the tools they used on a daily basis directly to the performance support content they needed.

The determination was made to update the existing legacy system and embed the performance support in the call center software. A primary issue was what to do with the old performance support content. Further, with advances in user contributed content, there would be no need for the knowledge managers who input information into the legacy performance support system. The shift in approach would require business process reengineering and redefining or even eliminating knowledge managers' roles and responsibilities. The goal of the new internal performance support was to eliminate the visibility of the performance support system and integrate it so that it was embedded in the employees' everyday work interfaces. How to seamlessly migrate almost 20,000 pages of content presented another challenge.

The solution was to create the new internal system then roll it out one division at a time. The metrics to evaluate the new system's performance included:

- Reducing average handling time in the call center (this is the amount of time a customer service representative is on the phone with a customer). To date, the data indicate that the new system reduced handling time by about 5 to 7 percent.

- The second indicator was to increase "first call resolution" (FCR). FCR is the resolution of the problem on the first call rather than the customer having to call back again about the same problem. There are no data on that at present.

- The third metric can't be measured yet. It is connected to another feature of the new performance support, which is to provide an external page that is tied into the performance support tool from which customers could get their answers without needing to have direct contact with a customer service representative. This would result in a reduction in total call volume to the call center. As mentioned above, this has not been implemented yet, so there are no metrics.

The advantages to the organization that result from implementing the new system are:

- Reduced training time
- Fewer costs associated with instructor time, travel, facilities, etc.

- More accurate information than, for example, a job aid, which would have to be continually updated to accommodate the ongoing changes in the industry
- Customer representatives having access to a robust body of information at their fingertips

Frank Nguyen, PhD, is the emerging technologies manager at American Express, Incorporated. His doctorate is in Educational Technology.

Mobile Electronic Performance Support

In an article written in 2008, Marci Paino and Allison Rossett state that many users of performance support systems want their support to "go with them wherever they go" (42). The authors indicate that technology is moving toward integration and omnipresence of performance support. Well, in the following case, mobile and integrated performance support is a reality.

A Korean insurance organization instituted a mobile EPSS to support their sales staff (Kim 2011). In order to sustain their talented sales associates and improve their performance, the organization developed a sophisticated mobile EPSS called a Technology-Enhanced Learning Environment (TELE). The in-house EPSS was made available to the sales associates over their Personal Digital Assistants (PDAs). Since sales associates work outside the office and cannot access legal, regulatory, and process information, a mobile performance support environment was better-suited to their work.

The TELE has a variety of functions. Frequently asked questions were converted to modular e-learning materials made available through the EPSS and accessible to sales associates on their PDAs. Many tasks have EPSS tools that can be accessed on handheld devices. Embedded coaching tools provide assistance with tasks such as contract writing by providing a diagram of the contract process as well as contract writing instruction using a "wizard." Calendars of personal schedules can be shared using the EPSS and sales persons can also connect to the customer database, where the associates can find client information.

This powerful mobile application has made a huge difference in the performance of the sales associates. It should be noted, however, that a sophisticated EPSS of this nature must have appropriate leadership support. Additionally, the initial cost for establishing a mobile EPSS can be very high. Thus, it makes sense to focus on a single practice area, such as establishing EPSS for a specific job, to mitigate the costs of a full-scale rollout for all functional areas (Kim 2011).

Electronic Performance Support Development and Lean Six Sigma Processes

There are a variety of approaches to the management of an electronic performance support system project. They should have some standard features, which we delineated above. Embedded in that approach are definitions of existing processes, performance metrics, and evaluation measures to ensure that the EPSS has met desired objectives. Another concern is that the EPSS development effort conform to quality measures and build them into the system.

One process that emphasizes the same objectives of measurement and quality is the *Lean Six Sigma* quality improvement method. While it is beyond the scope of this chapter to examine in great depth the Six Sigma movement, it does bear emphasis and an explanation of its unique relationship to EPSS development.

Lean Six Sigma is a process improvement program that emerged from the total quality management movement. Dr. W. Edwards Deming, an American statistician who led the quality movement in Japan, said that most quality problems are in the process, not the person. Later in life he stated it was more than likely that 96 percent of problems are built into the way work is done, with only 4 percent of business problems being the fault of individual employees! (Deming in George, Rowlands, and Kastle 2004, 19).

The Six Sigma process is based upon data and facts. The goal of the Lean Six Sigma process is to delight customers and improve processes. The approach involves identifying variations and defects and improving process flow. Because variation impacts the ability of an organization to meet customer needs, the ideal is to eliminate variation, and the way to eliminate variation is by improving process flow and speed. Eliminate the unnecessary complexity that adds cost and time and results in enormous waste; improve work processes, and organizational performance will improve.

The intersect between Six Sigma and EPSS design is the goal of assessing the process and identifying potential areas for improvement in flow and speed before designing the EPSS system. Further, since the EPSS may replace training and the Six Sigma approach is appropriate for workplace training design and development (Baun and Scott 2010), the Six Sigma can impact the EPSS design as well.

In both Lean Six Sigma and the EPSS project management process, there is a detailed examination and evaluation of business processes. In both cases, the starting point is to analyze the existing processes and identify possible improved efficiencies before proceeding with the design effort. This is how the EPSS design process can positively impact organizational learning and performance.

Whatever the net impact upon the organization, EPSSs are bound to influence the business processes and may actually create a need to modify business processes. The use of such performance support systems tends to redefine the nature of work activities. Job responsibilities and roles change, because a given individual is likely to be able to carry out a more diverse range of tasks, with more competency, than he would without the EPSS.

The importance of pointing out this overlap in processes is this: When instituting a new EPSS, the project manager must identify any ongoing process improvement and problem solving efforts (including Lean Six Sigma). These may alter the EPSS design. Waiting until after the fact requires reworking and changing the EPSS.

You can realize benefits both to process improvement and the quality of the EPSS by instituting the Six Sigma approach *before* designing and instituting the EPSS. Retrofitting an EPSS simply wastes time, effort, and money.

Tips and Tools for Using Performance Support Systems

- Use performance support systems when you need immediate performance with minimal external support.

- The development process for a performance support system is complex and expensive, although in most cases the rewards over time exceed the costs.

- It is a good idea to build best practices into the performance support system.

- Continuing savings occur over the life of the system in the form of reduced time for the worker to perform operations, reduced overtime, reduced calls to the helpline, and less downtime.

- An EPSS development effort involves representatives from a number of different parts of the organization, including the target audience, information technology, systems engineering, training, communications/publications, (performance technologist for maintenance).

Electronic Performance Support and the Learning Organization

An electronic performance support system should enable an individual to reach the required level of performance in the fastest possible time with the least personal support. This improved performance impacts the organization and its learning capabilities. Electronic performance support systems can impact the learning organization in three primary ways:

- Individual learning—Using performance support, the worker may change his behavior after receiving negative or corrective feedback, review EPSS modules on the job just before using them, and review modules off the job when mistakes would not be dangerous and costly.
- Generation of new knowledge—Using performance support system, the worker develops new techniques, methods, and procedures on the job that were not part of her original knowledge base.
- Knowledge capture—The performance support system captures new knowledge through some formal process (electronic messages, shared databases, interview, expert workers).

Conclusion

A performance support system can be a cost-effective way to provide the right information to the right user at the right time. The design is labor intensive, but the rewards can be improved performance for the labor force as a whole, and for new hires a shorter time from hiring date to productivity.

Communication Technologies

CHAPTER 11

Groupware for Collaboration

The reality of virtual teams and the growth of communities of practice spurred technology innovations in communication and collaboration. Groupware is a software that is designed to help groups work together by facilitating the exchange of information among group members who are not colocated (*http://searchdomino.techtarget.com*). Groupware enables ongoing virtual communication and collaboration.

In this chapter we will describe a variety of groupware products. We will address their benefits and point out potential pitfalls. The link between groupware and both social learning and communities of practice is established and provides a context for the use of groupware. Additionally, we will explore the impact of groupware on workplace policies.

What Is Groupware?

Groupware is a term for collaborative software (also referred to as *workgroup support systems* or simply *group support systems*) designed to help people involved in a common task to achieve their goals. Often, groupware incorporates video, chat, Instant Messaging, polling capabilities, emoticons for feedback, hotlinks for virtual tours, and whiteboards, as well as presentation software. It may rely upon both telecommunications and the Internet or strictly the Internet. The goal in using groupware is to enable interaction between individuals or groups that are not colocated. The level of sophistication of the groupware varies from the basic teleconference all the way to the use of telepresence. Let's examine the range of groupware options.

Teleconference

At one end of the groupware spectrum, there is the teleconference. We are all familiar with that form of collaboration. For these simpler versions of groupware, typical peripherals include a telephone and phone connection.

When the phone transmission takes place over the Internet, the voice message may travel over the phone lines or over the Internet. *Voice over Internet Protocol (VoIP)* is a technology that allows you to make voice calls using a broadband Internet connection instead of using a regular (or analog) phone line. Some VoIP services may only allow you to call other people using the same service, but others may allow you to call anyone who has a telephone number, including local, long distance, mobile, and international numbers. Also, while some VoIP services only work over your computer or a special VoIP phone, other services allow you to use a traditional phone connected to a VoIP adapter.

As the technology becomes more sophisticated, groupware systems may require peripherals such as a webcam and/or microphone attached to the computer, with software to enable the interaction online.

And at the most sophisticated level, such as telepresence, the technology requires accommodations or rooms that provide high-end video uplink/downlink equipment. Let's look next at a couple of the more sophisticated (compared to the teleconference) groupware products, starting with video teleconferencing.

Video Teleconferencing

A *video teleconference* is a set of interactive telecommunication technologies which allow two or more locations to interact via two-way video and audio transmissions simultaneously. It has also been called 'visual collaboration' and is a type of groupware.

Historically, the main use for video teleconferencing has been within the corporate environment for one-to-one business meetings. Because of the requirements for dedicated camera, audio, and networking equipment, it was usual to set up dedicated rooms for the purpose of holding video conferences.

Before the availability of high-bandwidth Internet connections, signals were carried over point-to-point connections established via ISDN lines. ISDN are similar to telephone connections in that the calling party would "dial up" the destination station and pay for the length of time the call was open. Because of the high bandwidth requirement, multiple connections were usually required, making it very expensive to hold international video teleconferences.

With the advent of web-enabled video conferencing, the desktop use of webcam and computer with Internet connection has made video conferencing more cost effective. Using web-enabled video conferencing, the users see and hear each other as they interact. A simple example of this form of video conferencing using the Internet is offered through the open-source product named Skype.

Web Conferencing

Web conferencing is where a presenter can deliver a presentation over the web to a group of geographically dispersed participants. The terms "web conference" and "webinar" are used interchangeably to refer to the same type of service. In its simplest form, the presentation is not interactive. Participants can see what's on the screen but cannot make changes.

Multifaceted Groupware

Another form of groupware relies upon VoIP and has other supportive features, including the incorporation of presentation software and social media. Elluminate Live!, Eduplex Interactive, GoToMeeting, and WebEx are popular groupware products.

As an example of groupware, Elluminate Live! offers a variety of features. There is a whiteboard on which the presenter can draw or write text. Presenters can import a Microsoft PowerPoint presentation, link to streamed video, access a demonstration website to share information, and share their computer screen for everyone to see. Elluminate Live! allows for interactivity using text-based chat, voice interaction (using a microphone), and video of the speaker (enabled by webcam). Participants may raise a hand for recognition, register a reaction using emoticons, and respond using the speaker-initiated polling feature in addition to using the microphone or webcam.

This learning and collaboration tool helps participants to go beyond web conferencing with web, audio, video, and social networking solutions for the twenty-first century. Eduplex Interactive (*www.eduplexinteractive.com*) is a groupware that uses video conferencing and is adapted for mobile use.

Telepresence

Telepresence is an example of a high-end groupware product that includes high-definition video technology to display life-sized, three-dimensional video for a conferencing experience closest to the in-person experience. Telepresence gives the appearance that all participants are present in the same room. The user's position, movements, actions, voice, and so on, may be sensed, transmitted, and duplicated in the remote location. This is a high level of videotelephony that uses greater technical sophistication and improved video and audio than is used in traditional videoconferencing.

BAE Systems' Managed Telepresence: Case Study

Bharat Amin

BAE Systems, Inc., the U.S.-based segment of BAE Systems plc, is headquartered in Arlington, Virginia. The U.S. entity, which has 52,000 employees, comprises approximately one half of the company's global workforce and is structured in five sectors. With 17,000 employees located in fifty-six sites, including the United States, Sweden, the United Kingdom, and South Africa, and markets in more than two dozen countries, the U.S. company's Land & Armaments (L&A) sector is a global leader in the design, development, production, and support of armaments. The range of armaments involved includes life support and upgrade of armored combat vehicles, tactical wheeled vehicles, artillery systems, and munitions, as well as military and law enforcement products.

BAE Systems Land & Armaments leaders often spent days traveling to periodic, face-to-face meetings. "It was almost ten years ago that I first recognized the need for videoconferencing as a business tool," said Linda Hudson, president and CEO of BAE Systems, Inc. The need became more apparent when air traffic was halted in the spring of 2010 as volcanic ash descended on Europe.

BAE Systems Land & Armaments chose AT&T Telepresence Solution* to manage its widely dispersed operations and enable engineering teams and business leaders to collaborate and solve problems. "Connecting our employees and bridging the distances between our home markets is a key capability which has been rolled out through our World-Class IT infrastructure Initiative. The AT&T Telepresence Solution is a critical component to enable this capability. Our teams experience an in-person meeting without having to travel frequently," said Bharat Amin, VP and business technology officer for Land & Armaments.

Unlike traditional single-camera video conferencing, AT&T Telepresence Solution replicates the in-person feel and nuances of communication possible in a face-to-face meeting. Employees are now able to sit across the table from "actual-size" video of colleagues around the world on ultra-high definition screens with wideband audio and communicate in real time across the AT&T global network.

Travel savings rapidly offset the cost. Additionally, BAE Systems realizes less tangible benefits. Employees who participate via telepresence recapture wasted travel time and can apply it to more productive tasks. Executives become more accessible, resulting in faster decision making. The technology mitigates travel risks. Finally, the decrease in travel reaps positive environmental benefits, enhancing BAE Systems' green initiatives though lowering CO_2 emissions.

Uses range from conducting monthly and quarterly executive meetings to running implementation sessions following a recent reorganization to engaging engineering staff in biweekly collaborative meetings. The ability to connect intercompany enables stronger relationships between customers, partners, and suppliers. On several occasions, BAE Systems Land & Armaments has used this technology to interview potential candidates for employment (internally and externally) within the United States and between the United States and the United Kingdom. With a minor kit update, the telepresence rooms can be converted to high-definition-quality digital media recording studios, allowing the company to record and publish digital media.

In the initial phase of this implementation, Amin calculated that the AT&T Telepresence Solution would deliver significant financial returns for the business. Installed, monitored, and managed entirely by AT&I, the system is user-friendly enough that employees are able to arrange and carry out their own conferences without additional support from IT. Amin calculates that if six individuals from each of the seven U.S. sites traveled to the U.K. for a meeting (as was conducted via telepresence for the ribbon-cutting ceremony), it would cost $220,000 in airfare, require 862 hours of employee travel time, use 347,000 in air miles, and contribute to the emission of 277 metric tons of carbon dioxide. The BAE Systems Land & Armaments business case estimates that using telepresence across the company will reduce travel costs by 10 percent, enough to repay the investment in 1.2 years. Clearly, the cost savings are significant, and they will increase as company use grows and employees further embrace the enhanced collaboration capabilities of this technology.

Bharat Amin, of BAE Systems, Inc., is vice president and business technology officer for the Land & Armaments sector. Amin is responsible for overseeing all aspects of the information management and technology functions for the sector. He has more than twenty-five years of IS/IT leadership and management experience in the consumer goods and aerospace and defense industries.

Why Groupware?

Groupware lends itself to numerous applications. Because such a variety of products exists, groupware can satisfy simple to complex requirements and budgets. There is a wide range in price based upon the level of complexity, from free, open-source products to telepresence products that, installed, may cost hundreds of thousands of dollars. The point is that there is groupware that can meet the needs of your organization. Collaborative software can be chosen based upon budget; in other words, financial constraints should not prevent organizations from using groupware. Further, a number of learning theories, processes, and best practices can be tied to groupware, legitimizing it as a learning media.

Social Learning Theory

Social learning theory (Bandura 1977; Vygotsky 1978) focuses on the social context in which people learn, that is, how they learn through interacting with and observing other people. People can learn from imitating others (thus the importance of role models and mentoring). Immediacy is another aspect of social learning, where immediacy means behaviors that are verbal (giving praise, soliciting viewpoints, using humor, offering self-disclosure) or nonverbal (eye contact, facial expressions, gestures). Researchers have found that immediacy leads directly or indirectly to greater learning (Swan and Shea 2005).

Social learning can be facilitated through web-enabled video conferencing groupware; the learners experience immediate feedback through that media. The experience of "social presence" can be accomplished through teleconferencing or videoconferencing. However, the media that are richer in facial and verbal expression are optimal for social learning (Swan and Shea 2005, 243).

Communities of Practice (CoPs)

Communities of practice are "groups of people who share a concern, a set of problems, or a passion about a topic, and who deepen their knowledge and expertise in this area by interacting on an ongoing basis" (Wenger, McDermott, and Snyder 2002, 4). Communities of practice typically meet on an ongoing basis. Communities of practice have a long and robust history starting in ancient Rome with corporations of craftsmen, continuing in the Middle Ages in the form of guilds, and revived in this Internet age.

With regard to technology, practitioners must use familiar, work-related technologies in order to sustain a community of practice (Wenger, McDermott, and Snyder 2002, 197). The "best media" tend to be those that enable shared workspaces for synchronous electronic collaboration enhanced by visuals (198). Shared workspaces are areas that are hosted by a web server, where colleagues can share documents and information, maintain lists of pertinent data, and keep each other up to date on the status of a given project (*http://office.micro-soft.com*). In other words, CoPs thrive when members use a technology that allows them to communicate synchronously (by voice or text) and be able to see some visual at the same time. This is because communities of practice rely upon robust communication. Groupware is one medium that fits the requirements for a CoP.

Virtual Teams

Virtual teams are teams that communicate and collaborate across time, distance, and departmental and organization boundaries (Mittleman and Briggs 1999, 246). In the mid-twentieth century, virtual teams were a novelty. By 1998, it was estimated that a total of more than one hundred thirty million people were connected to the Internet around the world (246). This surge in connectivity via the Internet laid the groundwork for virtual teams.

Daniel Mittleman and Robert Briggs in Sundstrom's book *Supporting Work Team Effectiveness* (2002) state that the following technologies are the most important and widely used for virtual teams:

- Audio communication system
- Video communication system
- Real-time data communication such as chat
- Different-time data communication, including e-mail and bulletin board software
- Electronic whiteboard
- Keypad voting system
- Document saving and retrieval
- Calendaring

In short, in order to collaborate, virtual teams rely upon internal communication process support, external communication process support, process structure tools, task structure tools, and task support (Nunamaker et al. 1997). A wide variety of groupware products exist, offering all of the above features. Groupware can support virtual teams!

Citing scholarly literature is important because the studies follow strict research protocol, so the conclusions are tested and peer reviewed. This makes the conclusions more reliable than, say, those found in marketing materials. Technology selection should rely upon logic, not fads. The articles above demonstrate the "fit" and appropriateness of groupware as a technology that can support social learning, communities of practice, and virtual teams.

GoToMeeting is a groupware product that usually serves as an online meeting program enabling individuals, business, and organizations to collaborate and communicate through the Internet (Safko 2010). Some of its features include presentation capabilities, audio, chat components, screen sharing, slideshows, and document sharing and editing, as well as meeting recording. It can be used for a variety of collaborative purposes, including social learning, virtual teams, and building communities of practice, but it also adapts well to product demonstration or proposal writing or other applications that rely upon the services it offers. The point is that some groupware is more robust than others. You can be creative in its uses.

Tips and Tools for Choosing Groupware Products

Thinking about groupware, but would like to experience it first? Try out these free or shareware services:

- Free teleconferencing and recording tool
  www.freeconferencecall.com
- Free Skype video teleconferencing
  www.skype.com
- Eduplex Interactive groupware (shareware)
  www.eduplexinteractive.com

Groupware and Presentation Software

Microsoft PowerPoint is not the only presentation software in existence, although it is widely used as a business application. An open-source software called Prezi allows you to have some flexibility to give your presentation a whiteboard look rather than a sequential slide presentation. Just as you write things on the whiteboard as the topic emerges, Prezi enables you to sequence your visuals and text as if you were using a whiteboard. Go to *www.prezi.com* for an example of another way to look at presentations.

Ideas can also be presented using narration with visuals. Microsoft Photo Story is a free application that allows users to create a show-and-tell video presentation from their digital photos. The resulting video is in .wmv format and can be played on a personal computer using Windows Media Player. It can also be converted to other formats using third-party software for that purpose. To access the Photo Story free application, go to *www.microsoft.com*.

Additionally, the iSpring shareware (free trial software) can be used to convert a PowerPoint presentation to a flash movie, which can then be uploaded to the Internet. Go to *www.ispringsolutions.com* to access this software.

The advantage of a video presentation is that it can be converted to the proper format to publish or share on a DVD, in a learning content management system, or—if it is in a compatible format—on a website. An interesting example of this video presentation approach, entitled "The Good Life (2008)," can be found at *www.youtube.com/watch?v=McvCJley78A&feature=related*.

One thing to remember about presentation slides: they are no substitute for well-designed, online training. Training requires a needs assessment to design a sound instructional experience with measurable results. Never confuse presentations with training.

Groupware Benefits and Pitfalls

Groupware offers a variety of benefits, many of which have been covered in previous sections. The software allows users to give slide presentations, use drawing tools, conduct demos, and collaborate in real time on projects. The groupware can support a wide variety of applications, everything from training in a social learning context to collaboration of virtual teams to promotion and coordination of communities of practice. There are also cost benefits to groupware. As companies try to save money, groupware allows organizations to cut down on the cost of travel both in real dollars and lost productivity (Agnvall 2009, 74).

The drawbacks of groupware are less obvious. As with any other technology, it is important to select groupware that is best-suited to and compatible with the technology infrastructure, organizational context, and culture. Additionally, design groupware-enabled interaction with the features of the tool in mind. Training may be needed in order to enable all of the stakeholders to be on the same footing with the same level of functionality. Planning for using the groupware is of the essence.

Failing to choose groupware that can be used by all, disregarding the need for initial training on the groupware, and/or a lack of preparation for and adjustment of the presentation approach to maximize the features of the groupware can cause even the best groupware to be underutilized.

When using groupware, here are some guidelines to keep in mind. If the groupware does not have a video component, introduce yourself before speaking. As the presenter, avoid long presentations; it's easy to lose your audience. Regularly gauge participant involvement by asking questions and polling for response. Document the audience input and questions, then ensure that you respond to each question. Try to engage the audience by using polling features, roll call, questions, and similar techniques to increase the social presence and sense of immediacy.

Thinking about Using Groupware? Consider This ...

When you examine groupware for adoption by your organization, you must first do your due diligence. Consider your answers to the following questions:

- How will your company use the groupware?
- Where will the software be rolled out in its pilot form, and what will the process be after that?
- Are all of the computers used by employees compatible with the software?
- Who will use this tool for remote collaboration, and will all users be in-house or will collaboration include clients?
- Is security important, and, if so, how will the groupware provider address that need? Or will security issues be handled in-house?
- Will firewalls conflict with the technology when installing new software?
- Do the employees have all of the hardware and peripherals needed to use the groupware?
- How many participants will you have and how often? Does number of participants impact cost, or is it a flat fee?
- How complicated is the installation, and will the users need assistance?

Your answers to these questions will clarify whether groupware is a viable collaboration tool for your organization.

Conclusion

Groupware offers powerful conferencing, collaboration, and synchronous communication capabilities. Groupware comes in a variety of forms, each of which has its benefits and shortcomings. When determining whether or not groupware is appropriate, always consider your audience … their level of comfort with the technology as well as their access to it, existing infrastructure, and the costs.

CHAPTER 12

Social Networks and Organizations

S ocial networks first appeared as a nonbusiness application, but they are quickly finding a place in the business realm (Boyd and Ellison 2008). Organizational applications of social networks are still in their infancy. There are both negative and positive ramifications for organizations that use social networks. Legal implications of social network usage are also catching up to business practices, and doubtlessly businesses will find it necessary to adopt policies that guide both the company and individual employees in the use of social network sites. Forecasts of trends in the use of social networks appear in this chapter as well as in chapter 18.

What Are Social Networks?

Social networks refer to the online clustering of individuals into groups, like small rural communities or a neighborhood subdivision, if you will. The in-person version of networking offers endless professional and personal benefits. Now take that online, and you have a powerful tool. The Internet is filled with millions of individuals who are looking to meet other like-minded people. *Social network services* (SNSs) connect individuals of similar interests regardless of their geographical locations. The topics and interests exchanged on social networks are varied and rich. In this chapter, we will use the term "social networks" to refer to "web-based services that allow individuals to (1) construct a public or semipublic profile within a bounded system, (2) articulate a list of other users with whom they share a connection, and (3) view and traverse their list of connections and those made by others within the system" (Boyd and Ellison 2008, 211). We understand that the term "social networking sites" also appears in public discourse, and the two terms are often used interchangeably. To narrow the scope of this chapter and to maintain the early definition of social networks, we will use that term.

Different categories of social networks exist. Facebook is a social network website where you can create profiles, exchange private or public messages, join friends, and so on, and is used by many as a personal space. LinkedIn is considered by many to be a business social network, but neither service is limited to one context or another. Fast Pitch! recently entered the professional SNS arena. Also, MySpace is an earlier online social network service that some use for business purposes. On each of these social network sites, users create a profile and then interact with other users, creating new relationships and maintaining existing ones.

These social network sites can be used in a number of ways. For instance, MySpace offers a tool called MySpace MyAds, which allows users to run effective online marketing campaigns within their social network. Entertainment features can be added, such as the popular video-sharing website YouTube. They must be compatible entities, however. MySpace also has a MySpace Developer Platform that allows users to design their own applications.

Common uses for social network services include marketing through advertisements. Politicians use social network sites to target and attract voters (Safko 2010, 463). Organizations use SNS to review applicant credentials and stay connected with business professionals (American Institute of Certified Public Accountants "Recruiting for Small Firms" 2008, 40). Social networks are also used for building communities of learning and for training (Bingham and Conner 2010).

Social Network Uses at Maastricht University, Netherlands: Case Study

Miriam Pinckaers, Bart Rienties, and Guy Vroemen

The introduction of social network services (SNSs) such as Facebook and LinkedIn have attracted millions of users who have integrated SNSs into their daily practices (Rienties, Tempelaar, Pinckaers, Giesbers, and Lichel 2010). The majority of SNSs serve primarily social purposes or tasks and aim to connect users with friends, relatives, and acquaintances. *Professional SNSs* such as LinkedIn are used for chiefly business purposes, and aim to: (1) connect experts; (2) share information about, and collaborate on, business cases and work fields; and (3) exchange job- and function-related information. This case study examines how Maastricht University in the Netherlands is actively helping students to develop a strong online identity and employability record by providing a social media and LinkedIn workshop conducted by We4people.

LinkedIn is the largest professional SNS currently available. Christine Fountain (2005) argues that the use of personal contacts in an online setting could be helpful for obtaining information about a job opening. Students and professionals actively construct public profiles in SNSs in order to increase their attractiveness and visibility for organizations; this then becomes a part of their job search strategy. Most profile information on LinkedIn forms, in essence, an online curriculum vitae that can be shared with network relations, enabling users to add communities of practice to their profile to reflect their interests and expertise. Evidence shows that most students and graduates are unaware that companies search for the online identity and networks of applicants.

Christine Fountain argued that "new communication technology might be help-ing people to find jobs … because it facilitates the personal communication between friends and acquaintances that often provide information about jobs" (2005, 1255). That is, LinkedIn can be used for several informal job search strategies, which includes the use of personal contacts, such as relatives, friends, and coworkers, who act as referrals and pro-vide inside information on job openings. The job searcher typically meets these personal contacts in a context unrelated to the search for information about job openings. This informal strategy saves on search costs when compared with more traditional channels, such as browsing through vacancies in various newspapers, in this way contributing to job-finding. The strength of a social relationship or tie affects job searchers by the amount and quality of information about job openings available to them. Job searchers who use weak social ties, such as acquaintances or former colleagues, rather than strong social ties, such as close friends and family, are more effective in gathering and getting access to information on available jobs. Weak ties, together with the interaction of a wide range of users in LinkedIn, might provide additional information and opportunities related to jobs. Moreover, LinkedIn can provide bridges for job searchers to valuable embedded resources and to distant parts of their social networks that may contain unique and valuable job information. During Maastricht's Social Media and LinkedIn Workshop, the focus is on raising awareness of how to actively create and sustain an online portfolio that maximizes the potential of the graduates' network.

Our research (Rienties et al. 2010) highlights that professionals use LinkedIn in completely different ways than do students. We discovered that 50 percent of stu-dents were members of LinkedIn, while 85 percent of professionals were members of LinkedIn. On average, LinkedIn members have 104 contacts in their account with, on average, twenty-seven close contacts. Professionals who have more contacts and weak ties in LinkedIn can provide more relevant new information than students. Thus, this indicates that professionals have broader networks, but they actively maintain and cherish their professional networks. Probably because one-third of LinkedIn profes-sionals receive job information via LinkedIn, they find it worthwhile to invest in their online presence. Furthermore, most professionals receive information about job open-ings by two or more SNS contacts on a monthly basis. In other words, professionals are actively using LinkedIn and their networks to share relevant job information with their connections.

Having a lot of LinkedIn links (contacts), in addition to having sufficient weak links who have powerful connections, increases the chance that LinkedIn users receive relevant job information (Rienties et al. 2010). Therefore, in the Social Media and LinkedIn Workshop, students learn best practices of professionals who actively and creatively use their LinkedIn profiles to enhance the visibility of their skills, expertise, and networks. By raising awareness and encouraging students and graduates to actively maintain their online presence and create powerful networks, Maastricht University is enhancing the employability of its students.

Miriam Pinckaers is senior HRM advisor at TNT Post at The Hague and graduate of International Business of Maastricht University. She is interested in change management, employee motivation, education and development, and absenteeism policy.

Bart Rienties, PhD, is lecturer, Higher Education, at the Centre for Educational and Academic Development at University of Surrey. He conducts research on work-based and collaborative learning environments and focuses on the role of social interaction in learning.

Guy Vroemen is an entrepreneur, managing director, and co-owner of the franchise company We4people. We4people delivers services and marketing support for entrepreneurs in recruitment and secondment (temporary transfer within an organization).

Social networks rely upon a variety of tools embedded in the service itself with the goal of connecting people. Interaction occurs through the use of e-mail, blogs, instant messages, text, podcasts, photographs, and video for social, professional, and business purposes. The goal is to build trust within a specific community.

The term *mashup*, with regard to social networks, means assembling unique items to create something new (Bingham and Conner 2010, 16). There are basically four different types of SNS mashups. These are role, workgroup, content, and management mashups. Definitions appear below:

- *Role mashups* occur when the roles online are blurred. So, a person could be both a teacher and learner or a creator and a recipient at the same time. These role changes make work nonlinear and collaborative.
- *Workgroup mashups* occur when people instantly team up with people everywhere, collaborating outside the boundaries of hierarchies and location.
- *Content mashups* occur when we access information retrieved from external data sources to create entirely new and innovative content and functionality.

- *Management mashups* are what leaders use to convey their ideas and vision, using a variety of communication methods such as blogs, e-mail, newsletters, video, and podcasts to connect with others.

The authors of the book *The New Social Learning*—Tony Bingham and Marcia Conner—think of these mashups as different ways to learn. The pair present an interesting argument that new training events using SNSs take advantage of these mashups as opportunities for "incidental learning, learning from interacting with others, and learning along the way in the course of work" (2010, 21). How novel. A caution, however, is necessary: you can never be assured that the information you have accessed via your social networks is accurate.

Types of Social Networks

The many online SNS communities can be broken down into major categories, including informational, professional, educational, academic, training and development, and news-related (*http://socialnetworking.lovetoknow.com/ What_Types_of_Social_Networks_Exist*). Within each of these major categories, there are many thousands of communities filled with active members who dedicate a fair portion of their day to participating in those social networks. It is certain that many others will surface in the next few years, as their popularity seems to be increasing.

Informational Social Networks

Informational communities are made up of people seeking answers to everyday problems. For example, when you are looking for the best arborist in order to plant appropriate trees for your climate in your backyard, you may perform a web search and discover countless blogs, websites, and forums filled with people who are looking for the same kind of information. Informational communities are often linked to businesses like service organizations, retailers, and other companies that are using social networks as a way to interact with customers. Forbes stock-picking community and e-HOW (which includes "how-to" information written by members) are two informational social networks.

Professional Social Networks

Professional social networks can help participants to advance within their career or industry. They help participants network and find new connections that they would not have otherwise discovered. Through those contacts, professionals can also gain new ideas. LinkedIn is a business network, and LPN is a Latino professional network.

Educational Social Networks

Educational networks are where many students go in order to collaborate with other students; they can perform research, ask questions of another student or an instructor, or interact in classroom forums. Educational social networks often rely upon blogs and classroom forums to exchange information and ideas. The Student Room is a U.K.-based student community, and ePALS School Blog is a service that connects students from around the world to promote world peace.

Academic Social Networks

ARPANET, the U.S. Department of Defense's original network, eventually morphed into a large network that is used not only for military purposes, but for collaboration within the scientific community. Social networks provide an obvious benefit for academic researchers to pursue research interests with experts and other like-minded professionals. Connotea is a collaborative research network service and Academici is for academics and academically interested friends and Edutopia is an academic service.

Training and Development Social Networks

Social networking as a training method is cost effective and makes it possible for learners to access course content when they need it. Learners participate with others in order to make sense of new ideas. Social networking leaves a digital audit trail, documenting the learning. Learners may use embedded blog posts to share best practices, techniques, or insights directly inside the course. Additionally, chat and "friending" other classmates allows professionals to build their professional networks. The social networking interactions can be archived and referenced at a later date. Typically these are developed in-house.

News-Related Social Networks

Another popular social network is the type with "community content." These are large content websites where members are allowed to make comments, post news stories, or anything else. When hosting these types of sites, they need to be monitored; when they are not monitored, the conversation can be filled with self-promotion and advertisements, rendering it unattractive to readers. Triond, AllVoices, and NowPublic are three such news-related SNSs.

Other tools also enable people to enter social networks. *Twitter* is a more recent new media as a social networking and microblogging service that allows a user to update friends by sending short messages called *"tweets."*

Microblogging differs from traditional blogging in that its content is typically much smaller, in both actual size, number of words allowed, and the full file size. A microblog entry could consist of nothing but a short sentence fragment, an image, an acronym or embedded video. As with traditional bloggers, microbloggers write about topics ranging from the simple, such as "what I'm doing right now," to the thematic, such as "French cooking." Commercial microblogs also exist to promote websites, services and/or products, and to promote collaboration within an organization. We will talk about microblogging, blogs, and other social media in more depth in chapter 14.

Why Organizations Use Social Networks

Social networks are appealing for many reasons. For organizations, there are a variety of uses, as Lon Safko points out in *The Social Media Bible* (2010):

> Social networks develop the trust that ultimately creates influence among your consumers. By developing and cultivating networks, your organization can create an opportunity to develop the trust that may result in more sales (21).

The social network has completely changed the way people interact. With a tool that powerful and undeniably appealing—which engages millions of people in one place, at one time, with common interests—organizations need to understand it and join in the conversation!

Business Applications

When social networks began, they tended to be used for sharing photos, videos, and gossip. However, social networks have grown into a mainstream business network. Social networks have a variety of applications that are valuable to organizations. These applications have been widely touted in support of social networks, and they are increasing in number. Organizations may also create their own organization-based social network, which is what EMC Corporation has done.

EMC Corporation's Social Network

EMC Corporation, headquartered in Hopkinton, Massachusetts, is a U.S. Fortune 500 and S&P 500 provider of information infrastructure systems, software, and services. Its flagship product, the Symmetrix, is the foundation of storage networks in many large data centers. EMC's social network, called EMC/ONE, became the mouthpiece for the chief financial officer to broadcast cost-cutting measures (Roberts 2010). In response to the mandates, the employees subsequently used EMC/ONE to start a forum for workers to share and discuss ideas for cutting costs (54). When the CFO learned about the forum, he read the postings and decided to adopt many of the ideas. The forum became a collaborative tool for thousands of employees to receive the cost-cutting message and to contribute to the pool of ideas about cost-cutting measures—a win-win situation on both counts!

Brainstorming is another potential application of social networks. Additionally, social networks can be used for strategic planning. Organizations may use social networks for the purposes of creating contacts among employees or finding out who is available to staff new projects. Recruiting can be done through social networks, and branding and customer contact may also occur in social networks. For internal benefits, social networks can facilitate knowledge management, informal learning, and collaboration, as well as support dispersed project teams (Roberts 2010).

Some other uses for social networks within an organization include:

- Finding translators for dealing with customers located in other regions of the globe
- Replacing the barrage of internal e-mails
- Connecting new hires with other new hires, mentors, managers, and team members (Arnold 2010)
- Dialoging about common issues and innovative ideas
- Sharing documents between project team members or others within the organization
- Training and employee development

Training may offer the most novel application of social networking. Paula Ketter asserts in *T+D* journal (2010) that training social networks are the wave of the future. How does it work? Capitalizing on the social learning theory (see chapters 4 and 11), employees can create learning events on social networking sites, where control of learning shifts from a designated instructor to anyone in whom the learner has confidence. In such an environment, Tony Bingham and Marcia Conner state in their book entitled *The New Social Learning*, "Everyone shares the responsibility for educating one another and giving each person an opportunity to seek focused help" (2010, 58).

According to Daniel Pink, in his foreword to *The New Social Learning*, traditional training approaches do not evaporate with the advent of social learning, rather "social learning can be used to supplement instruction. The collaboration and cocreation ... blur the boundary between instructor and instructed" (Pink 2010, xiv). Social networks allow us to "discuss, rate, rank, prioritize, link, and converse in text with anyone, at any time" (Bingham and Connor 2010, 152). Social networks have impacted the role of instructor and learner in ways that e-learning and other media have not.

Social networks change the context for learning. We can no longer expect people to sit still and listen. The new learning environment relies on real-time participation, real-time focus, real-time innovation, real-time contribution, real-time connections, and real-time evaluation. With everything taking place right now, there is no one individual who can currently satisfy all of these requirements. So the roles of instructor and learner are shared and constantly shifting.

Social Networks and the Portal

Interestingly, many organizations are turning to their portals to enable social networks (see chapter 6 for information about portals). The advantage of the Facebook-like directories available through the portal and internal social network sites is that employees can share expertise, join communities of practice, or simply connect with other employees (Zielinski 2010).

At the individual level, employees may personalize the sites to post contact information, areas of expertise, job skills, and project experience. This information can then be used for myriad other possibilities, such as project staffing, partnering mentors with employees, or creating a pool of individuals with specific functional expertise.

Tips and Tools for Social Networks

- Examine the social network use and policies of other organizations in your industry
- Determine whether social networks can be of benefit to your organization
- Identify whether there is an organization policy regarding the use of social networks on the job by employees
- Create a policy statement for employee use of social networks

- Draft a business case in support of an organizational implementation of a social network, if it is appropriate for your organization
- Communicate the organizational policy toward social networks at an organizational level and at the individual employee level.

Benefits and Potential Disadvantages

The benefits of social networks can be measured. Bill Roberts (2010) of the Society for Human Resource Management (SHRM) cited a study done by Towers Watson & Co. in 2009 that examined thirty-two organizations representing five million employees around the globe. Towers Watson reported that companies that used effective communication strategies—including social networks—posted higher returns for shareholders than companies with the least-effective strategies. Similarly, *McKinsey Quarterly*, in a recent survey of 1,695 executives across industries, regions, and functional specialties, noted that 69 percent of respondents reported measurable business benefits from social networks.

There are some perceived—and real—disadvantages to social networks. Employers fear that employees visiting social sites while working can lower productivity or jeopardize corporate data. In a study of four different countries (the United Kingdom, the United States, Germany, and Japan), overall usage of social sites during work hours has grown 19 to 24 percent. Also worth noting is that laptop users who can connect to the Internet outside the company networks are more likely to share confidential information than those who are always connected to a company's network (Wright 2010, 20).

Further, there are risks of identity theft for those who use social networks (Schreft 2007). Users are prompted to provide personal information, and every bit of personal information that an identity thief obtains can be used to fill in the blanks and possibly steal an identity. Social security numbers can be determined from date of birth and mother's maiden name, which can be gathered through automated searches of public records. Or publicly available information from the U.S. Social Security Administration can be matched to the issuing state and date, age range, and activity status (6). Clearly, identity theft should be a concern for social networker users.

Employers are using social networks to review and vet potential hires, even though that practice may have legal implications from a discrimination standpoint (SHRM, "Hear What's Happening in Workplace Law?" 2010). By reviewing social network sites, employers get a fuller picture of an employee's online persona and behavior. Hiring managers examine sites for the potential new hire's sense of propriety and for his ability to separate his work life and behavior from his personal life.

Some social network's privacy settings have shortcomings. Facebook tells its users that individuals should have control over their information and who sees it, however the site does occasionally update its settings which may disrupt your privacy settings, so it behooves users to periodically review their privacy settings. Facebook has basic visibility rules that allow friends and people in network to see a user's profile (Brandenburg 2008). Social networkers cannot and should not ignore the current threat to their online privacy.

Nevertheless, it is a bit of a bind. Perfect privacy settings could impede the very interactions that social networkers seek. The solution to privacy threats will eventually be resolved by the courts and legislature. Until such time that clear mandates are established, common sense dictates that social networkers err on the side of caution, both in their use of social networking sites and in what they post on these sites.

Technology Standards and Policies

Lisa Guerin (2009), employment law attorney and editor at Nolo, provides some guidelines for establishing an organizational policy about social networking services in the workplace. We summarize her recommendations below:

- Determine your current practices and whether they are working. Examine the company handbook to see if there are policies in place. Does your organization dictate employees sign acknowledgment of the policies?
- Talk to management in your IT department to establish what technologies your organization supports and what it prohibits. During that discussion, be sure to ask the IT department the following questions: Does the organization have the capability of reading employees' e-mail and tracking their Internet use? What websites does the organization block? What hardware does the company provide to employees (cell phones, laptops, smart phones, etc.)? What guidelines are provided for use and what is the definition of misuse?
- Consult with the organization's lawyers to find out whether there are any special industry-wide or company-specific issues or concerns to address. What is the organization's technology history (including misuse)? Ask about national laws pending or on the books that need to be taken into consideration when writing policy.

- Talk with those in your organization at the management level and ask what technological resources they use in their respective departments. Find out who purchases and owns the equipment.
- Interview the employees to find out what they use. Are there any informal practices that employees use to circumvent company policy?
- Draft policies based upon your findings. Be sure to generate specific policy statements for each technology. Company policies should even include guidelines for some technologies that are not available!
- Keep it simple and explain the policy in terms the employees will understand, not legal terms. State the purpose of the policy.
- Get some feedback on the policies for the purposes of review and revision from employees, managers, and people in the Information Technology Department.
- Revise the policies based upon constructive feedback, then offer them for review to the organization's attorneys.
- Distribute policies along with an acknowledgment form. Tell employees to read the policies and *sign an acknowledgment form*. The signed acknowledgment form ensures that the employees know the policy.
- Enforce the established policies. If they are not put into action, you will negate all of your hard work. Further, you become legally vulnerable if you do not enforce the policies. (Reprinted with permission from the publisher, Nolo, copyright 2010, *www.nolo.com*)

A Sample Social Network Use Organizational Policy

The following is an example of an organization policy regarding use of social networks:

Do not blog, post, or make inappropriate comments. If your blog, Internet posting, or social networking activities are clearly not appropriate as an employee or representative of a(n) [organization name] affiliate (i.e., not consistent with the mission, vision, and values of [organization], or would negatively impact our brand or reputation), you should not refer to [organization] or its affiliated organizations in the posting. If you are about to publish something that makes you the slightest bit uncomfortable, review these guidelines. If you are still unsure, and it concerns [organization] affiliates' business interests or operations, feel free to discuss with your manager or your Human Resources representative.

Let's review a standard social network policy that makes sense for this technology. To avoid potential misuse of social network sites for personal entertainment rather than the organization's benefit, two policies may be appropriate. An employee use policy in an organization that regularly accesses social network sites for screening potential applicants may look something like the following.

Here is a sample privacy policy for organizations reserving the right to monitor: "Internet use is not private. We reserve the right to monitor employee use of the Internet at any time. Your use of the Internet, including the sites that you visit, the amount of time you spend online, and your communications, are not private" (Guerin 2009, 74).

Here is a sample privacy policy for companies that monitor regularly: "Internet use is not private. Our organization uses monitoring software that tracks the sites an employee visits and how much time is spent at a particular site. You should not expect that your use of the Internet—including but not limited to the sites you visit, the amount of time you spend online, and the communications you have—will be private" (Guerin 2009, 74).

These specific policy examples provide full disclosure of the organization's intent, with no room for speculation on the part of the employee. Failure of an employee to comply with the policy, once the acknowledgment statement is signed, is basis for action. For more suggested policy statements, see Guerin's very useful book *Smart Policies for Workplace Technologies*. (Reprinted with permission from the publisher, Nolo, copyright 2010, *www.nolo.com*)

Legal Considerations for Social Network Use

The laws regarding social network use, like those regarding the use of some other new technologies, have not caught up with the technology. The rule of thumb—when using SNSs within your organization—is to consider the laws of the land where the organization is headquartered. In the United States, it is important to examine state laws as well federal laws when writing policy. Unfortunately, as new technologies emerge or increase in sophistication, there are cases where the law has not kept pace. In these cases, organizational policies should anticipate potential issues. The employee's required behavior becomes a matter of ethics and etiquette. As stated above, HR professionals must encourage their organizations to provide clear and comprehensive policies regarding employee use of technologies on the job.

Conclusion

Social networks provide valuable services when used appropriately in the workplace. Common uses for social network services include marketing, communicating a message, reviewing applicant credentials, building communities of learning, and training. There are many different types of social networks, and they serve different purposes. New applications for SNSs continue to emerge. Since the laws have not kept pace with this technology, if your organization is using SNSs, then be sure to institute a policy regarding acceptable and unacceptable uses of social networks in the workplace.

CHAPTER 13

Technology-Enabled Evaluation and Feedback

I t is important to evaluate HR interventions of all kinds in order to examine their effectiveness and whether they have accomplished the stated goal. One facet of the evaluation of HR interventions involves gathering feedback. This can be a tedious process when it is not assisted by technology. There are several technologies that can be used to assist with collecting feedback from learners and employees. Online evaluation and survey tools, as well as response systems and feedback-gathering technologies, are introduced in this chapter.

Evaluation in Organizations

There are many different forms of evaluation. In this chapter, we examine some of the most important aspects of evaluation and feedback methods and technologies. What is evaluation? Darlene Russ-Eft and Hallie Preskill state in their book *Evaluation in Organizations* (2001) that:

> Evaluation collects data, which is turned into information that, when used, becomes knowledge at the individual level. If shared with others in the organization, that knowledge may then lead to organizational-level learning (7).

Evaluation occurs within and outside organizations in many forms, such as product evaluation, service evaluation, process evaluation, program evaluation, course evaluation, and assessment of individual performance.

Why do we evaluate? What are our reasons? We evaluate because:

- Evaluation measures quality
- Evaluation contributes to organization members' increased knowledge
- Evaluation helps prioritize resources
- Evaluation helps plan and deliver organizational initiatives
- Evaluation helps organization members be accountable
- Evaluation findings can help convince others of the need or effectiveness of various organizational initiatives

Evaluation is an important thing. It usually takes one of three forms: developmental evaluation, formative evaluation, and summative evaluation.

Developmental evaluation is equivalent to a needs assessment, where the evaluator determines what the need is and contributes to the design of a solution. The *formative evaluation* occurs during the development or improvement process, and it is conducted more than once, with the goal of improving the program, process, or product (Scriven 1991). The *summative evaluation* occurs upon completion and determines the merit, worth, or value of the thing being evaluated.

So what does all this have to do with technology? When conducting any form of evaluation, technology can improve and facilitate the evaluation process. The limitations of technology to assist in the evaluation effort are simply based upon the technology infrastructure available to those involved in the evaluation.

The specific technologies used matter less than the fact that some evaluation and feedback-gathering activities are conducted and the results analyzed. Use of technology needs to be closely related to quality assessment in an organization, and evaluation should include processes such as needs analysis, quality specifications, and measurement procedures. Technology can make these processes more organized and efficient.

Evaluation is particularly important in the context of technology; you do not want to use a technology simply because it is trendy. The technology itself should be evaluated to determine whether it is meeting the organization's needs. Additionally, the target audience involved in an evaluation effort must be adequately supported in the use of the chosen technology. Always be open to the idea that another technology may be a better fit. With those caveats in mind, let's examine some tools that can assist evaluators.

Evaluation Tools

There are a number of different evaluation tools that can be used to gather feedback. Traditionally, the most commonly used approaches include surveys, focus groups, and interviews. Additionally, there are a number of different sources from which evaluation information can be obtained, such as archival data, observation data, and computer-based tests. Looking at these individually, there are pros and cons to each.

Archival data are currently available documents and records. There are two types: archival data that are unmodified and modified archival documents and records (e.g., monthly or quarterly reports, technical assistance logs). Depending upon the availability and security surrounding these resources, they can sometimes be difficult to obtain. Archival data relevant to HR might be stored in an organization's data warehouse, customer relationship management (CRM) or human resource information system (HRIS) databases, and may be accessed using data-mining techniques.

Observation of someone performing the task in natural settings provides excellent firsthand information for evaluating the success (or lack thereof) of a program. There is an alternative, which is observation conducted in artificial or simulated situations. Simulated environments suffice when there is limited access to the natural setting or the costs of conducting observation in the real situation are too high. To capture and analyze the user response in a simulation or in a live situation, use of video technology can assist in the observation process as long as there is a knowledgeable person who can set up and execute the videotaping of the observation event.

Probably the most commonly used evaluation tools are surveys and questionnaires. Given the current technologies available, surveys and questionnaires are quite easy to design and administer. This form of assessment may be used for a number of different evaluation purposes, from organizational assessments to screening individuals in a recruitment center to end-of-course evaluations. *Survey software* can be used to create the survey, administer it, collect the resulting survey data, and analyze the data.

Individual and focus group interviews can be used for gathering a lot of data in a short period of time for the purposes of evaluation. This form of data collection is well suited to groupware technology (see chapter 11 for more information on groupware). The interviewer can use teleconferencing, webconferencing, video conferencing, or telepresence as a method to conduct these information-gathering sessions. Typically, the interviews are typed up, and the text may then be analyzed using data analysis software tools such as Atlas Ti, Nvivo, or Xsight.

How do you choose the appropriate tool for conducting an evaluation? Start by determining what is being evaluated, and then choose the evaluation method and the evaluation tool from there. Most HR professionals evaluate learning, performance, and change initiatives (Russ-Eft and Preskill 2001, 64). We will focus on those areas in this chapter.

Presuming you have identified the evaluation model that you will use, the following set of preliminary questions can help determine what method, and ultimately the type of instrument and technology, you will use for data collection:

- What skills does the evaluation team (as a whole) have for collecting certain kinds of data? For instance, can your evaluation team create an online survey or a videotape? If you need to simulate the context for the task, does the team have the resources and skills to accomplish that?
- What kinds of data or methods do stakeholders prefer or find most credible? Do they prefer statistical or qualitative data?
- What level of intrusiveness will the organization accommodate for the evaluation?
- How will you ensure the appropriateness of the instruments you use?
- What is the schedule for the evaluation, and which methods can be implemented successfully within this planned timeframe?
- How will you ensure objectivity by the evaluators?

Whatever methodology you decide upon, it can be supported by technology. In fact, technology can make the data collection and analysis process easier, faster, and probably cheaper. It is worth repeating, however, if the participants are required to respond using a certain technology, they must have access to the technology and knowledge about the technology to complete the evaluation.

Evaluation Technology Tools

What tools are appropriate to assist with your evaluation efforts? The table that follows can be enhanced as new technologies emerge. We adapted the following chart from Russ-Eft and Preskill (2001, 179–180) to demonstrate technologies that could support the evaluation method. This list is by no means exhaustive:

Data Collection Method	Optional Technologies
Currently available archival data (documents and records)	Employee record databases (accessible using application software) and queries
	Organization's website or HRIS database and queries
	HRIS database
	Library document databases or online articles and search engine

Data Collection Method	Optional Technologies
Modified archival data (documents and records)	Learning management system, financial system, HRIS
	Help desk data records or incidences (recorded online) or customer relationship management (CRM) data
Observation in natural settings	Digital text
	Archival documents, e.g., customer service records or feedback forms in a CRM database
	Handheld mobile device to record an audio file
Observation in artificial or simulated settings	Handheld mobile device to record digital video, digital audio, or documented in digital text
Surveys and questionnaires	E-mailed survey, online survey
	Website response survey, online or e-mailed survey
Tests	Taken on PC and submitted by e-mail or offered using assessment software
	Offered through LMS or at a test site; submit online for analysis by contracting organization
	Tests offered at end of CBT training; analyzed using software
Individual and focus group interviews	Videoconferencing (recorded), groupware, use of a virtual space, audio-recording microphone and recording software, converted to text for analysis using software
	Teleconferencing with option to record

Surveys and Questionnaires

Surveys are a widely used approach for collecting evaluation data. A leader in online survey development, Donald Dillman, provides insight into how to design an effective survey instrument for administration over the Internet. The caveat is this: this tool is appropriate only for an audience that uses computers on the job, supporting the caveat to select the instrument best suited to the audience and how they do their work.

Survey Design

Although this book does not deal with how to perform an evaluation, the design of online surveys is relevant. The following are important online survey design considerations:

- Use a variety of sources for possible items
- Use respondents' nomenclature
- Avoid using "and/or" questions
- Include three to four items to measure the same variable
- Keep the survey short

- Include brief instructions
- Use consistent wording and formatting
- Ensure the format is conducive to data entry
- Pilot test with more items than necessary
- Statically analyze the pilot data
- Revise survey (Russ-Eft and Preskill 2001, 254–255)

Survey Delivery

Surveys can be designed for delivery using a free online tool (i.e. Survey Monkey or Zoomerang) or they may be offered through another system (i.e. a learning management system [LMS]). Surveys for training courseware, including the end-of-course evaluation, may be quantitative surveys, qualitative surveys, or a mix of the two.

Online survey tools typically have features that allow you to analyze the survey data. Survey reports can be produced in a variety of forms, including tables and charts. It is particularly important to be able to customize the reports to gather the best data.

The quantitative survey is a familiar approach to course evaluation. On a scale of one to five, students may respond, with five being extremely effective and one being not effective at all. Another approach to the same topic is to have students evaluate their own knowledge about specific topics before and after the course. This form of self-evaluation is particularly effective when the course is a constructivist design (see chapter 3 for an explanation of constructivism).

Another format for a survey is the qualitative survey. This is where the respondents provide their responses in a free-flowing written format. Respondents are anonymous and heir comments should appear in random form as separate entries in the report.

Survey Administration

Once the design is complete, the best practice for survey administration streamlines the process. Don Dillman—considered an expert in online survey administration—in his book *Mail and Internet Surveys* (2000) suggests an approach to administer online surveys:

- Send a brief notice letter to respondent a few days before the questionnaire.
- Send a thank-you postcard a few days to a week after the questionnaire.
- Offer a replacement questionnaire to nonrespondents two to four weeks after the previous mailing.
- Make a final phone contact after the fourth effort.

E-mail Survey Administration

If the survey is not online but rather is attached to an e-mail, Dillman (2000) provides us with guidelines on implementation, which can be summarized thus: "Use a multiple contact strategy" (367).

The form of communication both before, during the period of administration, and after survey administration can be enabled by technologies that include e-mail, online newsletter, websites or portals, and company-wide intranets. Further, the communication of the results to company executives can include use of groupware and presentation software. This is especially helpful if the executives are not colocated for the briefing.

While the format for the online survey may not have changed much from the paper-based version, the delivery mechanisms available—for communication about the survey, delivery of the survey, and follow-up—have changed.

Tips and Tools for Online Surveys

- Surveys must be designed with forethought, using survey design best practices.
- Surveys must be delivered according to a plan.
- A variety of online survey development and delivery tools exist, some of which are free and easy to use.
- Beware that free online survey tools do not have the database and report-generating flexibility of surveys that are tied to a powerful corporate database.
- The following online survey development and delivery tools are free (open source) or shareware (available for trial). Use these to experience the technology:
  - *http://freeonlinesurveys.com, www.smart-survey.co.uk/*
  - *http://express.perseus.com*
  - *www.zoomerang.com*
  - *www.surveymonkey.com*

Data Collection Using Mobile Technology: Case Study

Joel Selaniko

As mentioned earlier (see chapter 5, on mobile learning), people in some areas of the globe do not have reliable Internet access through a personal computer. However, that reality does not need to limit access to information or prevent us from using technology to collect data. In fact, with the aid of handheld devices such as mobile phones, the Internet-in-the-Sky, and a Global Positioning System, evaluation data can be collected. This type of mobile technology is currently being used in the medical field in some African nations, for example, when widespread disease prevention is the goal.

One example of survey software for use on a mobile device is DataDyne's EpiSurveyor. DataDyne's software can be used to create custom forms in a simple desktop application, deploy them to one or more mobile devices, collect the data from the field, and send it back to a PC for analysis. EpiSurveyor is a powerful and easy-to-use tool that has been used in a number of situations. One case in point is the use of DataDyne's EpiSurveyor tool, along with mobile technology, to gather medical data in Zambia. Another reasonable case where EpiSurveyor could help is in humanitarian emergencies.

Often, in widespread emergencies, standard evaluation measures are bypassed in favor of real-time evaluation (Walden, Scott, and Lakeman 2010). *Real-time evaluation* (RTE) involves gathering information immediate information about the use of resources, the progress of activities, and the way the activities are being carried out. The evaluation is carried out while the program is being implemented, with near-simultaneous feedback to the program for immediate use. The method was popularized in the 1990s in Darfur and Chad. Implementers use a set of benchmarks against which progress is measured. The accepted methodology calls for a team of two to four people drawn from different departments within the organization to visit a disaster-affected area. The team interviews individuals and groups—from nongovernmental agencies to local authorities to international organizations, as well as the affected population. Because timing is of the essence, the interviews take place shortly after the disaster. Then the recommendations are reported in the country of the disaster at a time that is convenient, so everyone can agree on the recommendations through a consensus approach. Later, evaluators follow up to find out which recommendations were used.

In the RTE approach, online surveys have been used effectively. In studies of RTE responses over the period of July 2006 to February 2008, there was a 48-percent response rate to the online surveys (Walden, Scott, and Lakeman 2010, 286). One of the more recent recommendations involving online surveys is to use handheld mobile devices to gather the information. In so doing, the evaluator eliminates the need for a PC in regions where, particularly in cases of a recent disaster, Internet connections may be intermittent at best.

Joel Selanikio, MD, is a practicing pediatrician, former Wall Street consultant, and former CDC epidemiologist with a passion for using technology to address inequities in health and development. Named by *Forbes* as a notable innovator of 2009, he was awarded both the Lemelson-MIT Award for Sustainability and the Wall Street Journal Technology Innovation Award for Healthcare.

Audience Student Response Systems (SRS)

Another way to gather feedback is through immediate methods. There has been a long-standing tradition in the training world of relying on student satisfaction surveys (often called "smile sheets") and tests of knowledge gained as the primary measures of training effectiveness. While high student satisfaction ratings and evidence of knowledge gained are both helpful indicators, they represent two measures. Neither provides much useful information relative to performance improvement. To make good decisions about the use of training technology and to determine the learning outcomes associated with them, HR professionals need to adopt more sophisticated and immediate measurement processes.

Research has shown that a key trait common to highly regarded instructors is their ability to engage students, keeping the students alert, focused, and involved. One method for accomplishing this is to provide interesting sessions, creative activities, and open discussions that encourage all employees to participate. In the classroom, a technology that is on the rise is the student response system, or SRS.

SRS relies upon a wireless response system that allows instructors to pose a question to which students respond by using a handheld response pad (called a clicker) to send her information to a receiver. Learners can answer questions that are multiple choice, true-false, yes-no, or survey-style questions presented to the class by the instructor. The instructor has the receiver attached to a computer.

Here is how it works. The system's software program is loaded onto the instructor's computer. The instructor presents a question and indicates the response choices. For instance, the instructor may display multiple-choice questions on-screen. The student presses the button on the clicker's wireless keypad, indicating the response she thinks is correct. This sends either an infrared or radio signal to a receiver attached to the instructor's computer. The computer records and/or displays the response per the instructor's preference (Hoffman and Goodwin 2006). The instructor may display the results in graph form to provide immediate feedback to the class. Students build confidence by knowing they answered correctly. Incorrect answers can be identified anonymously and corrected.

This learner response system is highly effective in large classes, where interaction typically cannot occur because of the number of students. It is an easy-to-use feedback device that enables the instructor to gauge the students' understanding of the material. The literature indicates an 80 percent "clicker satisfaction rate" reported by student surveys in the United States and Canada (Taylor in Morse, Ruggieri, and Whelan-Berry 2010). Many Fortune 500 organizations regularly use these devices for their face-to-face training classes. This active form of learning enhances student outcomes (Presby and Zakheim 2006).

The advantage of the clicker system is that it transforms classroom learning into a more interactive experience. The system is directly linked with increased attention because students are benefiting from instant and direct feedback. Further, it allows the instructor to gauge immediately the level of student mastery of content. Finally, the system generates a variety of class reports in PDF format while quantifying and analyzing student data in a timely and comprehensive manner (Ribbens 2007).

Building a case for this response system is not a difficult endeavor. The training needs are minimal, and no instruction is necessary for trainees to begin using the system. It is a simple "point and shoot" function. Training for instructors is minimal as well: They have to create a class roster and allow for anonymous responses, as well as learn to create a lesson and multiple-choice questions to use during the class. The instructor must learn to link each class lesson with its corresponding class roster and class session and learn to program software reporting capabilities (Hoffman and Goodwin 2006). These challenges are easily surmounted, to the benefit of the students.

The costs of student response systems outweigh the negatives. For a standard lecture set of fifty student remotes and one instructor remote, as well as one received software CD and two custom cases, the cost is about $2,000 (Smartroom Learning Solutions 2010). This is a viable alternative to standard face-to-face lectures and presents an innovative feedback mechanism in the classroom.

Conclusion

A number of innovative and usable feedback and evaluation devices exist. Evaluation takes many forms and serves a variety of purposes. Technology can be used to assist with the data-gathering and processing aspect of evaluation. Further, even face-to-face observations can be facilitated by technology. Employee feedback is often gathered through surveys conducted within an organization, and survey design, administration, and data analysis can all be facilitated through the use of technology. During a training session, feedback can be gathered from learners using a student response system that features a handheld device. The instructor can analyze that data for feedback on the students' understanding of the materials and her effectiveness in conveying the information. In-class tests can be administered online rather than as paper-based tests. All of these evaluation and feedback technologies can benefit the manager in search of reliable feedback and evaluation data. The instruments and tools discussed in this chapter should assist the HR manager to find new, unique, and cost-effective methods to gather important and useful data.

CHAPTER 14

Social Media

The social media technologies identified in this chapter pertain to communication. Social networks have their own unique chapter because of their varied and diverse applications that extend far beyond social media.

When we refer to social media, we are using the following definition: *social media* are the technologies we use to reach out and connect with other humans, create a relationship, build trust, and be there when the people in those relationships are ready to do business with our organization (Safko 2010, 4). Or another way of putting it is that social media are tools for communication and collaboration.

This chapter describes a variety of social media, provides examples, notes legal or regulatory issues, and offers some proven and powerful suggestions for applications. Best practices for implementing a social media organizational policy appear here, but we will not provide a list of laws and regulations. This is because the laws have not yet caught up with these technologies, which is all the more reason to use caution and common sense when implementing them. Social media offer some interesting possibilities for corporate, education, nonprofit, and government organizations.

Social Media ("New Media")?

In 2009, the Singapore group entitled REACH (Reaching Everyone for Active Citizenry @ Home) created an entire brochure describing "new media" that all citizens of Singapore should understand. The list included, but was not limited to, those media that appear below (REACH 2009). Some we have already discussed, but others have not been described before this chapter.

The new media that we will address in this chapter are:

- *Blog*—Derived from "weblog." It is the equivalent of an online journal.
- *Photo sharing (e.g., Flickr)*—A website where users may share photos and videos.
- *Podcast*—An audio or video file distributed over the Internet by syndicated download to portable media players and computers.
- *RSS*—Really simple syndication, a format for delivering regularly changing web content such as new headlines and notices.
- *Microblogging (e.g., Twitter)*—A social networking and microblogging service that allows a user to update friends by sending short messages called "tweets."
- *Vodcast*—The online delivery of video clips through web feeds.
- *Video sharing (e.g., YouTube)*—A video-sharing website where users can upload, view, and share video clips.
- *Wiki (e.g., Wikipedia)*—A website or similar online resource that allows users to add and edit content collectively.
- *Widget*—A small, specialized application that offers access to frequently used functions such as the weather, time, and a calculator.

The New Medium!

Let's start with Vin Crosbie, whom *Folio* magazine called the "practical futurist," and his comments about changes in communication, because they provide a context for this chapter. According to Crosbie, the phrase "new medium" has a significant history (2002). The "old mediums," which have been around since prehistoric times, are interpersonal communication and mass communication.

From ancient times, the primary medium for communication was interpersonal contact, people talking directly to each other. The *interpersonal medium* delivers a message that is unique and individualized, one to one. A second ancient communication medium was the *mass medium*. Used by tribal leaders, kings, priests, and others, the "mass" medium was a form of delivery where the communicator delivered a singular message to a group of recipients such as one person addressing the masses using verbal communication and a very loud voice, one to many. Enter the *"new medium."* This form of communication allows for individualized messages to be delivered simultaneously, using technology, to an infinite number of people, and each of the recipients has reciprocal control of the content, from many to many. This mode of delivery, many-to-many, emerged in the late twentieth and early twenty-first centuries, and Vin Crosbie proposes that it has revolutionized communication.

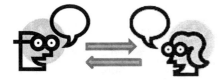

Interpersonal Medium: One to One

Mass Medium: One to Many

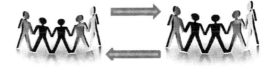

New Medium: Many to Many

FIGURE 14-1   New Medium

Media that capitalize on this "new medium" of communicating earned the label "new media" or "social media." In 2007, the journal *Corporate Communications* defined "new media" as blogging, ... wikis, podcasts, and social networking sites" (AIMIA 2007). New media implement a many-to-many communication method. These new web-enabled services were originally used by corporations to communicate with existing customers, communicate a corporate image, communicate internally, and communicate with new audiences and representatives of new markets (Hearn, Foth, and Gray 2008).

You will notice that we have a separate chapter for social networks. We determined that the topic of social networks needed a chapter of its own because of its history as a precursor to the "new" social media (Boyd and Ellison 2008). While we labeled many of the social media as communication technologies, the lines between communication technologies and social networks are becoming increasingly blurred as the technologies evolve. For in-depth coverage of social networks, see chapter 12.

New, Social Media—Descriptions

Each of these media is described in this section, and an example of its application provided. Further, where there are open-source websites available, you will also find them mentioned here. The value of open-source products is that they allow the user to try out the technology, experiencing it firsthand without making a commitment.

The applications for social media are limitless. New business uses continue to surface. However, there are some issues to be aware of before implementing new financial strategies involving new media. Where there is reason for caution, we will provide information. So let's look at them one at a time all the while considering practical applications of the media that you may want to implement within the context of your organization.

Blogs

A *blog* (short for weblog) is usually a web-based publication similar to a journal. It is maintained by an individual who regularly enters, or posts, commentary, thoughts, and ideas. The writer also may include photos, audio, video, or graphics. These entries appear in reverse chronological order. Usually, blogs are subject-oriented. *Vlogs* are blog sites that primarily use video, while linklogs are blogs that provide links to other sites. The Gartner Research Group indicates that there may be as many as 200 million former bloggers who have abandoned their blogs (cited in Safko 2010). Blogging may or may not be on the wane, but it is so prevalent that it should be understood.

For a sample blog, or to start your own blog, you may go to *www.blogger.com* or *http://wordpress.com*. There is a journal-like entry, and that original entry usually has a theme. Other writers then attach their comments by posting to the original entry. You can add a "tag" after the title of your post; the tag is a keyword or phrase indicating the topic of the entry. You may also see other bloggers' entries that have similar keywords by clicking on the keyword in the list of key words and phrases on the side of the screen. Bigger tag font size indicates increased use of that tag.

Blogs may be used for a number of purposes. As mentioned earlier, they typically revolve around topics or themes. However, organizations are becoming more adventuresome and savvy about the use of blogs. One business application for blogs is to allow interaction with customers and potential customers. It is also a media that enables branding and control of the message. Further, it can be a revenue generator as a soft sell tool. Or the blog may be used to provide customer service. The customer inquiries are filed by the Public Relations team and can be analyzed for relevant content and patterns. A positive aspect of blogging for work purposes is that it can be used to convey policy changes, explore new product/service possibilities, and contribute to informal learning.

A drawback to blogs, in general, is that not all of the information may be accurate. Blogs are not peer-reviewed to ensure quality and accuracy. Thus, you cannot always control what is learned and whether or not the learned information is correct.

Similar to a blog, a *moblog* combines mobile technology with a blog. The content is posted to the Internet from a mobile device using mobile browsers to publish to any blogging platform with mobile posting compatibility. This gives the user real-time access to information. It is useful to travelers, tourists, or people who do not have reliable Internet connectivity. Remember, however, that the moblog is not a password-protected environment.

Photo sharing—Flickr

There are many photo sharing websites, of which Flickr is one. Flickr deals with visual content in the form of photos and videos. The intent is to distribute visual content through as many venues as possible (Safko 2010). There is a collaboration feature in Flickr that allows friends and family to participate in the organization of the photo and video files (not streaming video). Photos and video are posted and visitors may add comments. These pictures can be printed in a variety of formats (such as postcards). Probably the largest user group is those who are artists or photographers.

Many contributors allow use of their pictures through *Creative Commons licensing*, as long as you give proper credit. The original set of Creative Commons licenses all grant the same "baseline rights," such as the right to distribute the copyrighted work worldwide, without changes, at no charge. There are several types of Creative Commons licensing dealing with different levels of attribution and right to change the item.

Before organizations decide to use Flikr or other photo-sharing technologies, they must consider whether there is a need for copyright and/or legal permissions attached to the material they post. Of course, the photo sharing site can also be used for internal or not-for-profit purposes. For instance, team-building or morale-enhancing efforts may rely upon a display of (flattering) photos of the employees participating in team or organizational activities.

Podcast/Vodcast

Podcasting is a free method of distributing digitized audio and video programs over the Internet. An MP3 file is a highly compressed audio format that has become the standard for Internet audio (Safko 2010). The term podcast is something of a misnomer, as it implies that this media can be used only on a particular type of equipment. The term "podcasting" is a combination of the words *iPod* and *broadcasting*. It was originally a general term for audio files made available for use on computers and mobile technologies. Additionally, there is also a video version, called *vodcasting*, which uses video files distributed over the Internet and downloadable to media players and computers.

The production of a podcast is quite simple, and it can be done for free. Using free software on a computer or downloaded from the Internet and a microphone connected to the computer, anyone can create and save a podcast. One site that enables podcast creation is *www.audacitysourceforge.com*. The resulting audio files can be saved in different formats depending upon the venue in which they will be used. They are portable. Podcasts are different from podcasting.

Podcasting is the process of creating an audio show of some sort available in MP3 or WAV format. Podcasts are designed to include talk shows, tutorials, music, or other audio content. Podcasts, like blogs, can be RSS-fed (see "Really Simple Syndication (RSS)") so that the listener gets regular updates. The feed allows podcasting (distributing your podcast worldwide) each time you publish a new one (Safko 2010). Qualified institutions can also post directly to iTunes U, which is primarily an educational site for podcasting lectures, speeches, and other audio messages.

Podcasting has many uses. Audio is a powerful communication method, especially for narrative-based content. Interviews are well suited to podcasts. Role plays as podcasts or vodcasts illustrate positive, realistic handling of situations. Storytelling to share anecdotes of everyday events can offer a powerful inducement to use this tool (Halls 2010). There are also video podcasts. These are called *vodcasts*.

Educators and trainers find that podcasts can supplement, duplicate, or replace face-to-face lectures. Podcasting enables anyone to create and deliver self-published materials and is particularly relevant as a training medium, as it can be used to deliver learning to a dispersed audience. Many experts use podcasting as a way to distribute their knowledge and build a loyal following. Podcasts can be used on social network sites or distributed using a Really Simple Syndication (RSS) feed.

Really Simple Syndication (RSS)

The acronym *RSS* stands for *Really Simple Syndication*. RSS is a family of web feed formats used to publish frequently updated digital content, such as blogs, news feeds, or podcasts. Users of RSS content use programs called feed readers or aggregators. The user subscribes to a feed by supplying their reader with a link to the feed. The reader then checks the user's subscribed feeds to see if any of those feeds have new content since the last time it checked, and, if so, retrieve that content and present it to the user.

RSS has several advantages: Users can be notified of new content without having to actively check for it. For instance, updates to blogs can be automatically sent to users. The information presented to users in an aggregator is typically much simpler than most websites. This spares users the mental effort of navigating complex web pages, each with its own layout. Media files can be automatically downloaded without user intervention. Podcasting from a server requires an RSS.

An RSS feed can be used behind firewalls. News updates, stock prices, and commodities can be sent out through the RSS. The business applications are obvious. For instance, for those working with banks or the stock market, this information is invaluable. Similarly, farmers could use an RSS feed to check future weather conditions or commodity prices. As mentioned earlier, podcasting is enabled through RSS formats. Organizations may find this a useful technology for notifying clients and/or potential customers of important information. Organizations can push their new information to readers, and, unsurprisingly, news agencies often use RSS feeds. A website that is available to help you set up an RSS feed is *www.FeedBurner.com*.

Microblogging—Twitter

Microblogging grew out of traditional blogging. As writers migrated away from long, e-mail-type messages, they posted condensed entries called microblogs. Twitter is a microblogging and social networking service that communicates using short, text-based messages.

Due to the limit on the number of characters one can use in a text message, shortened expressions, acronyms, and symbols emerged. For a list, do a search on useful-internet-slang-and-acronyms. Many professionals bemoan the impact of this new form of communication on business writing. All we can say is, oh well.

Twitter was one of the first providers of the microblog; this service allows its users to send and receive messages, known as tweets, of 140 characters or less. The messages can be displayed on the user's preferred technology. Technologies compatible with Twitter include cell phones, websites, personal digital assistants, the Twitter website, RSS, SMS, e-mail, and social networking sites (Safko 2010).

Many consider tweeting to be the preferred mode of thought leaders and the technologically savvy, but it is quickly becoming everyman's tool. It is quite popular, in part, because of the ease of creating a micropost. Additionally, the potential audience goes far beyond mailing lists (Freeman 2009).

The advantages of tweeting from a business perspective are overwhelmingly in favor of the tool. Twitter helps industry professionals share information, gain access to thousands of others of like mind, and connect with customers. Hash tags offer a way to create a keyword category and allow others to search for and find your updates; simply including a hashtag—a pound sign (#)—in front of a word in your tweet makes the word a searchable term. Recruiters are using Twitter to search bios for keywords and geography to find people who have particular skills (Fox 2010). Industry professionals can share information, advertise specials, and gain access to a knowledge base that is inaccessible without the microblogging tool.

As essentially open e-mails to the world, Twitter messages can be sent anywhere, and they can be seen by anyone, thus users must also be aware that there is no protection of the Twitter information. You can use the privacy setting, but it is not fail proof and messages can be forwarded.

Some organizations and countries do not accept or allow the microblogging technology. At the time of this writing, China does not allow access to Twitter, although other internal microblogging sites have developed as an alternative to Twitter (MacLeod 2010).

Short message service, or *SMS*, is a mobile data and Internet communications service that offers a worldwide system of short message services (SMS), along with multimedia messaging. It is available on cell phones and other handheld devices. Due to the billions of cell phones in use, SMS is the most ubiquitous messaging system on the planet. Typing text messages ("texting"), which are limited to 160 characters in length, can be done on basic cell phones with only numeric keys. Messages are sent to regular telephone numbers or to shorter numbers for commercial use (see short code).

This technology has inspired and enabled one of the largest mobile communities in existence. Once you have registered as an SMS user, you can regularly send messages using your cell phone. The service itself is free, with charges levied by country and service provider.

SMS has many purposes: It is an entertainment tool as well as an interpersonal communication tool. More importantly, SMS has recently been used for social awareness and to send warnings of dangerous conditions such as flash floods, tsunamis, earthquakes, and so on. It is easy to keep in touch with colleagues, friends, and family using SMS.

DatAgro—Supporting Agricultural Production with SMS: Case Study

Joel Selanikio

Sometimes a little bit of information can make a world of difference. To those who are geographically and digitally isolated, the most basic information is often hard to come by—even though these populations increasingly own basic mobile phones with voice and SMS capability. To provide these communities with the vital information they need, DataDyne launched the Mobile Information Project (MIP), a text message communications platform that allows anyone to subscribe to free information channels on even the most basic cell phones. MIP also enables any organization to create an information channel. The DatAgro project, which uses MIP technology, is taking advantage of the high penetration rate of cell phones in Latin America to allow rural farming cooperatives, beginning with those in Chile, to define the types of information most critical to their lives and livelihoods (such as weather and agricultural information), and to receive it via text messages.

The MIP software platform is a hybrid of web and SMS technologies and takes advantage of the high penetration rate of web access among ministry personnel and program managers, and the high penetration rate of cell phones among rural populations. MIP allows program managers to create and manage their communications via a website, and then to transmit their messages to rural or poor populations via SMS, a technology with high penetration in poor and rural communities. MIP allows those managers to enter their own informational messages, and also text-based Internet information (from RSS feeds, Twitter feeds, etc.), and then transmit this information to those who have SMS but no Internet access. This aspect of the project, which allows transmission of news and information to *any* mobile phone, enormously expands the population able to benefit from the worldwide library of information available on the Internet.

The Chilean agriculture cooperative Coopeumo is made up of 346 small-scale farmers in the Cachapoal Valley, two hours south of Santiago, Chile, who grow maize and other crops. The project enables these rural farming cooperatives to use text messaging to access locally relevant information that improves productivity—including market prices, local weather reports, agricultural information, and news reports. In less than a year, the DatAgro service has already had significant success with the Coopeumo farmers. One member, Hugo Tobar, says his entire crop for 2009 was saved by an SMS message. Just before he intended to plant, he received a message that urged him to wait because of impending bad weather. Thankfully, he did wait, because for the next week there was torrential rain that would have washed his seedlings away. Hugo's story demonstrates how a little bit of timely information can help farmers plan and adapt quickly to changing circumstances. The DatAgro project has used MIP technology to cost-effectively connect rural Chilean farmers to the wider world, to which they were previously connected economically but disconnected informationally:

> [Coopeumo farmers using DatAgro] can find out information about prices: supply prices, product prices, the weather, and what's going on in international

markets. It's because today, everything that goes on outside Chile affects us too. When there's an excess of production in one place, the prices go down here. When demand goes up in China or India the prices here get better. Everything is related in this connected world, and small-scale farmers aren't left out of that reality.

— Ricardo Danessi, Executive Manager, Coopeumo

The success of MIP has led to the program's expansion: In Peru, MIP is used in the SaludMóvil project to provide continuing education to maternal and child health workers in rural areas via text messaging, and in Honduras the platform is used in the PreveMóvil project to send youth-oriented prevention messages to youth at high risk of HIV and other sexually transmitted diseases. And further expansion is certain to follow.

Joel Selanikio, MD, is a practicing pediatrician, former Wall Street consultant, and former CDC epidemiologist with a passion for using technology to address inequities in health and development.

Video Sharing—YouTube

What an interesting tool YouTube has become! Events that once would have been relegated to one area of the world now impact those around the globe through this visual media. *YouTube* is a free service, a place to discover, watch, and share videos. Once you join the website, it recommends videos that you might like based upon your profile of interests and past choices. An account allows you to:

- Upload and share your own videos with the world
- Comment on, rate, and make video responses to your favorite videos
- Build playlists of favorites to watch later

The business application for YouTube is where things get interesting. The videos can be integrated into a variety of sites, including personal profile pages, websites, and portals. Though primarily an entertainment site, YouTube is revolutionizing the way media companies do business through its video identification program. This program uses the "claim your content" platform, which encourages users to "identify content and attribute it to its owner and apply the content owner's policy" (Safko 2010, 532). So, with YouTube in video ads, organizations can market products, services, and other entertainment options.

Attorney Lisa Guerin, in *Smart Policies for Workplace Technologies* (2009), offers legal advice on how to write company policy regarding video websites such as YouTube. From a policy stance, Guerin indicates that YouTube presents a number of issues. Consider your organization's technology capacity and limits, because YouTube and other streamed video and audio services can quickly overload your company's systems and bring down the Internet connection.

Based upon the organization's capacity to accommodate heavy technology use, provide clear guidance in the policy statement about use of YouTube and other streaming audio or video. If your company has blocking software to certain sites, you need to make that statement as well in the organization's policy statement. Indicate clearly the sites that are off limits, and even if the site is not blocked by the software, make clear that employees should not attempt to access them. As in all organizational policy statements, be specific with your policies (Guerin 2009). (Reprinted with permission from the publisher, Nolo, copyright 2010, *www.nolo.com*)

Wikis

The *wiki* may appear under social media or social networking; it fits into both categories. We have placed it in this chapter because it is a new form of social media that can be used in portals and other communication venues. What is a *wiki*? It's a website that allows people to collect and edit ideas in one place at any time. It is user-generated content that allows contributions based on an author's expertise and knowledge. The content can then be edited by subject matter experts.

Probably the best-known wiki is Wikipedia. This is a wiki that allows subject matter experts to contribute on the same types of topics that appear in print encyclopedias. It is overseen by a nonprofit organization that provides a platform for the world's largest online user-generated content encyclopedia. The millions of articles included in Wikipedia are written by volunteers and experts around the world and edited by those with access to the site. It is the largest, most popular general reference work on the Internet.

Some of the complaints about Wikipedia can be generalized to the technology as a whole. Directly from the Wikipedia site, critics of Wikipedia in particular state that it contains bias and inconsistencies, and favors consensus over credentials in its editorial process. This makes its reliability and accuracy suspect. It is susceptible to vandalism and may be polluted by unverified information. The vandalism, however, is generally short-lived, as there is oversight, and errors are quickly corrected.

Businesses are using wikis in conjunction with their knowledge management systems to gather, update, and maintain a body of information on an area of expertise. Because a wiki can be open to the public or restricted to members or employees, there are proprietary issues that may accompany its use. It is also valuable to organizations for retaining corporate information for collaboration and for training. Wikis are used to showcase the collective knowledge of the employees on a variety of topics from the esoteric to the mundane (for example, how to fix the copier if it is jammed). It is a free resource tool that is easy to use.

There are, however, some cautions regarding the use of a wiki for organizational purposes. Most prevalent are the security issues posed by wikis. Because wikis are an "open" set of documents that are generally accessible to the employee base, they are vulnerable to mistakes and vandalism. Of course, one extreme example of the potential misuse of wikis occurred in the case of WikiLeaks.

In case you are unfamiliar with *WikiLeaks*, it is an international non-profit organization that publishes submissions of private, secret, and classified media from anonymous news sources and leaks. Launched in 2006 and run by The Sunshine Press, the website handled and stored more than 1.2 million documents within a year of its launch. WikiLeaks was originally started as a user-editable wiki site, but it no longer accepts either user comments or edits. In 2010, WikiLeaks released more than 250,000 State Department cables that embarrassed many high-ranking officials in countries around the globe (Pelofsky and Colvin 2010). The ethical issue involved here revolves around the fact that the information was classified and it had not been declassified when the material was posted.

To avoid theft and publishing of private information, it is very important for organizations to have clear policies in place regarding misuse of proprietary and/or confidential information. Again, a good reference on this topic is *Smart Policies for Workplace Technologies* (2009) by Lisa Guerin. The author provides sample policy statements and legal precedent. While it is unlikely that policy statements will stop theft, they do provide a legal position for prosecuting those who abrogate the policy.

There are free wiki sites for those with less-nefarious intent. We encourage you to go to one of these to test out the wiki and how it works. One such site is *www.wikispaces.com*.

And another, more sophisticated version of a wiki can be accessed through the following site: *www.mygads.com*.

Wikis are great collaborative tools for generating company ideas, documenting brainstorming sessions, working together on a document, and other joint efforts. But, as with most new technologies, there are reasons to proceed cautiously when setting up company wikis.

Widgets

Widgets are applets (small applications) that can be placed on your blog, website, or social network and embedded in other applications; they can be very useful, especially for marketing purposes. Widgets relay short messages, including the same type of information transmitted in an RSS feed. Social media widgets can be used in all of the ways cited below:

- Maps/mashups
- Calendars/events
- Polling/surveys
- Chat/real-time
- Videos
- News information
- Feeds/RSS
- Forms/databases (*http://derekshowerman.com/2009/08/11/5-must-have-social-media-widgets*)

Thousands of social media widgets surface daily. Some are better than others. Derek Showerman, director of Digital Marketing at Environmental Data Resources, recommends the following widgets as some of the best. Why not try them?

- JS-Kit Echo—a commenting tool for use with testimonials
- Share This—enables the content of a page to be e-mailed, sent via IM, and posted into social media channels
- Freedzilla RSS—for the posting of the latest news
- FriendFeed—allows you to document and show your social activities
- Tweetizen—posts a Twitter group within a website

Tips and Tools for Using Social Media

Before developing policy or implementing social media within your organization, you should experience the environment firsthand. The following is a set of free, open-source tools that you may use to try out the features of each of the social media types described in this chapter.

- Blog—*www.blogomonster.com/blogo.php*
- Photo sharing—*www.flickr.com*
- Podcast
  - How-to—*www.apple.com/itunes/store/podcaststechspecs.html*
  - Creating a podcast—*www.audacitysourceforge.com*
- RSS—*www.reuters.com/tools/rss*
- Microblog—*http://twitter.com/*
- Vodcast, how-to—*www.macworld.com/article/46066/2005/07/howtovodcast.html*
- Video sharing—*www.youtube.com/*
- Wiki—*http://pbwiki.com/*
- Widget—*www.widgetbox.com/tag/free*

Legal, Regulatory, and Policy Issues for Social Media

Legal and Regulatory Issues

The emergence of social media as a widely used communication tool has had unintended consequences in the workplace. These cannot be ignored, as employees may visit social media sites on employer time. However, according to John Lyncheski, in his article on social media and its legal ramifications, only about one in five employers has policies governing social media access and use (Lyncheski 2010). The purpose of policies about social media is to strike a balance between a congenial workplace that allows social media and one that protects confidentiality, security, and the employer's legal interests. The legal implications are complex and varied. For instance, consider each of the following questions regarding blogging:

1. Should bloggers who gather and report news be considered journalists under reporter-privilege laws?
2. Should bloggers who post messages anonymously that others consider defamatory be able to keep their identities unknown?
3. Can public employers discipline their employees for making critical or off-color comments about their workplace or fellow employees?
4. Should bloggers be subject to campaign-finance laws?
5. Do some bloggers take First Amendment freedoms too far by engaging in what First Amendment Center Ombudsman Paul McMasters has termed a "blog-mob mentality"?

John Lyncheski indicates that significant legal issues arise when interpreted with regard to the following laws and regulations:

- The Fair Credit Reporting Act requires that consumer reporting agencies adopt reasonable procedures "in a manner which is fair and equitable to the consumer with regard to the confidentiality, accuracy, relevancy, and proper utilization of such information" in accordance with the requirements of this title (*www.ftc.gov*).
- Stored Communications Act passed by Congress regulates when an electronic communication service ("ECS") provider may use the contents of, or other information about, a customer's e-mails and other electronic communications to private parties (*http://ilt.eff.org/index.php/ Privacy:_Stored_Communications_Act*).
- Federal Computer Fraud and Abuse Act (CFAA) generally prohibits unauthorized accessing of a computer; it is a criminal statute that contains a civil enforcement provision, the primary focus of which concerns outside attackers, i.e., traditional hacking.
- Health Insurance Portability and Accountability Administration's (HIPAA's) Secrecy Rule—The HIPAA Secrecy Rule ensures that a patient's personal and private healthiness information isn't freely allocated to anybody, interpreted to include prohibiting posting or distribution using a social media venue (*http://www.hhs.gov/ocr/privacy/hipaa*).
- Federal Trade Commission regulations as they apply to social media, prohibits "endorsements" and "comments about a related party's product" on a blog or social media site (Lyncheski 2010, 33–34).

It doesn't take much for damage to occur through an intended (or unintended) disclosure of proprietary information using social media. Surprisingly, the interpretation of the law can favor the employee rather than the employer. One critical way in which organizations can protect themselves is if they have a clear policy statements regarding employee use of social media.

Impact on Policy

Under each of the technologies described earlier, where there are specific associated policy issues, we have stated them. However, there are general policy recommendations that can serve as the overarching theme for policy development. Combining the contributions of attorney Lisa Guerin (2009) and author John Lyncheski (2010), we developed the following guidelines for the policy content:

- Make clear the right of the organization to monitor all use of technology and communication made or received on the employer's equipment, from office-based hardware to employer-provided cell phones or laptops.
- Clarify monitoring policies in no uncertain terms, to remove expectation of privacy. Remember: in the United States, you have the right as an organization under the National Labor Relations Board to impose a complete ban on employee use of employer technology for personal or nonbusiness communications (not enforced discriminatorily).
- Build FTC (Federal Trade Commission), FCF (Federal Computer Fraud) and HIPAA guidelines into your social media policy.
- Delineate that employees must obtain approval for any postings regarding the employer's facility, services, or residences.
- State clearly that employees are prohibited from disclosing or posting any proprietary, confidential, or intellectual property information. Make clear that, in any organization-related postings, employees must reveal their relationship to the organization in any statements about the employer's services or products.
- Clarify to employees that they will be held accountable for any infraction in terms of laws, rules, and regulations (this includes anonymous postings).

HR-Intersect and Social Media

Given the broad range of application for social media, the groups with which HR must collaborate depends upon the application. Organizational groups that may be involved in the design, development, and implementation of social media range from the Legal Department to Marketing to Information Technology to Communications. Be prepared. As long as you know the issues and the design considerations of the technology you're planning for, you will know who needs to be involved.

Conclusion

Social media are varied and powerful. They can be used in many different ways, from enhancing the organization's portal to meeting collaboration to contributing to knowledge management. They can enliven presentations, personalize learning, equip novices with expert advice, and document innovations. New social media offer great opportunity, but with that opportunity comes responsibility as well. It is the responsibility of the organization to be aware of legal and regulatory issues surrounding social media in order to design effective stance policies about the use of social media in the workplace.

Knowledge Management

CHAPTER 15

Organizational Learning, Knowledge, and Technology

Thomas Stewart, in *Intellectual Capital: The New Wealth of Organizations*, writes, "Simply put, knowledge has become more important for organizations than financial resources, market position, technology, or any other company asset" (1997, ix). In today's turbulent, competitive environment, knowledge is seen as the key driver and ultimate resource for organizational success. And how an organization uses technology to manage that knowledge has emerged as the most important discriminator between success and failure in an intensely competitive global economy.

Organizational Learning

Organizational learning is the process of using knowledge with the potential outcome of becoming a "learning organization." The effort of capturing, acquiring, storing, and sharing knowledge is futile if the organization has no capacity to learn.

Dave Schwandt and Michael Marquardt, in their book *Organizational Learning: From World-Class Theories to Global Best Practices* (2000), specify some ways in which an organization can implement processes that generate organizational learning. A modified approach offers practical steps toward jump-starting organizational learning.

1. Gather information about the organization's predisposition toward learning. Some general examples of questions include:
   * What are the processes used to scan the environment and benchmark best practices in the industry?

- What kind of information does the organization generate?
- Does the organization support experimentation? If so, what role does experimentation play in developing new information?
- To what extent are employees involved in decision-making processes?
- Does the organization evaluate the success of technical methods and approaches? What methods of evaluation does it use?
- To what extent are performance data available?
- How is leadership defined in the organization?
- How are knowledge and information shared?
- How are success and failure documented?
- What are the formal mechanisms to distribute technical knowledge?
- How is information about technical expertise stored?
- How do employees access this information when they need it?
- What value is placed on learning? On performance?

2. Convert the answers and new information into meaningful knowledge. The answers to the preceding questions generate new information about the organization and its disposition toward learning. Remember that information is not knowledge. Knowledge requires understanding and assigning meaning to the information after reflecting upon it.
3. Analyze and reflect upon the answers to these questions. Once the questions are answered, where do you start with the information that you have gathered about your organization and its disposition toward learning?
   - Identify key elements that contribute to learning within your organization and those that undermine learning.
   - List and prioritize those learning-enabling characteristics. Take action. Create a corporate learning model to enhance business results. Use the answers to these questions and others, as well as your reflections, to generate a plan. Then do something. You may find that your approach toward promoting organizational learning will involve technology.

These steps move you toward establishing an organizational learning strategy.

Technology and Organizational Knowledge

Ikujiro Nonaka, one of the world's leading authorities on organizational learning and knowledge management, proclaimed that a company's ability to create, store, and disseminate knowledge is absolutely crucial for staying ahead of the competition in areas of quality, speed, innovation, and price (2008). He notes that technology is essential to developing and implementing the mechanisms necessary for an organization to assemble, package, promote, and distribute the fruits of its thinking and learning. Only through the use of technology will a company be able to transform knowledge into corporate power. Unfortunately, however, most companies are incompetent at managing knowledge. It is totally uncharted territory. Although managing knowledge is different from managing cash or buildings, it is perhaps as important, if not more so.

Hierarchy of Knowledge

Certain types of knowledge are more valuable to an organization because of their strategic and cascading importance. Often, the more valuable the knowledge, the more difficult it may be to capture, store, and disseminate throughout the organization. It is wise for HR leaders to be aware of the hierarchy of knowledge as shown in Figure 15-1, which demonstrates how knowledge can range from less to more breadth, depth, meaning, conceptualization, and value.

Let's examine briefly each level, beginning at the bottom.

- *Data* include texts, facts, interpreted images, and uninterpreted numeric codes without context and therefore without meaning.
- *Information* is data imbued with context and meaning, whose form and content can be applied to a particular task after being formalized, classified, processed, and formatted.
- *Knowledge* comprises bodies of information, principles, and experience that actively guide task execution and management, decision making, and problem solving. Knowledge enables people to assign meaning to data and thereby generate information. With knowledge, people can deal intelligently with available information sources and then take action.

Hierarchy of Knowledge

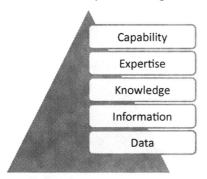

FIGURE 15-1   Hierarchy of Knowledge

- *Expertise* is the appropriate and effective application of knowledge in order to achieve results and improve performance.
- *Capability* encompasses the organizational capacity and expertise to create a product, service, or process at a high level of performance. It requires the integration, coordination, and cooperation of many individuals and teams. Capability is more than just current performance; it is the ability to learn, innovate, and create.

Knowledge can also be classified in a number of other ways, for example:

- "Know what": Knowing which information is needed
- "Know how": Knowing how information must be processed
- "Know why": Knowing why certain information is needed
- "Know where": Knowing where to find certain specific information
- "Know when": Knowing when certain information is needed

Karl Wiig (1997) distinguishes types of knowledge in yet another way:

- *Goal-setting or idealistic*: Vision, "care why" knowledge, or self-motivated creativity
- *Systematic*: "Know why" knowledge for acquiring systems understanding
- *Pragmatic*: "Know how" knowledge for acquiring advanced skills
- *Automatic or tacit*: "Know what" knowledge for routine working

A Systems Model for Managing Knowledge

Let us now look at a comprehensive systems approach to managing corporate knowledge, which involves six stages that examine the transition of knowledge from source to use:

1. Acquisition
2. Creation
3. Storage
4. Analysis and data mining
5. Transfer and dissemination
6. Application and validation

Organizations will be able to manage their knowledge efficiently and effectively when these six stages are ongoing and interactive. They are not sequential or independent: information should be distributed through multiple channels, each with often differing timeframes. The management of knowledge must be subjected continually to perceptual filters as well as both proactive and reactive activities. Successful learning organizations systematically and technologically guide knowledge through each and all of these six stages.

Knowledge Acquisition

People increasingly need an overwhelming volume and variety of knowledge from all over the world in order to adequately perform their work. Organizations build their knowledge bases by collecting information from many internal and external sources.

Internal Collection of Knowledge

One major complaint of workers is that their organizations do not tap a significant portion of their knowledge. Companies are often startled to discover the amount of intellectual capital present in the brains of their own employees; this is what Ikujiro Nonaka (2008) calls "tacit knowledge." Sources of tacit knowledge include an individual's expertise, memories, beliefs, and assumptions, all of which may be valuable to the organization. This kind of knowledge is usually difficult to communicate or explain but can result in tremendous benefits to companies.

Organizations may also adopt either an active or a passive mode of scanning their internal environments. On the one hand, they may allow information to percolate up or trickle down through the organization; on the other, they may actively scan their own internal environments for information, reflect on it, and convert it into usable knowledge. An excellent example of the latter approach is 3M Corporation, which has developed its ability to ascertain information from scientists within the organization. Through flexible structuring and reinforcement of the value of sharing work data, the company has benefited from a wealth of information, which in turn has been converted into innovative knowledge and marketable products.

The ability to learn from activities in other parts of an organization can become a principal source of added value for corporations. Organizations may acquire knowledge internally by tapping into the knowledge of their staffs, learning from shared experiences, and implementing continuous change in their processes. There are a number of external sources for acquiring knowledge as well.

External Collection of Knowledge

The pace of change is so rapid today that no single organization can ever control all effective operating practices and good ideas. Being a marketplace leader requires an organization to look outward for constant improvement and new ideas. The old school of thought, which held "if it isn't invented here, it can't be any good," is a curse in today's high-velocity markets. Organizations don't need to reinvent what others have done: today's rallying cry is "acquire, adapt, and advance." Companies can capture external information using some of the following methods:

- Benchmarking other organizations
- Attending conferences
- Hiring consultants
- Reading newspapers, journals, and websites
- Viewing television, videos, and films
- Monitoring economic, social, and technological trends
- Collecting data from customers, competitors, suppliers, and other sources
- Hiring new staff
- Forming joint ventures
- Building alliances

Knowledge Creation

The January 15, 2011 issue of *The Economist* observed that organizations that are clever and create knowledge are the first and, at that time, the only organizations to grow during the recent U.S. recession. Knowledge creation and companies that are innovator and not imitators are becoming ever more critical in the increasingly competitive global economy.

Knowledge can be created through a number of processes ranging from daring innovation to painstaking and diligent research. It can also arise from the "uncanny ability people have to see new connections and combine previously known knowledge elements through complex inductive reasoning" (Wiig 1997). The kind of knowledge discovered through problem-solving, experimental, and demonstration projects might be most valuable for organizations.

Whereas knowledge acquisition is generally adaptive, knowledge creation is generative. Creating new knowledge involves not only group-developed external information but tacit and highly subjective individual insights and intuitions as well. It is about using ideals as well as ideas to fuel innovation. Creating new knowledge is traditionally thought to be the province of the research and development department, but the task truly belongs to every unit and person in the organization.

For example, at National Semiconductor, management knows that it must shape and move knowledge throughout the organization if it is to be a leader in shaping and moving technologies. The company has initiated ongoing efforts to identify best practices and new concepts from all over the world, which are then systematically disseminated organization-wide. National Semiconductor uses the following keys to encourage innovation:

- A corporate culture that emphasizes diversity in ideas, skills, and people and that makes innovation a top corporate goal
- Open attitudes that tolerate risks and convert failure to a learning opportunity—in other words: projects fail, people don't
- A clear, funded, and supported innovation process
- Corporate labs where development of patents and other intellectual property is highly valued
- Project champions who work with small, dedicated, multifunctional teams
- A workplace that stimulates new ideas and does not minimize any contribution
- Innovation measurement performed at all levels and considered important to corporate success
- Reward systems that provide clear-cut, significant, and timely benefits— such as money, position, or control—for innovators

Four Patterns of Knowledge Creation

Ikujiro Nonaka, professor of management at Hitotsubashi University in Tokyo, writes that "successful companies are those that consistently create new knowledge, disseminate it widely throughout the organization, and quickly embody it in new technologies and products" (1995, 96). He goes on to state that knowledge creation should be at "the epicenter of a company's corporate strategy" (96). Nonaka has identified four patterns of interaction between tacit knowledge and explicit knowledge for building or augmenting organizational knowledge. Tacit knowledge is the knowledge we hold inside and may have difficulty expressing. Explicit knowledge is formal, systematic, easily shared knowledge, such as product specifications, scientific formulas, and computer programs. The four patterns of interaction between tacit and explicit knowledge are:

- *Tacit to tacit:* This form of knowledge growth occurs when an individual passes on knowledge to another individual, as in a master–apprentice relationship. By working closely with the master, the apprentice absorbs the master's tacit knowledge. This is a limited form of knowledge creation because the knowledge of both people is never made explicit and cannot be leveraged by the organization as a whole.
- *Explicit to explicit:* This kind of knowledge comes from combining and synthesizing existing explicit knowledge, as when the company controller gathers and synthesizes company information. This pattern represents a limited form of creating new knowledge because it uses learning that already exists.
- *Tacit to explicit:* This pattern of knowledge creation occurs when an individual takes existing knowledge, adds his or her tacit knowledge, and creates something new that can be shared throughout the organization, as when the company controller comes up with a new system of budget control.
- *Explicit to tacit:* This form of knowledge creation takes place when new explicit knowledge is internalized by the members of the organization to create new tacit knowledge, as when the controller's new budgeting process becomes the company's standard way of doing business.

In the knowledge-creating company, all four patterns exist and work dynamically together in a kind of knowledge spiral. These patterns become a powerful force for creating new knowledge as the various interactions generate much personal, group, and organizational commitment and energy.

Knowledge-Creating Activities

An organization may engage in a number of activities to promote knowledge creation, including action learning, experimentation, reflection on past experiences, and scenario planning.

Action Learning

The *action learning* approach to knowledge creation involves a group of people working on real problems, learning while doing so, and incorporating that learning to more quickly and creatively solve problems and develop breakthrough strategies (Marquardt 2011, Marquardt and Yeo 2011). Action learning builds on the experience and knowledge of an individual or group by adding skilled, reflective questioning that creates new knowledge. As strategies are adopted, additional reflection on the results develop additional new learning and creative ideas.

Experimentation

This form of knowledge creation is motivated not by current situations or difficulties but by opportunity and expanding horizons. Examples of experimentation include the development of original innovations through research and development, pilot projects, and autonomous, on-the-side research efforts (for example, Lockheed Martin's "skunk works" is a preeminent research and development operation that, throughout the Cold War and beyond, produced a variety of high-tech surveillance and stealth weaponry). Experimentation may take the form of ongoing programs or one-of-a-kind demonstration projects.

Ongoing programs involve a continuing series of small experiments that are designed to produce incremental gains in knowledge. This form of knowledge creation is the mainstay of many programs for continuous improvement and total quality and is usually found on the shop floor. Learning organizations such as Corning and Chaparral Steel have successfully created new technologies through this technique.

Demonstration projects are usually larger and more complex; they generally require holistic, system-wide changes undertaken with the goal of developing new organizational capacities. David Garvin, Professor of Business Administration at Harvard Business School, notes that demonstration projects share a number of distinctive characteristics:

- Systematic principles and approaches that will be adopted later on a larger scale
- Learning by doing and making midcourse corrections
- Severe tests of commitment for employees who may be wondering if rules and operations have, in fact, changed
- Development by multifunctional, multilevel teams
- Explicit strategies for transferring learning required to produce significant effects (1993, 83)

Knowledge Creation from Past Experiences

Organizations can create valuable knowledge by reviewing their successes and failures, subjecting them to systematic assessment, and transferring and recording what is learned in a way that will be of maximum benefit to the organization. According to David Garvin (1993), research on the development of new products shows that the knowledge gained from failure was often "instrumental for organizations in achieving subsequent success. In the simplest terms, failure is the ultimate teacher" (89).

Boeing is one learning company that expects its managers to systematically think about the past and learn from successes and mistakes. The company's 737 and 747 planes were introduced with serious problems. To ensure that those problems would not be repeated for the upcoming 757 and 767 planes, Boeing commissioned a high-level employee group, called Project Homework, to examine the development processes of the 737 and 747—as well as the 707 and 727, two of the company's most successful planes. After three years, the group identified hundreds of improvements that were then transferred to the 757 and 767 start-ups. Guided by the review, Boeing was able to produce the most successful, error-free launches in its history.

Knowledge Creation from Future Learning/Scenario Planning

Knowledge can also be created by planning for the future, and developing ideas and strategies that will enable the organization to be successful in an uncertain future. This creative process is called scenario planning. Scenarios constantly rephrase possible pathways into the future. Planning, when based on forecasts from history, can be accurate when times are stable. But because the global economic environment is turbulent and volatile, scenario planning has proved to be a valuable and knowledge-creating way to look toward the future.

Knowledge Storage

Before organizations begin to store knowledge for later retrieval, they must identify important information and determine the best method for retaining it. Organizations give meaning to data through reflection, research, and experimentation. Knowledge storage utilizes technical systems, such as records and databases, and human processes, such as collective and individual memory and consensus. A knowledge storage system should have:

- A structure that permits the system to find and deliver information quickly and correctly
- Categories such as facts, policies, or procedures divided on a learning-needs basis
- Ability to deliver requested information in a clear and concise form
- Content that is accurate, timely, and consistently available

Knowledge storage systems are not new. In fact, the concept first emerged in the 1980s. The thought was that after data were in place and catalogued, managers could help themselves to whatever slice of the data pie they needed at that moment. The idea sounded good. In practice, however, the size and complexity of the resulting *data warehouse* meant that maintenance costs were too high for everyone except a few banks and airlines. A data warehouse is similar to a database, but it is organized and designed for the user to make powerful queries whereas an application database is built primarily to maintain records.

Within the past few years, the concept of data warehousing has reappeared, and it is now traveling quickly around the world. Why? The answer has to do with competition as well as dramatic reductions in cost and increases in the power of today's computers. Thus, comprehensive repositories—online, computer-based storehouses of expertise, information, experience, and documentation in which knowledge is collected, summarized, and integrated across all sources—are emerging in organizations around the world.

In chapter 7 we talked about databases. In this chapter, we just introduced the term data warehousing. Because both are relevant to the discussion of knowledge storage, and because there are significant differences between databases and data warehouses, let's quickly discuss the two. First the commonalities: Both are databases, and both have some tables containing data. If you look deeper, you'd find that both have indexes, keys, and views. So how is the data warehouse different from a database? And if the two aren't really different, why not just run your queries and reports directly from your application databases?

Well, to be fair, that may be just what you are doing right now, running some end-of-day (EOD) reports as complex SQL queries and shipping them off to those who need them. And this scheme might just be serving you fine right now. There's nothing wrong with that if it works for you.

The primary difference between your application database and a data warehouse is that while the former is designed (and optimized) to record data, the latter has to be designed (and optimized) to respond to analytical questions that are critical for your business. It is basically a difference in level of sophistication. Further, the data warehouses of this generation can handle a lot more information (*http://it.toolbox.com*).

Modern database (DB) machines—that are not application databases dedicated to, for instance, an HRIS—include Oracle Exadata VI and Netezza produced by Netezza (Velicanu, Litan, and Mocanu 2010). The important fact about these powerful machines is that they can store a huge volume of highly complex data, much more than a typical database for an application such as an HRIS.

In the new economy based on knowledge, capacities for storage, queries, and data analysis are critical for any organization. When the volume of information is very large, the use of a database machine—hardware and software that are specialized for storing, accessing, and interpreting data in real time—offers a competitive advantage (Velicanu, Litan, and Mocanu 2010, 42).

Further, with a storage system an organization is capable of retaining knowledge. That knowledge then becomes company property; it doesn't go home at night or become lost to the company when an employee leaves. Unfortunately, this intellectual capital, although far more important than physical material, may be scattered, hard to find, and liable to disappear without a trace because it is not stored. So storage is obviously important, but what kinds of knowledge should be stored?

Which Knowledge to Store

Thomas Stewart (1997) has proposed five general categories for knowledge storage.

- Corporate yellow pages: Capabilities of employees, consultants, and advisers to the organization—who speaks Thai, who knows JavaScript, who has worked with certain clients.
- Lessons learned: Checklists of successes, mistakes, or failures that might be applied to other projects.
- Competitor and supplier intelligence: Continuously updated company profiles and news from commercial and public sources and wire services, call reports from salespeople, attendees' notes from conferences and conventions, an in-house directory of experts, and news about regulations.
- Company experiences and policies: Process maps and workflows, plans, procedures, principles and guidelines, standards, policies, performance measures, stakeholder and customer profiles, products and services (including features, functionality, pricing, sales, and repair).
- Company products and processes: Technologies, inventions, data, publications and processes, strategies and cultures, structures and systems, effective organizational routines and procedures.

How to Store Knowledge

Knowledge is nothing more than unusable data unless it is coded and stored in a way that makes sense to individuals and their organizations. Many companies are overwhelmed, inundated with the vast amounts of data that clutter up the information highway. Irretrievable, distorted, fragmented, or inaccurate information will not produce learning. To determine what data can be used, organizations must determine what is of value and then code the data based on learning needs and organizational operations. In addition, companies must establish well-defined criteria for identifying new knowledge, develop plans for formulating knowledge, and select efficient storage locations. Store acquired learning by methods that enable workers to:

- Decide which coworkers might have the knowledge needed for a particular activity
- Decide which coworkers would be interested in a lesson learned
- Enter a lesson learned into the corporate memory

For example, Cigna Corporation, a leading insurance company, knows that excellence comes from making knowledgeable choices. Cigna realizes that significant latent knowledge and expertise exist throughout the organization but, until recently, the company did not have a good means of extracting and publishing this know-how. The company assigned home-office managers the job of building and maintaining a knowledge base—basically a collection of checklists, rules of thumb, formal guidelines for risk assessment, and names of experts. The collected knowledge was installed in the software used by underwriters to process applications. Now, if a nursing home in California wants insurance, the custom-built software tells the agent the location of the nearest geological fault line along with estimates of its threat level provided by the company's experts. When new information comes in, if it is sound, the managers evaluate it and promptly add it to the database.

Challenges in Storing Knowledge

It is important to repeat that knowledge storage involves both technical and human processes. As organizations become physically and geographically diffused as well as more specialized and decentralized, their storage systems and memory may become fragmented, and the corporate benefits of the knowledge may be lost. And as work becomes more computer oriented, information from different occupational specializations is potentially available across functional boundaries. Networked information technology must be utilized so that fragmented information can be reinterpreted and readily exchanged internally and externally.

Given the fact that new technology is able to store and provide more information, consideration must be given to the potential of data deluge or information overload. The amount of information stored should not exceed the company's human capacity to process it.

Analysis and Data Mining

Over the past thirty years, organizations have become skilled at capturing and storing large amounts of operational data. Until recently, however, we have not seen corresponding advances in techniques for analyzing these data, to reconstruct, validate, and inventory this critical resource. Manual analyses with report and query tools are still the norm, but this approach fails with increased data volume and dimensionality. New approaches and tools are therefore needed to analyze large databases and interpret their contents.

Data mining is the latest analytical tool to enable organizations to find meaning in their data. By discovering new patterns or fitting models to data, employees can store and later extract information to aid in developing strategies and answering complex business questions. Software is being developed that can analyze huge volumes of data and identify hidden patterns. Whereas OLAP (online analytical process) can answer the questions managers ask, data mining software answers the questions managers haven't even thought of yet.

There are several data mining tasks, such as classification, regression, clustering, summarization, dependency modeling, and change and deviation detection. Data mining methods include example-based methods, decision trees and rules, nonlinear regression and classification, probabilistic graphical dependency models, relational learning, and intelligent agents.

Data Mining Tools

Data mining tools are software components and theories that allow users to extract information from data. The tools provide individuals and companies with the ability to gather large amounts of data and use it to make determinations about a particular user or groups of users. Some of the most common uses of data mining tools are in the fields of marketing, fraud protections, and surveillance. A growing number of data mining tools are being developed for navigating data, discovering patterns and creating new strategies, and identifying underlying statistical and quantitative methods of visualization. Platforms to support these tools, techniques for preparing the data, and methods for quantifying the results are also emerging.

Who Benefits from Data Mining

Data mining is being utilized by a growing array of organizations.

- *Retailers*: The universal adoption of electronic point of sale (EPOS) and the spread of loyalty cards are fueling rapid need for knowledge analysis.

Key benefits are the abilities to understand customers' buying behavior and rapidly identify unprofitable lines. W. H. Smith is reported to have weeded out twenty thousand of its least profitable products as a result of knowledge analysis, and the biggest U.S. retailer, Walmart, is investing in the world's largest data warehouse to handle data on customer buying patterns from its nine thousand stores worldwide.

- *Financial services organizations*: These institutions have long seen the potential of knowledge analysis to obtain an integrated view of their customers. High-payoff areas include targeted database marketing-and-risk analysis. Capital One Financial Corporation has virtually revolutionized the credit card business by using data mining to do highly sophisticated customer profiling and targeting. As a result, it has been able to develop a portfolio of literally hundreds of segmented credit card products.

- *Manufacturers*: Some of the latest data mining techniques are being used by manufacturers. Downtime—for instance, when a paper roll breaks in a paper mill—is expensive, but by analyzing the data from previous stoppages, companies have been able to predict the combinations of circumstances that are likely to result in downtime. Organizations then match this knowledge with current operational conditions and act to avoid potential breakdowns, which represent prevention rather than a cure.

- *Telecom companies*: These firms generate huge volumes of customer and operations data. Telecom operators analyze call data in ever more sophisticated ways for the purposes of determining competitive pricing, developing new price tariffs, and designing highly segmented marketing campaigns. Knowledge analysis technologies have also been applied to improving network utilization; for example, a company can analyze the amount of uncompleted calls to specific customers that may result from an insufficient number of lines.

Knowledge Transfer and Dissemination

Knowledge transfer and dissemination involves the organizational and technological movement of information, data, and knowledge. An organization's capacity to move knowledge is also the capacity to transfer and share power and is indispensable for corporate success; knowledge must be disseminated accurately and quickly throughout the organization, or the company fails.

Knowledge retrieval may be either controlled or automatic. Controlled retrieval utilizes individual and group records and memories; automatic retrieval is triggered by various events or situations. Carl Weick (1993) warns that information retrieved from organizational memory may bear little resemblance to the original material due to the transformational nature of storage and retrieval processes, the normal integration of human memory, the impact of perceptual filters, and the loss of supporting rationales. It is therefore important to develop a corporate memory and design processes that ensure accurate and timely knowledge retrieval.

Accessing required information just in time extends an individual's long-term memory and reduces workload memory requirements. The corporate knowledge base consolidates information in a central location, thus liberating a person's working memory from such menial data as resource location. This creates the right conditions for rapid sharing of knowledge and sustained, collective knowledge growth. Lead times between learning and knowledge application are shortened throughout the organization. Human capital will also become more productive through structured, easily accessible, and intelligent work processes.

When structuring knowledge, it is important to consider how and why the information will be retrieved by different groups of people. Functional and effective knowledge storage systems are categorized with the following elements in mind:

- Learning needs
- Work objectives
- User expertise
- Function or use of information
- Location and method of information storage

Several companies have made great strides in developing their knowledge-sharing systems. Accenture, for example, uses Knowledge Xchange, which allows more than fifty thousand professionals around the world to utilize the system to access knowledge bases and share knowledge. Chevron employs intranets, groupware, data warehouses, networks, bulletin boards, and videoconferencing to distribute stored knowledge. In addition, Chevron utilizes knowledge bases, lists of experts, information maps, corporate yellow pages, custom desktop applications, and other systems. Verizon uses CYLINA (Cyber-spaced Leveraged Intelligent Agent), which acquires knowledge through interactions with large numbers of users. The company supplements this approach with Auto-FAQ, a system that helps users retrieve knowledge from CYLINA in response to their questions.

Formal Transfer of Knowledge within the Organization

Knowledge may be transferred intentionally by a variety of means. Written methods include individual communications such as memos, reports, and open-access bulletin boards, as well as internal publications of all kinds, using video, audio, and print media. Internal conferences, briefings, mentoring, and training with internal consultants or perhaps in formal courses offer additional opportunities for exchanging information. Job rotation or transfers can be planned to disperse knowledge to other areas of the organization, although large corporations comprising many divisions may provide short-term tours tailored for specific audiences and needs.

Informal Transfer of Knowledge within the Organization

Organizations may also transfer knowledge unintentionally in a number of ways. Routine job rotation, stories and myths, task forces, and informal networks all send knowledge to different areas of the organization. Much informal learning takes place as a function of daily and often unplanned interactions among people. The less intentionality or planning there is to the process, the more potential knowledge is lost.

Barriers to Sharing and Transferring Knowledge

Knowledge should be disseminated appropriately and quickly. However, three major conditions create bottlenecks in the timely and effective transfer of knowledge:

- Critical business processes are available only to a few people
- Knowledge is not available at the appropriate place and/or time
- Transfers and restructuring increase the difficulty of securing knowledge

Barriers to Retrieving and Transferring Knowledge

Four factors may limit the transfer of knowledge within organizations and thereby affect its availability, form, accuracy, and meaning:

- Cost
- Cognitive capacity of the recipient
- Message delay caused by prioritized sending
- Intentional or unintentional message modification or distortion of meaning

Knowledge sharing is critical to success for consulting firms such as Accenture. Previously, the company relied on individual and team knowledge sharing via a network of strong personal relationships. With the advent of technology, however, the firm extended its focus through groupware technologies and the creation of knowledge-sharing applications. In addition, Accenture created four interrelated teams to disseminate and diffuse knowledge:

- People Team, which continues to evolve the firm's understanding of the competencies, roles, rewards, measures, and learning needed to support knowledge sharing
- Process Team, which concentrates on knowledge-sharing processes and their integration into business processes, along with the functional requirements and design of KnowledgeSpace
- Technology Team, whose mandate is to define the technical architecture to support Accenture's knowledge-sharing needs
- Leadership Team, whose task is to implement the required structures, processes, and technology and to serve as role models

Technological Modes of Transferring Knowledge

A comprehensive, wide-scale transfer of knowledge is accomplished most efficiently through the intelligent use of technology, which makes knowledge available anywhere, anytime, and in any form. Information communications software—including e-mail, bulletin boards, and conferencing—enables interactions in person and among dispersed groups. It also provides an electronic learning environment in which all members have equal access to data and are able to communicate freely.

Search engines now allow for searches of all files located on a local area network or wide area network, using criteria found in many web browsers. Current groupware offers the incorporation of expert or decision-support systems into a standard graphical user interface and enables individuals to access imported knowledge as well as capture congenital and experiential knowledge within the organization.

As mentioned in chapter 12 on communication media and chapter 14 on social network services, these technologies have given rise to new modes of knowledge transfer. Information is shared through use of communication media such as blogs, wikis, RSS feeds, video, and podcasting. Social networks offer the advantage of documenting ideas and innovations, sharing expert knowledge, and forming networks of experts within an organization to quickly disseminate new ideas. Groupware, described in chapter 11, offers synchronous, web-enabled conferences to brainstorm, collaborate, or present new ideas. Even the virtual world Second Life, as described in chapter 3, offers opportunity for coaching, training, and mentoring, all of which result in knowledge transfer.

Knowledge Application and Validation

One of the most critical stages of the knowledge management process is the application and reapplication of valuable knowledge. This is accomplished through the continuous recycling and creative utilization of the organization's rich knowledge and experience. Technology enables optimum application of corporate knowledge.

A company's ability to provide customer service through diagnosis and troubleshooting is a good example of knowledge application and validation. The net positive results include:

- Savings in areas such as shipping costs of physically transferring knowledge
- Improved ability to tap into colleagues' knowledge
- Capacity to work globally
- Forum for mapping corporate brainpower
- Ability to cope with growth and staff turnover, as newcomers who quickly learn organizational knowledge can contribute to its success much more rapidly

Technology to Manage Knowledge

Throughout this book, we have presented ways and resources for using technology to manage the organization's intellectual capital. Technology provides organizations with numerous strategic opportunities to automate, educate, and transform themselves. Technology permits the redistribution of power, function, and control to locations where they will be most effective. The production, coordination, and management of knowledge is enhanced, simplified, and made cost-effective via technology. Technology allows organizations to break many old rules of managing change, development, and learning. Technology adds a number of capabilities related to knowledge management:

- Information appears simultaneously in as many places as it is needed
- Generalists are able to do the work of experts

- Organizations can reap the benefits of both centralization and decentralization
- Decision making becomes part of everyone's job
- Field personnel can send and receive information from any location
- Plans can be revised instantaneously

In chapter 16 we will address knowledge management from a system viewpoint. Remember that knowledge management systems should be designed and customized for your particular organization. As a customized system, it is as unique as the organization's culture, products and services, and technology infrastructure.

Technology and Knowledge Flow

Technology can be a key mechanism for improving organizational communication and knowledge transfer. Information technology in particular improves communication by blurring the boundaries within the company and increasing the range of possible relationships beyond hierarchies. It also permits easier direct communication across time and space by electronic bulletin boards, mail, and conferencing. Communications software creates electronic learning environments in which all members have equal access to data. With every personal computer networked through the mainframe, with relevant external systems, any person in the organization can take part in gathering and transferring knowledge. Remote access to national and global knowledge networks is available at any time.

Information technology reduces the number of management levels needed in the hierarchy, yet at the same time provides enhanced potential for span of control. Empowered with information, frontline workers gain increased autonomy. For example, Buckman Laboratories, a leading-edge chemical company, has made the front line the focus of almost all its knowledge management and e-learning. Cisco equips sales representatives on their way to client meetings with new product information via Internet, teleconferencing, and even wireless transmission.

Information technology contributes to flexibility. A computer-mediated communications system utilizes its own storage, processing, and retrieval capabilities for internal and external communications. Databases, texts, articles, reports, manuals, and directories can be held for quick and easy access by all workers. One hundred percent of Cisco Systems' sales and technical staff learn online. The company's approach keeps employees constantly up-to-date and has reduced training expenses by 60 percent.

Conclusion

Returning to the title of this chapter, we talked about organizational learning from the perspective of its basis: knowledge. You cannot have organizational learning without an agreed-upon foundation of knowledge. Knowledge builds upon itself if organizations follow the knowledge management systems model. Organizations that acquire knowledge, create knowledge, store, analyze, disseminate, apply, and validate knowledge will maximize knowledge assets. Technology can assist in each of these stages of knowledge management. In the next chapter, we will examine specific technologies that assist in managing the knowledge you have collected.

CHAPTER 16

Managing Knowledge

Knowledge management (KM) is neither a product nor a service, but rather a system. Philip Harris, in his book *Managing the Knowledge Culture*, defines knowledge management in the following way:

> Knowledge management is the facilitation and support of the processes for creating, sustaining, sharing, and renewing organizational knowledge in order to generate economic wealth, create value, or improve performance (19).

Knowledge management has become particularly important in order for organizations to obtain a leading edge. Executives need intelligent and insightful information to efficiently manage corporate operations and support decision making. Knowledge management offers a critical service to satisfy the need for good information (Kazemi and Allhyari 2010). Knowledge management provides a competitive advantage for organizations that invest in it. Knowledge management can help enterprises to integrate traditional resources and capabilities in unique and innovative ways. However, there are critical factors that impact the success or failure of a knowledge management system. For knowledge management system to succeed it must have:

- Top management and leadership support of the KM initiative
- Organizational culture that encourages knowledge sharing, creation, and contribution
- Flexible and informal organizational structure that facilitates internal communication and knowledge
- Alignment and support of the KM system with the organizational strategy and organizational needs

- Processes that capture or facilitate the building and dissemination of organizational knowledge
- Technology infrastructure that is integrated with current systems, effectively uses software tools, includes a database that is updated periodically, and protects the data security
- Employees educated on what knowledge management is, why a KM program has been initiated, how to contribute, and what they can get from it
- Measurement plan to evaluate the impact of KM
- Incentives to encourage employees to contribute to and participate in KM efforts
- KM team with specialized skills to effectively promote and drive KM throughout the organization

Without these elements in place, the knowledge management system may be useless. Further, if there is no measurement or evaluation effort, knowledge management may be perceived as just another management fad. Implementation of a knowledge management system must be intentional and follow best practices, and needs to include ongoing evaluation.

The knowledge management system may use a mix of many technologies described in this text. A knowledge management system can range in sophistication from a system that is reliant upon a master database or data warehouse (see chapter 15 for a description) to a system that is a partitioned, shared drive on a local area network. It may rely upon a human resources information system (HRIS) or it may be driven by direct input from individuals or both. Your organization and its needs will impact the design of a knowledge management program in your organization.

Knowledge Hierarchy

As mentioned in chapters 7 and 15, there is a knowledge hierarchy. At the bottom of that hierarchy are data, which provide the raw material for creating both information and knowledge. The higher an element is placed in the knowledge hierarchy, the more valuable the knowledge is to the organization. Data can include images, facts, numeric codes, and texts, but data are useless unless interpreted and put to use.

Information is data that has meaning to the user and has a context. It is useful because it is data that has been classified, processed, formatted, and accepted as relevant.

Knowledge is information that has been analyzed, understood, and interpreted. Knowledge creation occurs when people understand and interpret data (Linderman, Schroeder, and Sanders 2010, 702). Just capturing data is not sufficient for knowledge management. Data and information must be deciphered and translated in a way that is significant to the organization.

Knowledge can be transferred to other areas of the organization, which enables other employees to develop new proficiencies or expertise. *Expertise* is the appropriate and effective application of knowledge in order to achieve results and improve performance.

Capability is an organization-wide ability to produce a product, service, or process at a high level of performance. Capability carries with it an orientation to the future. Organizations benefit from increased capabilities.

How does an organization build its knowledge base? It can be done by creating a knowledge management system. Knowledge can be sustained through a process that involves acquiring, creating, storing, analyzing, disseminating, applying, and validating knowledge.

Tips and Tools for Knowledge Management

- Knowledge management requires forethought, planning, and involvement of upper management.
- When establishing a knowledge management system, it is best to provide access through a customized, internal portal.
- The knowledge management system relates to and supports organizational goals.
- Existing systems and expertise within an organization can be used to provide knowledge.
- Knowledge management systems need to be monitored and maintained to be useful.
- Gatekeepers and a knowledge management team can provide oversight and ongoing strategies to increase the usefulness of a KM system.
- HR must be a strategic partner in the knowledge management process as well as an advocate.

HR-Intersect and Knowledge Management

The knowledge management system can ultimately be used by every group within the organization. The more robust the design, the more people will want access to the KM system. Any group or division within the organization that will use the system should have a representative and advocate involved in its design. Of course, there will be ongoing interactions with the Information Technology professionals. But there may also be work with the financial and marketing departments as well as graphics and any other group in the organization who will benefit from the KM system.

Computer Systems That Impact Knowledge Management

Surprisingly, legacy systems can contribute to the knowledge management process. A legacy system is one that runs on obsolete and usually slow hardware. However they can be used to an organization's advantage when developing a knowledge management system because the lessons learned from past business endeavors may be stored in the legacy system. Further, with the advent of service-oriented architecture (SOA), those systems can now talk with the updated systems and that knowledge retained.

Three commonly used computer systems include learning content management systems (LCMSs), human resource management or information systems (HRMS/HRISs), and client or customer relationship management systems (CRMs). Each of these three computer systems can contribute to the knowledge base. The learning content management system captures knowledge through the courses offered and indicator of the knowledge deemed important enough to disseminate. The HRMS provides information about top performers who can be considered sources of knowledge. That knowledge can be shared over corporate intranet portals and linked to an HRMS. Further, the HRMS can cultivate knowledge by sharing directories or databases with contact information linked to knowledge providers via a knowledge map. The CRMs offers a wealth of knowledge in the feedback from clients.

Learning Management System

Chapter 3, which focused on e-learning, described *learning management systems* (LMSs) and *learning content management systems* (LCMSs) that are used to create, offer, manage, and evaluate training within organizations. LMSs/LCMSs are powerful tools that have revolutionized learning. Taken a step further, they can contribute to a company's knowledge base.

Caterpillar provides an excellent example of an organization with a knowledge management plan that pivots around learning and their learning management system. As a Fortune 75 company, Caterpillar is the world's leading manufacturer of construction and mining equipment, diesel and natural gas engines, industrial gas turbines, and is also a growing services provider through Caterpillar Financial Services, Caterpillar Remanufacturing Services, Caterpillar Logistics Services, and Progress Rail Services, with 2009 sales and revenues of $32.396 billion (*www.cat.com*).

Caterpillar's learning management system serves as the foundation for Caterpillar's knowledge management system (Glynn 2008). According to Glynn, "One of the most crucial roles is to link learning to the key enterprise business strategies. This alignment ensures success through continual learning" (40). The corporate university, nicknamed "Cat U," is responsible for:

- The enterprise learning strategy
- The enterprise learning budget
- The development, redesign, and retirement of learning
- The policies, processes, and standards for learning

Additionally, the university works with in-house resources to develop and implement learning that results from a specific business need.

By creating a connection between learning and knowledge management, Caterpillar has achieved extraordinary success. It is an organization that built its knowledge management system upon a learning management system.

Human Resource Management Systems and Human Resource Information Systems (HRMS/HRIS)

We examined the human resource information system (HRIS) in great depth in chapters 7 and 9. Personnel Software, Employee Software, HR Database, HR system—These were the common terms used to define what we know today as HRIS, HRMS, or HRM software, so we are going to refer to them together (*http://hrissoftware.org/hris-and-hrms-is-there-a-difference*). An HRMS/HRIS can also contribute to organizational knowledge, a role that develops when the database is actively used to aid organizational members.

For example, managers can gather compensation and incentive plans from the HR manager so that policies align throughout the organization. When areas of expertise are linked to personnel descriptors in the HRMS, that information can be used to find expertise within the organization for the purpose of sourcing projects, gaining insights on specific issues, staffing and writing proposals, creating communities of practice, and other important functions. Also, HRMSs that are linked to project management software can directly feed operational data that allow managers to monitor HR contact and performance. The HRMS can contribute to the overall knowledge management strategy in these ways and many more (Desouza and Awazu 2003).

Customer or Client Relationship Management (CRM)

Customer or *client relationship management (CRM)* involves using the CRM system technology to organize, automate, and synchronize business processes such as sales activities. It is useful for customer service and marketing. Salesforce, Microsoft, and SAP are three well-known CRM vendors.

A CRM system can supply valuable information for knowledge management by furnishing data that provide insight into the habits, preferences, and needs of the client. CRM systems can identify, draw, and help acquire new clients, cultivate and retain those the company already has, and reengage former clients, all while reducing costs of marketing and servicing the client. A CRM contributes to the knowledge management process because it provides client information including needs and preferences (Britt 2011). Avaya, Inc., is an organization that uses CRM as part of its knowledge management system.

Avaya Knowledge Management: Case Study

Kimberly Schuler

Avaya is a global leader in enterprise communications systems, with a long record of delivering excellent customer service. The company has been recognized by J. D. Power and Associates for providing "An Outstanding Customer Experience" for the past two years, so it is no surprise that enterprises of all sizes depend on Avaya for state-of-the-art communications that improve efficiency, collaboration, customer service, and competitiveness. Avaya's success can be traced in part to the company's approach to knowledge management. Avaya's knowledge management evolved over a period of years to where it is today.

The Handbook of Blended Learning, by Alan Chute, David Williams, and Burton Hancock (2006), featured a case study about Avaya's knowledge management system in which the authors detail the origins of the knowledge management movement at Avaya. Avaya embarked on a new approach for equipping its sales force in 2001, adopting an approach with a blended learning model to effectively disseminate customer relationship management knowledge. The leadership team commissioned the Avaya Customer Relationship Management Institute to create a repository of knowledge, skills, and experiences. A portal became the entryway to the KM repository. Through the portal, users accessed communities of practice, knowledge assets, courses, and affinity associations (contributors to the knowledge base).

Over the years, Avaya enhanced its internal portal to offer a broader range of resources to audiences that include both Avaya employees (associates) and partners. The revolutionary approach that Avaya adopted is to support customers while gaining valuable information about its customers, as well as information from its customers, so the company can better serve them. Much of the internal multimedia training using video- and audio-enhanced courseware is also available to customers. One of the key updates involves the use of multiple, audience-oriented portals that draw from a single document management system that supports:

- Advertising technology
- Enterprise resource planning applications
- New knowledge assets
- Advanced search engine
- Deep personalization

Through these targeted portals, Avaya's sales and marketing personnel have access to all of the knowledge assets, including video, white papers, audio files, and presentations—basically any information developed by Avaya. Avaya partners also have access to any of these assets that are suitable for external use. Even customers have access to selected resources. Using a common database, the system tracks downloads by the audience accessing the database in order to identify the information deemed most valuable.

A document management database coupled with a web publication service comprise the basis for knowledge management and delivery. Associates access an intranet portal to view all the assets that support company solutions, processes, policies, and communications. Upon log-in to this secure portal, associates receive updated banner ads and headlines carrying important current information. They can request Really Simple Syndication feeds of news, telephone information, and updates based on categories of information, which will then be proactively "pushed" to the employee's e-mail address as news arises. Further, employees may chat with executives and experts through the portal blogs and social media sites. They have access to an employee self-service center (ESC) for tasks such as payroll, time reporting, 401K, travel arrangements and reimbursement, and even current job opportunities. Many of the tools and resources necessary for the sales force are accessible using a powerful search tool. In fact, all of the resources of the knowledge management system are accessible through the portal.

To maintain the KM database and keep it useful, the portal is updated in real time each time a new document is posted. Gatekeepers ensure that the data are current. Those who choose to submit items to the knowledge database must insert content following template guidelines. Then a reviewer examines the submission for appropriateness. A select portal team vets all content for the portal and is responsible for examining of all of the content once a year. Asset owners are also prompted to update or delete their materials on an annual basis. Keep-or-discard decisions are based upon usage reports and owner input.

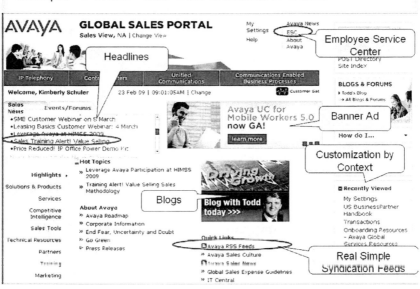

FIGURE 16-1 Avaya Knowledge Management Portal (Used with permission of Avaya)

Based upon a user-friendly interface, high-end technology, use of video, and customized assets available to both internal associates and external partners, the portal is the centerpiece of knowledge management at Avaya. It houses both the documents and the applications necessary for true collaboration and learning. But there are also several applications worth mentioning, as they support the dissemination of information among various Avaya organizations and resellers.

The customer relationship management (CRM) and partner relationship management (PRM) application is one such critical success feature of the Avaya knowledge management system. This web-based application serves as the foundation for both customer and partner relationship management at Avaya, allowing advanced collaboration between the Avaya sales force and their resellers. The CRM/PRM database takes the sales team one step further than the portal content, allowing users to rate/evaluate existing content and even publish their own content for others to share. This application also offers salespeople the ability to initiate special design, support, or pricing requests for each opportunity, offering a single process for internal and reseller sales staff to engage all of the resources necessary to close each opportunity.

Avaya has also integrated its own click-to-chat customer service application into the knowledge management system, capturing employee questions into a searchable database of frequently asked questions and answers for employee self-service. This in turn is used in the development of training sessions to target issues identified through this interactive medium.

Avaya's robust knowledge management system achieves the company's goal of providing valuable, practical information just-in-time at point-of-need, using the most advanced technology to serve both internal associates and external partners. This well-designed approach explains the overwhelming success of Avaya's powerful knowledge management system.

Kimberly Schuler, MBA, is director of Global Channel Communications at Avaya, Inc. Ms. Schuler, who has twenty-four years of experience in the communications industry, currently manages the strategic global communications for Avaya's extensive channel partner community, which includes more than ten thousand independent resellers and one hundred thousand partner associates.

Knowledge Management "Systems"

A variety of approaches appear in the literature for managing knowledge. The elements differ based upon the author and includes everything from cycles to process maps (Alee 2003; Harris 2005). Through analysis of these formats we can derive some elements of the knowledge management process that are common to all approaches. Simply stated, knowledge management systems must be able to create, store, acquire, use—by both analyzing and applying—and share knowledge. Technology assists with every step.

Creating Knowledge

Organizations have within their own confines the ability to create knowledge. Knowledge creation can be achieved through a number of different methods. Some of the approaches to knowledge creation mentioned in chapter 15 include:

- Performing research in the targeted area of knowledge
- Instituting problem-solving techniques
- Implementing action learning to address difficult, urgent problems
- Encouraging innovation
- Using demonstration projects
- Converting tacit knowledge to explicit knowledge

The outcomes of these efforts will result in new knowledge. Once that knowledge is created, however, it must be captured; otherwise, the effort expended is wasted.

Storing Knowledge—People and Technology

Capturing and storing knowledge the company creates requires a plan and some hardware. Typically, the explicit knowledge that is captured is stored in a database. We talked about databases in some depth in chapter 7, where we discussed HRIS selection and implementation. To capture and store knowledge, the organization may use databases and/or data warehouses. Knowledge management relies heavily upon technology to contain and retain knowledge.

Once knowledge is captured, it becomes company property, but someone must determine what knowledge to capture and store. Before instituting a knowledge management system, the organization should develop a strategy and identify the type of knowledge it needs to capture and save. The goal is to collect information of value to the organization, and this may vary according to the industry, as well as by the organization's competition, mission, and vision.

Acquiring Knowledge—Roles and Responsibilities

Any approach to knowledge acquisition should involve an oversight plan. The organization should establish a method for capturing and collecting knowledge. Some organizations have a review board that oversees the knowledge management system. Additionally, gatekeepers should be established and given the role of ensuring that the knowledge that is captured and stored is worthwhile and aligned with the organization's mission, vision, and goals. Clearly defined submission procedures (for submitting knowledge assets for the knowledge management system) serve to protect the quality of the knowledge.

Kevin Desouza and Yukika Awazu (2003) indicate in their article "Knowledge Management" that knowledge needs to be valued and rewarded in the organization in order to encourage contributions and to acquire knowledge from internal sources. When knowledge incentives are in place, employees are more likely to generate and disseminate knowledge for the benefit of everyone in the organization.

Human resource management systems can also play a role in promoting, identifying, replenishing, and protecting knowledge. To maximize the benefits from an HRMS, realign incentive schemes to accurately account for and capture vital knowledge contributions. Next, identify experts and knowledge providers in the HRMS through the use of directories or databases with staff identification information as well as knowledge provider information. These directories then serve as a type of knowledge "map," so that when employees are reassigned or moved within the organization, they can still be located and their expertise used.

Ensure that there is a process in place to evaluate and eliminate or replenish existing knowledge. This purging and updating process can be done based on how often the information is used. Someone must be assigned to regularly assess knowledge that is not used. That person should conduct routine maintenance to preserve the value of the knowledge. On a very practical level, instituting policies for capturing tacit knowledge gained from project debriefs and exit interviews and making it explicit are critical for retaining important institutional knowledge. Ensure that adequate security, backup, and control mechanisms are in place to prevent any intentional or unintentional deletion or depletion of knowledge. The HR manager can help an organization manage knowledge, and in so doing, the HR manager is redesigning her own role—making it critical to the effective management of knowledge within an organization.

As mentioned in chapter 15, an organization can acquire knowledge through a variety of means, including benchmarking other organizations, hiring people with necessary knowledge, gleaning information from newspapers and journals, and attending conferences. There are many ways to acquire knowledge, and certainly new media can help with knowledge acquisition.

Using Knowledge

It is not enough for knowledge to be acquired and stored: it must be used in order to make the endeavor of knowledge management worthwhile. Knowledge use depends upon employees having valuable stored information available (often in databases) and being able to access that information efficiently in order to use it. Two key technologies that assist in knowledge use are data mining and networks.

Data Mining

One way to use the knowledge that you have acquired is through the process of data mining, assuming that the knowledge management system is built around a database (see chapter 15 for more information). Data mining is the process of automatically searching large volumes of data for patterns, a process that can result in identifying previously unknown combinations of information that may be commercially useful. Data mining can help organizations find meaning in the data they have collected.

Knowledge Networks

Networks are the backbone of the knowledge management system: Knowledge is accessed and used via a network. Networks such as the Internet, intranets, local area networks (LANs), wide area networks (WANs), virtual private networks (VPNs), adaptive private networks (APNs), and cloud computing can connect the user to the knowledge. Each of these network types is defined below:

- Internet—A loose confederation of computer networks around the world that is connected through several primary networks.
- Intranet—A network that operates like the Internet, but which is restricted to users within an organization.
- LAN (local area network)—A network of computers sharing the resources of a single processor or server within a relatively small geographic area.
- WAN (wide area network)—A network of computers sharing the resources of one or more processors or servers over a relatively large geographic area.
- VPN (virtual private network)—A computer network in which some of the links between nodes are carried by open connections or virtual circuits in some larger network (for example, the Internet) instead of physical wires.
- APN (adaptive private network)—A new class of product with a unique strategy to leverage VPN technology to deliver enterprise WANs.
- Cloud computing—Internet-based computing services and storage provided on demand and as needed rather than through software (see chapter 7 for a more detailed description).

The network on which the organization runs allows employees to share knowledge. Typically, the choice of network has been made by the time the knowledge management system is conceived. However, you may have some input regarding network updates and flexibility within the existing infrastructure. Most organizations use Internet-enabled networks to access the knowledge that they have.

Sharing Knowledge

The organization's network is instrumental in sharing and transferring knowledge. Through technology, knowledge can be made available anytime, anywhere, and in any form. Of course, the Internet is critical to knowledge sharing. However, there are some other technologies that assist in knowledge sharing.

Electronic Data Interchange (EDI)

Electronic data interchange (EDI) is the structured transmission of data between organizations by electronic means. It is used to transfer electronic documents

or business data from one computer system to another. EDI is used extensively in the retail business, where the electronic communication of business
transactions—such as orders, confirmations, and invoices—between organizations is critical. It is also used by healthcare and food-related industries. Third
parties provide EDI services, helping organizations with different equipment to
connect. EDI implies direct computer-to-computer transactions into vendors'
databases and ordering systems.

EDI is not a new technology, although the Internet gave EDI quite a boost.
Rather than using privately owned networks and traditional EDI data formats,
the Web EDI enables quick and efficient data transport. Further, Web 2.0 has
super-fast, high capacity, with connections up to ten thousand times faster than
the average home hookup. So information travels much faster over Web 2.0.
In fact, Web 2.0 is revolutionizing the Internet and the way business is done.
This was predicted and it has come true. Web 2.0 is more secure, reliable, and
provides a huge spur to e-commerce. Most EDI products have been adapted
for a variety of platforms and browsers (Davidovich 2010). In the twenty-first
century, knowledge typically is shared over multiple platforms and using a
variety of browsers and EDI has benefitted. With the advent of cloud computing, this versatility is only likely to increase.

Networked Communities of Practice

Technology is not the only way that knowledge moves: It is also shared person
to person, in the form of communities of practice (CoP). However, communities
of practice can be assembled or facilitated by technology, as we have seen in
earlier chapters. Etienne Wenger, an expert on the topic, defines a *community
of practice* as a group of individuals who are informally bound by what they do
together and by what they have learned jointly through their association. A CoP
differs from a community of interest because of the shared practice (1998).

Wenger further explains that a community of practice generally has three
dimensions: first is the agreed-upon joint enterprise, next is the way the community functions, and finally is what it produces. As we saw in chapter 11, communities of practice can be facilitated through technology. Blogs, wikis, social
networks, and groupware—all available through mobile technologies—can be
used to establish, grow, and sustain communities of practice.

Electronic Records

Electronic records are superior to paper records in that they are easy to share
and use, and electronic record-keeping is having a positive impact upon

knowledge sharing. One discipline that is being transformed by electronic records is healthcare.

In the medical field, paper-based documentation has been an impediment to sharing knowledge. The twenty-first century, however, is seeing paper replaced. Healthcare providers are digitizing and storing health records rather than relying solely on paper. Electronic health records collect health information about individual patients or populations, and can be shared across different healthcare settings once they've been embedded in secure, network-connected, enterprise-wide information systems. The records may include everything from demographic information to medical history, immunizations, tests, and results to personal information and billing information. The gathering and sharing of this information makes it possible to create a complete patient profile.

The automation and sharing of healthcare information streamlines the process of diagnosis because the records offer real insight into patient care and organizational performance. Healthcare providers, researchers, and directors work more efficiently when they have access to comprehensive, holistic views of patient data.

The ultimate goal is to connect doctors, patients, and insurers so that they may share information seamlessly and securely. The move toward electronic medical records assists in this effort of sharing data, with the object of better leveraging and managing the resulting patient information.

Knowledge Management Legal and Ethical Challenges

Legally and ethically, however, limits to sharing knowledge exist. Let's start with the legal arena. In the area of medicine and health sciences in the United States, the Health Insurance Portability and Accountability Administration (HIPAA) Privacy Act is an ongoing concern for those involved in records management. This act is a federal law, part of which provided that the Department of Health and Human Services establish rules to improve the dissemination of healthcare information while protecting the privacy of individuals.

Those who work in the field of health sciences and medicine in the United States are very aware of this act and its importance. Any knowledge management system dealing with patient medical records must be secure and protected from piracy, invasion of malware, or any other threats to corruption or abrogated security of important and private medical data.

With regard to ethics and knowledge sharing, we mentioned earlier the issues surrounding social media. The case of WikiLeaks (discussed in chapter 14) demonstrates what happens when proprietary information or secure information is shared and security is breached. Protocols, clear policies, and secure systems must be in place to prevent this from happening. Information or knowledge that has been classified should be accessible only to those with proper clearance.

Knowledge Management Vulnerabilities

The issue of protecting private data is not limited to the healthcare sector; it has relevance for all industries. Three key areas of vulnerability for any computer or knowledge management system include the threat of piracy, potential invasions of privacy, and breaches of security involving online information. Each of these threats is explained later.

Piracy is the illegal copying of software or unauthorized use of material from computer or online sources. Some ways to prevent piracy include: obtain licenses, lock hard disks, limit access to information, and educate employees on the organization's policies. United States copyright laws make it illegal to put large portions of copyrighted text or images on the Internet (or to otherwise republish it). The fair use doctrine and the TEACH Act, described in detail in chapter 3, offer some limited exceptions to copyright. Most universities have university library representatives post copyrighted materials in a way that abides by copyright laws.

Privacy pertains to employee, member, or student information that is often kept in databases. In many databases, it is easy to track what the user is doing, but individuals must be warned that online actions are being recorded and may be examined. Any information captured without an established policy and employees' foreknowledge of that policy is considered an invasion of privacy. For organizations, this is an important aspect of software and Internet usage. The protection of privacy begins with an organization having a clearly stated policy regarding what can and cannot be shared.

Security of online information means keeping unauthorized people from accessing information. This can be prevented using firewalls. *Firewalls* are technological barriers designed to prevent unauthorized or unwanted communications between computer networks or hosts.

Other Threats to Knowledge Management Systems

Threats to knowledge management systems include computer viruses and worms. A *computer virus* is a small software program that is designed to spread like a highly contagious illness from one computer to another and to interfere with computer functions. A virus may corrupt or delete data on a computer, use an e-mail program to spread itself to other computers, or even erase everything on the hard disk. Computer viruses spread through infected attachments in e-mail messages or instant messaging messages. That is why it is essential that you never open an e-mail attachment unless you know whom it's from and you are expecting it. Viruses can be disguised as attachments of funny images, greeting cards, or audio or video files.

A *computer worm* is a malware program that self-replicates. It uses a network to send copies of itself to other computers on the network; it may do so without any user intervention. The worm is successful when there are security shortcomings on the target computer. Unlike a virus, a computer worm does not need to attach itself to an existing program. Worms almost always cause at least some harm to the network, even if only by occupying bandwidth.

It's Legal, but Is It Ethical?

In an article summarizing a dialogue about ethics in the workplace, a group of academic and business ethicists considered some of the dilemmas faced in a complex work environment. These dilemmas directly relate to knowledge management systems. The resulting list, cited below, delineates unethical behaviors that were agreed upon by these ethicists. It is **unethical** to:

- Sabotage systems/data of a current coworker or employer
- Sabotage systems/data of a former employer
- Access private computer files without permission
- Listen to a private cellular phone conversation
- Visit pornographic websites using office equipment
- Use new technologies to unnecessarily intrude on coworkers' privacy
- Create a potentially dangerous situation by using new technology while driving
- Use office equipment to network/search for another job
- Copy company's software for home use
- Wrongly blame an error on a technological glitch
- Make multiple copies of software for office use
- Use office equipment to shop on the Internet for personal reasons.

When an organization creates a sophisticated knowledge management system, employees may access the knowledge while multitasking and find themselves inadvertently compromising one of these ethical areas. An informed HR professional can protect an organization and its employees by establishing clear technology use policies.

Further, some basic practices should be disseminated to the employees. At very least, these should include prompts for employees to:

- Periodically change account passwords
- Run virus detection programs
- Establish and enact a file backup system

The bottom line is this: Be flexible with your solutions and have a variety of solutions to protect your knowledge assets. Provide a clearly stated policy for employees that establishes what is in bounds and what is out of bounds. Provide the necessary software to assist with malware protection and file backup.

Stages of Technology Support for Knowledge Management

A knowledge management system must be phased in, and the KM must have serious and dedicated technology support. The stages of support for the KM phase-in include:

Stage 1: Establish an installed, networked IT infrastructure for all employees

Stage 2: Create an enterprise-wide data, object, and knowledge repository

Stage 3: Automate and enable operations, management, and support activities.

Stage 4: Develop integrated performance support systems and knowledge discovery and data mining applications (Marquardt and Kearsley 1999)

It is apparent when examining these stages, that KM requires a long-term commitment of labor, intellect, and financial resources. The knowledge management system cannot simply be thrown together. Rather, it requires strategic planning that integrates the knowledge management system with the organizational goals, systems, infrastructure, processes, and training.

Conclusion

This chapter builds upon the previous chapter about organizational learning. We demonstrated the importance of knowledge management to organizations. First, we reviewed what knowledge management is, then we examined how knowledge can be created, stored, acquired, used, and shared. We offered a case study that represents a robust knowledge management system, to demonstrate how an organization designed and implemented an effective knowledge management system. Finally, we talked about potential threats to knowledge management systems.

CHAPTER 17

Human Resources and Technology: HR as Strategic Partner

This century marks a shift in the HR profession, from a predominantly administrative to a strategic role. Those HR professionals who understand technology will be at the forefront of this transition, leading the way. They will have the ability to collaborate with other department leaders and will understand the performance metrics and analytic tools used to examine and draw conclusions from HR data. Further, they will contribute to their organization's intangibles such as customer service, ethics, and social responsibility. Communicating throughout the organization will become paramount to the organization's success and a critical aspect of the HR function.

Focusing on trends such as workforce management, virtual teams, performance management, globalization, and management development will encourage HR professionals to widen their circles of influence rather than remain in an organizational silo. Most HR professionals already possess change management and communication skills; those will be used for consulting with other internal departments and building collaborative relationships. In this chapter we will point out several areas where HR can have a positive tactical impact.

Strategies that earn the HR professional a seat at the proverbial executive table include:

- Understanding business financials, performance metrics, and ROI
- Communicating regularly across business units
- Improving business processes
- Fostering relationships
- Developing the workforce

FIGURE 17-1   HR as Strategic Partner

- Dealing positively with intangibles
- Keeping current regarding professional developments

Many of these functions we delineated in earlier chapters. However, in this chapter we will pull them all together and cite previous content that addresses these functions in the text. Figure 17-1 highlights the topics we will explore.

Understanding Business Financials, Metrics, and Return on Investment

In chapter 3, we addressed the need to understand and calculate the cost benefits of implementing new technology. Similarly, in chapter 8, we discussed the selection process and the financials associated with outsourcing versus developing technology in-house, or the benefits of customizing an off-the-shelf product for something like a human resource information system. These decisions have financial implications. We cannot reiterate enough the need to get your hands dirty and do the math when it comes to technology decisions. In order to be taken seriously at the strategic level, you need to understand the financials associated with decisions that impact the entire organization.

HR managers who have human resource information systems and other technologies already in place should capitalize on the available information in ways that drive business performance. By analyzing the data in the HR databases and other sources, HR professionals can assist in higher-level decision making. Making use of data, metrics, statistics, and scientific methods enables HR professionals to gauge the impact of our practices on business goals. Some of the data that are useful in decision-making processes include analyzing turnover, identifying talent gaps, calculating return on investment, identifying valuable customer service data, and identifying compensation data (Roberts 2009).

Communicating Regularly across Business Units

Achieving global advantage depends on quick and accurate communication between far-flung offices, so HR professionals in global companies should make purchasing and the efficient use of computer and communications equipment a corporate priority. Communication can be enhanced by using identical computer software and information systems in all the company's offices, wherever they are located. The HR professional has responsibility for encouraging and training people throughout the organization to understand and apply the power of information technology and to ensure that the workforce is well equipped.

HR professionals can also make major contributions by developing a globalization communication plan that respects and appreciates cultural differences, acknowledging the difficulties and challenges of communicating across borders and cultures. To accommodate language differences, global firms should search for tools (e.g., portable computers, voicemail, learning management systems, and learning content management systems) that have translation abilities.

Internally, HR leaders can communicate new ideas and improve collaboration between business units by championing communities of practice (CoP) as well as communities of learning (CoL). Both require mutual engagement, a joint enterprise, and a shared repertoire of practices (Neff 2002). CoPs typically refer to groups of practitioners into which newcomers would enter and attempt to learn the cultural ways. A community of learning, on the other hand, is a group of people who, while sharing common values and beliefs, actively engage in learning together from each other. Led by HR professionals, both the community of practice and the community of learning will enable the exchange of ideas. This is an effective and positive way to build collaboration and learning into the daily business.

Social media tools like microblogging, chat, YouTube, wikis, and podcasting (described in depth in chapter 14) can assist the HR professional in building CoPs and CoLs and help an organization's staff to communicate across business units in an efficient manner. Additionally, social networks (see chapter 12) and groupware (see chapter 11) represent tools that can facilitate communication and build community.

Improving Business Processes

Throughout this book, we emphasize the link between technology and effective business processes. Pursuing these best practices situates the HR professional as a source of good ideas. Further, improving business processes is a competency that aligns with the responsibilities of the HR professional.

We also demonstrate technologies that can improve performance, and discuss when you would use them as well as how to implement them. For example, cloud computing is a technology that, once introduced, may improve business processes, result in greater efficiencies, and reduce the cost of doing business (see chapter 8). Mobile technology can provide access to training and communication tools in situations where limited Internet access exists (see chapters 5 and 11).

The use of Lean Six Sigma for eliminating error and increasing efficiencies is explained in chapter 10. This important process improvement philosophy emerged from the total quality movement and represents the leading edge in improving the quality of process outputs. Governance policies provide processes, structure, and tools (described in chapter 8) to manage large-scale technology projects, while the RACI Model (also presented in chapter 8) offers a unique way to establish roles and responsibilities for a large-scale IT implementation effort and conform to governance policies.

Business process reengineering (BPR) may be necessary when new technologies are instituted. It is the HR professional's responsibility to perform the "as-is" and "to-be" analyses that impact the redesign of workflow and to document the changes to job functions (see chapter 9). In managing these aspects of a new technology introduction, the HR professional significantly contributes to the organization at a strategic level.

Fostering Relationships

The workplace today relies upon collaboration among people who are working in different offices, sometimes continents apart, and also those who are working remotely, away from an office environment completely. Virtual teams are now commonplace. It is important for the HR leader to create an environment that cultivates collaboration and builds relationships. By partnering with team leaders, the HR professional may assist with recommendations to facilitate team collaboration. More importantly, HR can assist teams in developing online protocols and standards as well as team norms so that the virtual teams function in a healthy, productive manner (Gardenswarz et al. 2009).

E-collaboration occurs any time two or more people share complex information via the computer on an ongoing basis for a specific purpose or goal. Technology offers abundant opportunities for supporting the virtual team and virtual collaboration. An obvious fit between technology and virtual teams is the use of groupware (chapter 11) or any of the social networks or social media (chapters 12 and 14). When virtual teams function well, knowledge transfer is the result; this can be facilitated through technology such as a knowledge management system (see chapter 16). Using technology to increase knowledge and make information available online can also mitigate some of the administrative responsibilities of the HR professional.

Developing the Workforce

The workforce of the twenty-first century includes a broad mix of age groups; while there has always been a range of ages among those employed, the different expectations and technical abilities associated with age groups today present a challenge to HR professionals.

Workforce Age Demographics

Each age group presents a different set of needs and may have varying levels of comfort with technology. Characterizing these groups assists HR leaders in the process of satisfying, motivating, and rewarding them. Let's look at how the literature defines these age-determined categories. They are most commonly divided into

- *Baby Boomers* → (born between years 1951–1960)
- *Generation X* → (born between years 1961–1970)
- *Generation Y* → (born between years 1971–1988)
- *Millennials* → (born between years 1989–present)

One of the challenges of virtual teamwork has to do with the age group's perceived—and sometimes real—disposition toward using technology. Here is what the literature tells us about each of the above age groups and its characteristic response to technology:

- Baby Boomers—Introduced to television and global viewpoint; much more educated than the level of education required by available jobs; they were exposed to rapid technological change; while organizations saw the computer as productive and profitable, this generation experienced the computer creating meaningless jobs; they became disenchanted with technology; they prefer work that is active and autonomous and are willing to change jobs (much more so than their elders).
- Generation X—Tend to use technologies that support their lifestyle, such as online banking and shopping; have hectic lives, with careers and families, and enjoy the convenience of digital; the number of those reading blogs and using social media is rising, but they still fall behind younger people (Leggatt 2008).
- Generation Y—Spend more time online than Gen X; watch more online video and text message more often than the older generations; technology plays a major role in their entertainment and socializing (Leggatt 2008).
- Millennials—Like the Baby Boomers, who were greatly influenced by technology, they were exposed to rapid technological advances; they are highly educated; called "digital natives" because they adapt easily to technology; they are very mobile (Wesner and Miller 2008).

Other workforce cultural shifts offer challenges to virtual teamwork and technology adaptation: the growth of minorities in the workforce impacts communication and cultural differences; the increase in outsourcing highlights and exacerbates cross-cultural challenges; and changes to dominant business languages can cause communication challenges (Gueutal and Stone 2005). Keep in mind, however, that these workforce dynamics and stressors can be mitigated when Human Resource professionals help team members establish working practices that support communication and respect cultural differences. In fact, the HR professional should provide a model for a communication conduit.

The twenty-first-century worker has different expectations and needs, depending upon the demographic group to which he belongs. These expectations are neither good nor bad; they simply require flexibility and innovation on the part of HR professionals to address potential problem areas. Diverse workplace demographics result in different expectations from different employees; if these varying expectations are met, the result can be dramatic shifts in workplace practices and policies. For instance, if the workforce is primarily composed of Generation X and Generation Y employees, the rate of technology adoption may increase causing frequent changes to work processes. The HR professionals in that organization must be flexible, responsive, and creative to maximize the return on investment.

Management Development

In recent years, HR professionals have taken on a consultative, rather than an administrative, role. As consultants to the business units, HR professionals may identify issues and assist managers in developing their problem-solving skills. Management development can occur in any number of ways, including training. The goal, however, is for the HR professional to serve as a business partner rather than act as a "keeper of the policy" (Fox 2003, 34).

Behaviorism was the predominant adult learning theory during most of the twentieth century. Behaviorists believe that learning is built on three assumptions: (1) changed behavior indicates learning; (2) learning is determined by elements in the environment; and (3) repetition and reinforcement of learning behaviors assist in the learning process.

More recently, this learning theory has come under fire because of the limits of its usefulness when dealing with topics that require evaluation skills and judgment rather than simple recall and understanding. The complex business problems of the twenty-first century require that managers possess strong critical thinking skills. Consequently, newer learning theories have emerged to deal with more complex or ambiguous situations. Constructivism is among the newer adult learning theories.

Constructivism provides a potent and effective theoretical approach for adult learners. It is best used when there is no single right or wrong answer. The appropriate scenario for a constructivist approach is one where "the learner is exploring complex scenarios and applying problem-solving skills to ambiguous situations" (Rungtusanatham et al. 2004, 112). Constructivists believe that puzzlement stimulates learning and that the puzzle itself determines the nature of what is learned. The learning process occurs when the individual makes meaning from experience and reflects upon experience. Constructivists consider the individual as the center of learning; in this view, the point of learning is to enable people to "construct" or create new ideas based upon what they already have learned. As a consequence of the learner-centric approach, the instructor becomes a facilitator of learning who negotiates the meaning of the learning experience with the learner.

Constructivism impacts the design of management development activities in many ways. Suggestions for constructivist instructional design include:

- Anchor all learning activities to an authentic, larger task or problem
- Support the learner in developing ownership for the overall problem or task
- Design the task and the learning environment to reflect the complexity of the environment the learner will function in at the end of the learning

- Give the learner ownership of the process used to develop a solution
- Design the learning environment to support and challenge the learner's thinking
- Encourage testing ideas against alternative views and alternative contexts
- Provide opportunity for and support reflection on both the content learned and the learning process (Savery and Duffy 1995, 32–35)

When developing managers either through instruction, coaching, mentoring, or experiential learning activities, HR professionals can use these guidelines for insight into how to make the learning most effective.

Opportunities for combining technology with management development abound. The obvious ones are training enabled through the use of learning management systems and online learning (see chapters 3 and 4). However, performance support systems (PSSs) provide immediate assistance for those tasks that are rarely performed and very time consuming (see chapter 10).

Learning Transfer

Technology enables us to implement development techniques online, in an e-learning environment. Because learning that is situated in real work environments provides opportunities to learn in context (Raelin 1999), online learning is highly appropriate. Online learning facilitates learning transfer because most adults function in a networked, computer-mediated environment. Constructivism applied to e-learning engages the learners as coproducers of the course situated in a realistic learning setting. As you can see, technology offers an appropriate venue for management development using a constructivist approach.

Dealing Positively with Intangibles

The intangibles that Human Resource professionals can affect include risk taking, integrity, customer service, innovation, and social responsibility. As globalization increases, these intangibles—and the ability to influence them— change. Previously, we discussed the impact that HR professionals may have on intangibles such as business ethics (chapter 3 as well as all of the legal/regulatory issues mentioned throughout the book), customer service (chapter 16), and technical innovation (chapter 5). An intangible that we have not yet discussed, however, is social responsibility.

With globalization comes the need for HR professionals to promote sustainability and social responsibility. *Globalization*, simply described, is the process by which national and regional economies, societies, and cultures have become integrated through a global network supported by communication, transportation, and trade. The globalization of organizations as it exists today was not possible until technologies such as the Internet and videoconferencing were available. Corporations had for years recognized the power and benefits of being able to be both centralized and decentralized (that is, global) but could not put the theory into practice until the needed technologies emerged.

Globalization impacts organizations and the workplace in a variety of ways, including:

- *Information*—Increase in information flows between geographically remote locations
- *Creation of a global language*—English has become the "lingua franca" of globalization (Wikipedia 2011)
- *Competition*—Survival in the new global business market calls for improved productivity and increased competition, usually involving the use of technology
- *Spreading of world culture*—Growth of shared lifestyles and values
- *Technical*—Development of a global information systems, global telecommunications infrastructure, and greater transborder data flow

Globalization highlights the need for social responsibility. Not only should we, as HR professionals, care about the organization's success in a global economy, but we must consider the other cultures and people who are touched by the organization. As we gain in technical competence, we should offer assistance and give back. A consideration for global organizations is how to be socially responsible and benefit the communities in which we operate. Corporate social responsibility builds employee engagement when people are focused on something bigger than themselves (Wright 2009). In global organizations, the HR professional should spearhead the discussion about social responsibility as an intangible, yet critical, contribution.

Staying Current with Developments in the HR Profession

Society is undergoing dramatic changes, and Human Resource professionals stand at the crossroads of these changes. The workforce has become increasingly multifaceted in the last several years, and we are realizing that the twentieth-century way of doing things is no longer applicable. The changing world demands that we keep pace with the continually expanding competencies required of today's HR professional.

Throughout this book, we have suggested ways in which HR professionals can remain current and informed. Professional journals often provide relevant and valuable information; choose a peer-reviewed journal for the HR profession and subscribe to it. Reading journals regularly will give you new ideas, but there are also other practices that can help you stay current.

Professional social networks (see chapter 12) such as LinkedIn can be of great value. In these social networks, ideas are exchanged among professionals in the same or related industries. They allow you to make both local and further-flung connections. Job positions are posted on social networks, allowing you to take your career in new and unexpected directions.

As we in HR departments continue to be judged by how we contribute to the bottom line, more and more we are expected to be key players in ensuring the success of our organizations. We must know the business from all sides, and if we are to remain true to ourselves, our organizations, and our profession, this commitment to professional excellence will demand our best, every day, all day.

Professional associations provide members with the resources and the tools necessary to become leaders and decision makers within their organizations. Within professional associations, you will find others in the same position; they will understand the pressures and challenges you face. Not only will they understand, but they may have some answers to the dilemmas you face. At professional associations, ideas are shared, certifications are offered, tools are provided, books are suggested, and friends are made.

What associations exist for the HR professional? To some extent, that will depend upon your focus and location. Some HR professionals find themselves doing a lot of business process reengineering. Others specialize in business leadership. Some are benefits specialists or focus on processes to encourage and increase safety and security in the workplace. There are those who focus on learning, employee development, and performance improvement initiatives. Some of you do all of the above. Each of these facets of the HR profession has its own professional organization. You can do a search online to find one that satisfies your interests. Another approach is to join an organization that has it all.

The Society for Human Resource Management (SHRM) is the world's largest association devoted to human resource management. Representing more than 250,000 members in more than 140 countries, SHRM serves the needs of HR professionals and advances the interests of the HR profession. Founded in 1948, SHRM has more than 575 affiliated chapters within the United States and subsidiary offices in China and India.

Another organization that has a worldwide presence is ASTD (the American Society for Training and Development). ASTD is the world's largest association dedicated to workplace learning and performance professionals. ASTD's members come from more than one hundred countries and connect locally in more than 130 U.S. chapters and with more than thirty international partners. Members work in thousands of organizations of all sizes, in government, as independent consultants, and as suppliers.

The Academy of Human Resource Development is a global organization made up of, governed by, and created for the human resource development (HRD) community of academics and reflective practitioners. The academy was formed to encourage study of human resource development theories, processes, and practices; to disseminate information about HRD; to encourage the application of HRD research findings; and to provide opportunities for social interaction among individuals with scholarly and professional interests in HRD from multiple disciplines and from across the globe.

Human Resource People and Strategy (HRPS) is another association that provides a place for executives, practitioners, academics, and consultants to connect with colleagues who make bottom-line decisions about people and business results. Benefiting HR professionals for more than thirty years, HRPS has served as a vital gathering place for most of today's top thought leaders. Many of them continue to contribute to the HRPS journal, *People and Strategy*, as well as to its conferences, forums, and other events.

All four of these organizations offer tremendous resources, connections, conferences, certifications, and so on, with the goal of keeping HR professionals current and effective in the workplace. There are many more excellent HR-related associations. Find the one nearest you and get involved!

Tips and Tools for Becoming an HR Partner

- Grow in your understanding of business financials, performance metrics, and return on investment
- Use systems, queries, and analytics to examine relevant data for patterns and trends
- Assist with cross-division communication to eliminate organizational silos and encourage collaboration

- Seek to improve business processes and document those that exist
- Foster relationships throughout the organization and use technology to assist others to do so
- Set up business processes and training as well as make available tools that will improve performance
- Be proactive in your dealing with intangibles such as customer service, ethics, and sustainability
- Join an association for HR professionals such as SHRM (*www.shrm.org*), ASTD (*www.astd.org*), the Academy of Human Resource Development (*www.ahrd.org*), Human Resource People and Strategy (*www.hrps.org*) or the International Society for Performance Improvement (*www.ispi.org*), to name a few

Your Organization and Technology

Demographic changes within organizations—along with new approaches to managerial learning, management development, performance management, and globalization—have rocked institutions and disrupted the way they do business. Organizations must make deep and lasting modifications to the way they function in order to adapt. Technology will be involved in all future organizational functions.

Today, employees desire a more participatory approach to management. Technology will enable availability and communication between managers and their employees. Using tools such as groupware, social networking, and new media, managers can keep in touch with their employees and take an approach that supports a nonlinear, faster-paced, more casual style of communication.

Compensation packages will even be impacted by technology. There will be a shift toward flexible benefits that are customizable across all compensation areas. Performance will be assessed by metrics that can be captured in a performance management system. While salaries may not increase, the overall salary package will need to offer a variety of personal scenarios and accommodate a range of work styles. Human resource information systems will be used to handle many of these complexities. Increasingly, organizations will turn to an employee self-service approach to select benefits and handle other services typically in the HR domain. The use of performance support tools will replace some instruction that typically addresses training gaps.

Employees will work wherever and however they deem best. This may mean that they will work at home or at the ballpark or wherever they are comfortable. More than likely, the brick-and-mortar setup of the organization will change, with a pronounced shift toward telecommuting. Fewer organizations will invest in substantial office space, and more companies will encourage working from home. Employees will need connectivity with the organization's systems from a variety of venues: flexible connectivity will be critical.

Organizational culture will be part of an employee's attraction to a particular organization. HR must align organizational culture decisions with the expectations of the talent pool from which the organization must draw. The culture of the organization will become part of the organization's brand, and will either make or break the organization. The corporate culture will be conveyed through the organization's website or portal, advertising materials, its social networking presence, and other technology tools that can transmit images of the corporate culture to observers.

Organizations will treat employees as assets and value their input, and HR will seek to connect with employees through a variety of tools, including social media (such as blogs, chat, Twitter, YouTube), webcasts, videoconferencing, and other groupware. HR must assume responsibility for promoting a positive culture, where diversity is embraced, active participation in company decisions is encouraged, and a learning environment is cultivated.

These descriptions are not the future. They are the present. This is the role of the HR professional, to be a strategic partner dealing with this century's new challenges.

Conclusion

The workforce of the twenty-first century differs significantly from that of the twentieth century. Demographics, virtual teams, performance management, management development, and globalization are just some of the issues that demand attention. Technology plays a significant role in the way the HR professional handles these twenty-first-century challenges. The HR professional becomes a strategic partner by not shying away from the issues but rather welcoming the opportunity to contribute to achieving the organization's twenty-first-century mandates through strategic planning and appropriate use of technology.

CHAPTER 18

Future Trends for Technology and HR

Predictions about the field of human resource development (HRD) always include an expanded role for technology. One cannot dismiss technology as an underpinning of human resource development functions, and in fact, a review of current articles about trends in HRD unveils projections for technology growth in all of the major areas of HRD. We can conclude that technology will continue to play a major role in organizations, and HR managers—indeed all employees—must get on board. In the twenty-first century, those organizations that do not use technology to improve organizational, team, and individual performance will be left behind.

Organizational Trends in Human Resources

The organizational trends of the present require the support of technology. An article by Paula Ketter entitled "Six trends that will change workplace learning forever" notes an increasing move toward globalization and virtualization (Ketter 2010). These shifts require strategic planning on the part of organizations to handle the countless necessary adjustments resulting from cultural, technical, intellectual, and physical dynamics (Porter and Kramer 2006).

Who will be best prepared to lead in this environment? Organizations will need to emphasize new ideas to deal with new challenges if they are to produce leaders capable of handling the increasing complexity of the global workplace, and they will need to train managers in best practices to effectively supervise a diverse, global workforce. So leadership development and management training will be two other trends (Baker 2010).

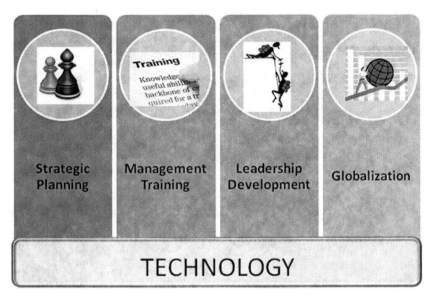

FIGURE 10 1　Future Trends in e-HR

Human resources professionals must adjust their approach to succeed in the future, and this includes rebranding the HR function. Technology will play a major role in reengineering HR functions.

HR Technology Trends

The Human Resources department of the future will require adjustments to the traditional approach for handling an organization's human resources. Four major changes expected for Human Resources in the twenty-first century are increased globalization, a more significant role in strategic planning, an emphasis on leadership development, and an emphasis on more effective methods of management training.

Globalization

It would be difficult to dispute the prediction made by Michael Marquardt and Nancy Berger that the potent energy of globalization has and will continue to impact "every aspect of the HRD profession" (2003, 283). Human Resource practitioners must be aware of the need "to increase the capacity of people to lead productive, complete, and fulfilling lives, regardless of where they live or work" (293). In fact, recent articles predicting future trends indicate that globalization underscores the role of HR to deal with increasing diversity, the need for inclusion, and the ability to surpass cultural barriers (Ketter 2010).

How do we go about accomplishing this goal? Marjorie Derven states in her article "Managing the Matrix in the New Normal" (2010) that we must teach critical behaviors. This includes collaboration, communication skills, conflict management, team alignment, emotional intelligence (what it looks like and how to improve), and building cross-functional networks. Include training as part of the onboarding process and address topics such as how to function in a matrixed, multicultural, virtual workplace.

Virtual teams composed of employees from countries around the globe are commonplace. Along with these diverse groups come some challenges; misunderstandings can arise when people misinterpret behaviors that belong to a different cultural context. While understandable, disagreements must be seen as opportunities to extend our understanding of other cultures and to adjust our conduct appropriately. And HR must be at the forefront, leading the way in problem solving, negotiating, and equipping others with the tools to deal with these issues.

In spite of recent economic downturns, technology continues to facilitate globalization (Mellina 2010). One impact of economic adversity is that it forces organizations to promote a culture of innovation. Technology usually accompanies innovation because it can provide cost-effective solutions and help overcome the challenges of collaboration across time zones. For instance, in a report by PricewaterhouseCoopers (PwC), predictions included a future where independent contractors organize themselves to form "guilds" (Fox 2010, 22). The guilds would handle their own health and retirement benefits as a community, rather than relying upon an organization to do so. In this scenario, the functions once handled by the Human Resources department of a single organization will be handled by a more diffuse association made viable mainly through virtual collaboration. We can expect to see more of this independent style of work and less that is driven by an organization because of the boundary-spanning capabilities of groupware and social media.

Strategic Planning

Strategic planning will be a major area of contribution by HR professionals. Michael Allison and Jude Kaye, in their book *Strategic Planning for Nonprofit Organizations*, describe strategic planning as:

> [A] systematic process through which an organization agrees on—and builds commitment among key stakeholders to—priorities that are

essential to its mission and are responsive to the environment. Strategic planning guides the acquisition and allocation of resources to achieve these priorities (2005, 1).

Human Resource professionals need to participate in strategic planning, because it is the responsibility of HR to assist in the recruitment, selection and hiring of employees with the appropriate skill sets who will best fulfill the organization's priorities, satisfy its multiple stakeholders, and create "the conditions where strategic objectives and resulting performance can be realized" (Garavan 2007, 26).

HR's strategic initiatives to empower the workforce must include just-in-time performance support for employees located around the world in a variety of time zones. As a result of the economic downturn, those who survived the reduction in workforce have learned to do more with less. Paula Ketter, in her 2010 article "Six Trends That Will Change Workplace Learning Forever," calls this current and future work environment "the new 24-7 world." The HR strategy evolving in tandem with this new work environment will need to include performance support systems, social media, and mobile learning as preeminent technologies that support workers around the clock. More than likely, these technologies will be enabled through cloud computing that lets the worker harness the power of the Internet through their personal computers (Ellis 2010). Mobile phones will be used for in-field performance support as well as to access current information just in time and to receive and transmit information in areas that do not have the technology infrastructure to support Internet. Not only are these technologies needed, but workers will demand this level of support, especially—as we have noted earlier—the Generation Y workers.

Corporate strategies will increasingly include corporate social responsibility. We can no longer pretend that our actions do not impact others. In this global society, multinational organizations have a responsibility to behave responsibly (Porter and Kramer 2006). HR can and should participate in this movement through awareness of industry CSR issues and innovative ideas to be socially responsible within the industry. This knowledge will establish HR as a strategic leader within an organization.

HR strategic initiatives will include implementing technological solutions to assist the future workforce. HR will need to lead the charge to revise and update business processes and policies so that they align with the new way of functioning in a global, 24-7 work environment.

Leadership Development

As indicated by Thomas Garavan, "Leadership is key to implementing vision and values and developing culture" (2007, 20). When so much depends upon those who lead in the twenty-first century, leadership development emerges as an essential component of any successful organization's overall business plan.

Dr. Tim Baker, in his article "Does the HRD Industry Have a Future?" (2010), asserts that the future must include a major shift in the way leaders are developed, changing from a top-down approach to a bottom-up form of leadership. The bottom-up approach relies upon greater involvement of stakeholders and employees, seeking their input in the direction the organization should take. This new form of leadership can be characterized as open and transparent, with everything from business operations to financials shared with employees at all levels (Li in Ketter 2010).

HR Leadership development efforts must emphasize a renewed commitment to ethics and integrity. It is HR's responsibility to make accessible through and/or embed in the technology systems the laws and regulations that should guide the leaders' actions so that there is no doubt about parameters. Through knowledge portals, performance support tools, and learning management systems, the appropriate legal and ethical guidelines must be made available and clear to both company leaders and employees. This built-in emphasis on ethics will protect both the organizations and their workers and can be assisted by technology.

Leaders must communicate clearly and use technology to assist them. Knowledge sharing tools, social media, and social networking sites give unprecedented opportunities for leaders to share their vision and strategy ... to inspire others. Leaders must use technology to make their ideas known. These collaborative and communication technologies make it possible to make an impact as a leader, even in a virtual space (Derven 2010).

In addition, leaders in the twenty-first century must be action-oriented and work well with teams rather than operating as autocrats or lone rangers. Emotional intelligence—essentially, the ability to assess and understand the emotions of oneself, of others, and of groups—will play a key role in twenty-first century leadership. It is much more challenging to encourage participatory leadership than it is to enforce a top-down approach; collaboration will have its own set of challenges that will require emotional intelligence for everyone, including the HR professionals (Mellina 2010, 13).

Metrics supported by data will demonstrate leaders' value to the organization. HR performance metrics are available through project management databases, HRIS, and ERP systems; they can be used to measure performance and productivity. In the past, HR professionals have not relied upon nor used metrics to their full capacity, but this must change.

Further, HR professionals should join professional organizations, where they can access information about technology best practices and benchmarking. In the future, these professional connections will become increasingly important as leaders continue the trends toward mobile communication and conducting business virtually. Technology will become progressively more critical to associations and professional organizations, who will reach their vast memberships via webinars, podcasts, groupware, social networks, and social media.

Action learning—in which participants learn through tackling urgent problems and use reflective questioning to find answers and take action—will increase as a leadership development method. Action learning is a valuable leadership option in these unnerving times. Further, because the global workplace makes it increasingly difficult to convene face-to-face for action learning sessions, HR professionals will conduct action learning sessions online as a viable alternative (Waddill, Banks, and Marsh 2010).

Management Training

Perhaps the largest impact of technology will be on management training. As mentioned earlier, organizations and universities will include experiential and workplace-relevant learning in their curricula (Kramer 2008). The design will be learner-centric, with emphasis on collaboration, critical thinking, and problem-based learning (Barut and Kanet 2003; Domans et al. 2002). And technology will enable participation in learning events.

Allison Rossett, arguably one of the most informed advocates of alternative learning formats and theories, predicts that the future of management learning is in collaborative and problem based training (Rossett and Marshall 2010). Others predict reliance upon engaging entertainment, games, and interactive simulations. By necessity, management education and training will become more process and participation oriented rather than static, closed, and rational. Adult learning theory promises the most substantial disruption to the management learning status quo. To develop effective decision making, curriculum designers will use a constructivist, problem-based approach rather than a behaviorist approach.

The technologies that will support learning in the future will rely more heavily upon social media, using shared virtual workspaces and wikis to deliver learning and development opportunities. There will be mobile options for delivery instead of relying solely on course delivery to the desktop. If organizations do not step up and provide updated learning environments using these tools, they will soon become irrelevant. Social learning will not replace traditional approaches, but it can supplement instruction with collaboration (Bingham and Conner 2010).

Conclusion

We hope that in reading this book, you have taken away this premise: technology is a powerful HR and organizational tool that must be thoughtfully examined and implemented in a way that creates advantage to the organization and its employees. Wise professionals will select and use technology wisely and never invest in a technology simply because it is the most current fad.

We will conclude, then, with your charge regarding HR technology:

1. Find the best technology resources (do your due diligence).
2. Collaborate with others within and outside the organization.
3. Question fearlessly.
4. Learn continuously.
5. Involve stakeholders in your technology decisions.
6. Keep up-to-date on current technologies.
7. Be aware of technology-related legal issues.
8. Contribute to technology-related efforts.
9. Join a professional association or community of practice.
10. Seek the good of the organization and its employees in all of your technology decisions.

If you follow these guiding principles, you will find yourself an active participant, rather than a bystander, contributing to—and leading—HR technology decision making.

Digging Deeper, by Chapter and Topic

Chapter 2: Technology in Workplaces around the World

The following texts may be of interest if you would like to pursue the topic of culture and organizations further:

- Conaway, Terri, and Morrison, Wayne A. (2006). *Kiss, bow, or shake hands*, 2nd ed. Avon, MA: Adams Media.
- Foster, D. (2002). *The global etiquette guide to Africa and the Middle East*. New York: John Wiley & Sons, Inc.
- Gannon, Martin. (1994). *Understanding global cultures*. Thousand Oaks: Sage Publications, Inc.
- Hofstede, Geert, and Hofstede, Gert Jan. (2010). *Cultures and organizations: Software of the mind*, 2nd ed. New York: McGraw-Hill
- Zweifel, Thomas. (2010). *Culture clash: Managing the global high-performance team*. The Global Leader. New York: Select Books Incorporated.

Additionally, the website below can be used to analyze the proper way to respond to cultural mores within specific countries:

- *www.geert-hofstede.com/geert_hofstede_resources.shtml*

Chapter 3: Technologies That Enable Learning

The following texts provide further insight into the topic of e-learning:

- Bonk, C., and Graham, C. (2006). *The handbook of blended learning*. San Francisco: Pfeiffer.
- Phillips, Jack J., Phillips, Patricia P., Duresky, Lizette Z., and Gaudet, Cyndi. (2002). Evaluating the ROI of e-learning. In *The ASTD e-learning*

handbook: Best practices, strategies, and case studies for an emerging field, edited by A. Rossett. New York: McGraw-Hill.

- Rossett, A., ed. (2002). *The ASTD e-learning handbook: Best practices, strategies, and case studies for an emerging field.* New York: McGraw-Hill.
- Rosenberg, M.J. (2001). *E-learning: Strategies for delivering knowledge in the digital age.* New York: McGraw-Hill.
- Rudestam, K.E., and Schoenholtz-Read, J., eds. (2002). *Handbook of online learning: Innovations in higher education and corporate training.* Thousand Oaks, CA: Sage Publications, Inc.
- Wiley, D.A., ed. (2002). *The instructional use of learning objects.* Bloomington, IN: Agency for Instructional Technology.

Chapter 4: e-Learning Technology Selection, Design, and Implementation: What Makes Sense

Adult Learning Theory and Instructional Design

- *Schools of learning*—Merriam, S.B., and Caffarella, R.S. (1999). *Learning in adulthood,* 2nd ed. San Francisco: Jossey-Bass.
- *Learning orientations*—Swanson, R.A., and Holton, E.F. (2001). *Foundations of human resource development.* San Francisco: Berrett-Koehler Publishers, Inc.
- *Cognitivist approach*—Gagne, R.M., Wager, W.W., Golas, K.C., and Keller, J.M. (2005). *Principles of instructional design,* 5th ed. Belmont, CA: Wadsworth/Thomson Learning.
- *Behaviorist approach*—Dick, Walter, and Carey, Lou. (1996). *The systematic design of instruction,* 4th ed. New York: HarperCollins. Mager, R.F. (1988). *Making instruction work.* Belmont, CA: David S. Lake Publishers.
- *Humanist approach*—Knowles, M.S. (1970). *The modern practice of adult education: Andragogy vs. pedagogy.* New York: Association Press.
- *Social learning*—Bandura, A. (1986). *Social foundations of thought and action: A social cognitive theory.* Englewood Cliffs, NJ: Prentice-Hall.
- *Constructivist approach*—Duffy, T.M., and Jonassen, D.H., eds. (1992). *Constructivism and the technology of instruction, a conversation.* Hillsdale, NJ: Lawrence Erlbaum Associates, Publishers. Bentzen-Bilkvist, Ann, Gijselaers, Wim H., and Milter, Richard G., eds. (2002). *Educational innovation in economics and business VII: Educating knowledge workers for corporate leadership.* Learning into the Future, Vol. 7. Dordrecht, Netherlands: Kluwer Academic Publishers.

Media Selection

Some excellent books and articles on the topic of media selection include:

- Anglin, G.J. (2005). *Instructional technology past, present, and future.* Englewood, CO: Libraries Unlimited, Inc.
- Dobbs, R.L. (2006). Development phase of systematic training: New technology lends assistance. *Advances in Developing Human Resources, 8*(4), 500–513.
- Leidner, D.E., and Jarvenpaa, S.L. (1995). The use of information technology to enhance management school education: A theoretical view. *MIS Quarterly, 19*(3), 265–291.
- Rungtusanatham, M., Ellram, L., Siferd, S., and Salik, S. (2004). Toward a typology of business education in the Internet age. *Decision Sciences Journal of Innovative Education, 2*(2), 101–120.
- Yang, J.F. (2006). The discussion of media selection and accessible equity in distance education. *Journal of American Academy of Business, Cambridge, 10*(1), 126–130.

Chapter 5: Leaders and Mobile Learning

Mobile Learning

The following websites provide more information about the design and availability of mobile learning solutions:

- *www.mlearning.com*
- *www.eclo.org/pages/M-learning%20Homepage.html*

Chapter 6: Human Resource (HR) The Portal

- Gueutal, Hal G., and Stone, Dianna L., eds. (2005). *The brave new world of eHR.* San Francisco: Jossey-Bass.
- Sullivan, Dan. (2004). *Proven portals: Best practices for planning, designing, and developing enterprise portals.* Addison-Wesley Information Technology Series. Boston: Addison-Wesley.

Chapter 7: HRIS Selection and Implementation Processes

- Kavanagh, M.J., and Thite, M. (2009). *Human resource information systems: Basics, applications, and future directions.* Thousand Oaks, CA: Sage Publications, Inc.

- Meade, J.G. (2003). *The human resources software handbook: Evaluating technology solutions for your organization.* San Francisco: Jossey-Bass/Pfeiffer.

Chapter 8: e-Recruiting

General e-Recruiting

- Reynolds, D.H., and Weiner, J.A. (2009). *Online recruiting and selection: Innovations in talent acquisition.* West Sussex, UK: Wiley-Blackwell.

Cloud Computing

- *www.ibm.com* (white paper on cloud computing)

Service-Oriented Architecture

- Carter, S. (2007). *The new language of business: SOA and Web 2.0.* Upper Saddle River, NJ: IBM Press.

IT Governance

- Bedell, M.D., Canniff, M., and Wyrick, C. (2009). Systems considerations in the design of an HRIS. In *Human resource information systems: Basics, applications, and future directions,* edited by M.J. Kavanagh and M. Thite, 45–76. Thousand Oaks, CA: Sage Publications, Inc.
- *www.isaca.org/Knowledge-Center/cobit/Documents/COBIT4.pdf*
- *www.enisa.europa.eu*

Corporate Governance

- Letza, S., Kirkbride, J., Sun, X., and Smallman, C. (2008). Corporate governance theorising: Limits, critics, and alternatives. *International Journal of Law and Management, 50*(1), 17–32.

Chapter 9: Handling HR Functions with an HRIS and/or Specialty Software

Employee Self-Service

- Kavanagh, M.J., and Thite, M. (2009). *Human resource information systems: Basics, applications, and future directions.* Thousand Oaks, CA: Sage Publications, Inc.

e-Assessment

- Gueutal, H.G., and Stone, D.L., eds. (2005). *The brave new world of eHR.* San Francisco: Jossey-Bass.
- Reynolds, D.H., and Weiner, J.A. (2009). *Online recruiting and selection: Innovations in talent acquisition.* West Sussex, UK: Wiley-Blackwell.

Time Tracking

- Meade, J.G. (2003). *The human resources software handbook: Evaluating technology solutions for your organization.* San Francisco: Jossey-Bass/Pfeiffer.
- Reynolds, D.H., and Weiner, J.A. (2009). *Online recruiting and selection: Innovations in talent acquisition.* West Sussex, UK: Wiley-Blackwell.

Performance Management

- Kavanagh, Michael J., and Thite, Mohan. (2009). *Human resource information systems: Basics, applications, and future directions.* Thousand Oaks, CA: Sage Publications, Inc.

Regulations and Legislation

- Isenhour, L.C. (2009). HR administration and HRIS. In *Human resource information systems: Basics, applications, and future directions,* edited by M.J. Kavanagh and M. Thite, 211–250. Thousand Oaks, CA: Sage Publications, Inc.
- Kavanagh, Michael J., and Thite, Mohan. (2009). *Human resource information systems: Basics, applications, and future directions.* Thousand Oaks, CA: Sage Publications, Inc.

Chapter 10: Electronic Performance Support Systems

Electronic Performance Support Design and Development

- Gery, Gloria. (1991). *Electronic performance support systems.* Boston: Weingarten Publications.
- Nguyen, Frank. (2011). Performance support. In *Trends and issues in instructional design and technology,* edited by R.A. Reiser and J.V. Dempsey. Boston: Springer.
- Nguyen, Frank, Klein, James, and Sullivan, Howard. (2005). A comparative study of electronic performance support systems. *Performance Improvement Quarterly, 18*(4), 71–86.

- Nguyen, Frank, and Woll, Craig. (2006). A practitioner's guide for designing performance support systems. *Performance Improvement, 45*(9), 37–48.
- Rossett, Allison, and Schafer, Lisa. (2007). *Job aids and performance support: Moving from knowledge in the classroom to knowledge everywhere.* San Francisco: Pfeiffer.

Performance Support Software

- Epiplex—Software product for developing an interface and creating wizards without touching underlying code. See the trial product available at *www.epiance.com*
- Procarta—A tool for modeling tasks. Available at *www.procarta.com*

Chapter 11: Groupware for Collaboration

Social Learning

- Bandura, A. (1977). *Social learning theory.* Englewood Cliffs, NJ: Prentice-Hall.

Virtual Teams

- Sundstrom, Eric. (1999). *Supporting work team effectiveness: Best management practices for fostering high performance.* The Jossey-Bass Business and Management Series. San Francisco: Jossey-Bass Publishers.

Communities of Practice

- Brown, John Seely, and Duguid, Paul. (2000). *The social life of information.* Boston: Harvard Business School Press.
- Wenger, E., McDermott, Richard, and Snyder, William M. (2002). *Cultivating communities of practice.* Boston: Harvard Business School Press.

Groupware/Webconferencing/Videoteleconferencing

- Agnvall, Elizabeth. (2009). Meetings go virtual. *HRMagazine, 54*(1), 74–78.
- Sundstrom, Eric. (1999). *Supporting work team effectiveness: Best management practices for fostering high performance.* The Jossey-Bass Business and Management Series.

Telepresence

- *www.ivci.com/telepresence-index.html*

Chapter 12: Social Networks and Organizations

Social Networking Technology

- Bingham, Tony, and Conner, Marcia. (2010). *The new social learning: A guide to transforming organizations through social media*. San Francisco: ASTD & Berrett-Koehler.
- Safko, Lon. (2010). *The social media bible: Tactics, tools, and strategies for business success*, 2nd ed. Hoboken, NJ: John Wiley & Sons, Inc.

Legal and Policy Considerations

- Guerin, Lisa. (2009). *Smart policies for workplace technologies: E-mail, blogs, cell phones, and more*. NOLO's Human Resources Essentials. Berkeley, CA: NOLO.

Chapter 13: Technology-Enabled Evaluation and Feedback

The following texts provide outstanding, authoritative information about the design and development of online surveys:

- Dillman, Don. (2000). *Mail and Internet surveys: The tailored design method*, 2nd ed. New York: John Wiley & Sons, Inc.
- Phillips, Jack J., Phillips, Patricia P., and Hodges, Toni. (2004). *Make training evaluation work*. Alexandria, VA: ASTD Press.
- Russ-Eft, Darlene, and Preskill, H. (2001). *Evaluation in organizations*. Cambridge, MA: Basic Books.
- Torres, Rosalie, Preskill, Hallie, and Piontek, Mary E. (2005). *Evaluation strategies for communicating and reporting: Enhancing learning in organizations*, 2nd ed. Thousand Oaks, CA: Sage Publications, Inc.

Chapter 14: Social Media

Social Media Technology

- Bingham, Tony, and Conner, Marcia. (2010). *The new social learning: A guide to transforming organizations through social media*. San Francisco: ASTD & Berrett-Koehler.

- Safko, Lon. (2010). *The social media bible: Tactics, tools, and strategies for business success*, 2nd ed. Hoboken, NJ: John Wiley & Sons, Inc.

Legal and Policy Considerations

- Guerin, Lisa. (2009). *Smart policies for workplace technologies: E-mail, blogs, cell phones, and more*. NOLO's Human Resources Essentials. Berkeley, CA: NOLO.

Chapter 15: Organizational Learning, Knowledge, and Technology

Organizational Learning

- Argyris, C., and Schon, D. (1996). *Organizational learning II: Theory, method, and practice*. PH OD Series. Reading, MA: Addison-Wesley.
- Schwandt, David R., and Marquardt, Michael J. (2000). *Organizational learning: From world-class theories to global best practices*. Boca Raton, FL: St. Lucie Press.

Action Learning

- Marquardt, Michael. (2011). *Optimizing the power of action learning*, 2nd ed. Boston: Nicholas Brealey Publishing.
- Pedler, M. (2008). *Action learning for managers*. Aldershot, UK: Gower.

Chapter 16: Managing Knowledge

Several excellent texts and articles deal in great depth with the topic of knowledge management. These include:

- Chute, Alan, Williams, David, and Hancock, Burton. (2006). Transformation of sales skills through knowledge management and blended learning. In *The handbook of blended learning*, edited by C. Bonk and C. Graham. San Francisco: Pfeiffer.
- Kazemi, Mostafa, and Allahyari, Maral Zafar. (2010). Defining a knowledge management conceptual model by using MADM. *Journal of Knowledge Management, 14*(6), 872–890.
- Harris, Philip Robert. (2005). *Managing the knowledge culture: A guide for human resource professionals and managers in the 21st century workplace*. Amherst, MA: HRD Press, Inc.

- Nonaka, I., and Takeuchi, H. (1995). *The knowledge-creating company.* New York: Oxford University Press.

Chapter 17: Human Resources and Technology: HR as Strategic Partner

The following documents further explore the topics of adult learners, generational differences, and technology:

- Gueutal, Hal G., and Stone, Dianna L., eds. (2005). *The brave new world of eHR.* San Francisco: Jossey-Bass.
- Rungtusanatham, Manus, Ellram, Lisa, Siferd, Sue, and Salik, Steven. (2004). Toward a typology of business education in the Internet age. *Decision Sciences Journal of Innovative Education, 2*(2), 101–120.
- Wesner, Marilyn, and Miller, Tammy. (2008). Boomers and Millennials have much in common. *Organizational Development Journal, 26*(3), 89–96.

Chapter 18: Future Trends for Technology and HR

The Future Role of Associations and Communities of Practice

- Meister, Jeanne, and Willyend, Karie. (2010). Looking ahead at social learning: 10 predictions. *T+D, 64*(7), 34–47.

Future Trends in Training

- Bonk, Curtis, Kim, Kyong-Jee, and Zeng, Tingting. (2006). Future directions of blended learning in higher education and workplace learning settings. In *The handbook of blended learning,* edited by C. Bonk and C. Graham.
- Ketter, Paula. (2010). Six trends that will change workplace learning forever. *T+D, 64*(12), 34–40.
- Swanson, Richard A., and Dobbs, Rita L. (2006). The future of systemic and systematic training. *Advances in Developing Human Resources, 8*(4), 548–554.

Recruitment and Selection in the Future

- Lukaszewski, Kimberly M., Dickter, David N., Lyons, Brian D., and Kehoe, Jerard F. (2009). Recruitment and selection in an Internet context. In *Human resource information systems: Basics, applications, and future directions*, edited by M.J. Kavanagh and M. Thite. Thousand Oaks, CA: Sage Publications, Inc.

Performance Management, Compensation, Benefits, and Payroll

- Bedell, Michael D., Canniff, Michael, and Wyrick, Cheryl. (2009). Systems considerations in the design of an HRIS. In *Human resource information systems: Basics, applications, and future directions*, edited by M.J. Kavanagh and M. Thite. Thousand Oaks, CA: Sage Publications, Inc.
- Fay, Charles H., and Nardoni, Ren. (2009). Performance management, compensation, benefits, payroll, and the HRIS. In *Human resource information systems: Basics, applications, and future directions*, edited by M.J. Kavanagh and M. Thite. Thousand Oaks, CA: Sage Publications, Inc.

Knowledge Management and Information Availability in the Future

- Harris, Philip Robert. (2005). *Managing the knowledge culture: A guide for human resource professionals and managers in the 21st century workplace.* Amherst, MA: HRD Press, Inc.
- Ketter, Paula. (2010). Six trends that will change workplace learning forever. *T+D, 64*(12), 34–40.

Evaluation in the Future

- Chapman, Diane D., Wiessner, Colleen Aalsburg, Storberg-Walker, Julia, and Hatcher, Tim. (2006). New learning: The next generation of evaluation? Paper presented at AHRD International Conference, Columbus, OH, February 2006.

Future Trends in Leadership Development

- Trehan, Kiran. (2007). Psychodynamic and critical perspectives on leadership development. *Advances in Developing Human Resources, 9*(1), 72–82.
- Waddill, Deborah, Banks, Shannon, and Marsh, Catherine. (2010). The future of action learning. *Advances in Developing Human Resources, 12*(2), 260–279.

Bibliography

Abdullah, A. (1996). *Going global.* Kuala Lumpur: MIM Press.

Agnvall, Elizabeth. (2007). Biometrics clock in. *HRMagazine, 52*(4), 103–106.

Agnvall, Elizabeth. (2009). Meetings go virtual. *HRMagazine, 54*(1), 74–78.

AIMIA (Australian Interactive Media Industry Association). (2007). Traditional media the early marketing adopters of YouTube and MySpace within entertainment industry. Accessed November 29, 2010, *www.aimia.com.au/*.

Alee, V. (2003). *The future of knowledge: Increasing prosperity through value networks.* Oxford, UK: Butterworth-Heinemann/Elsevier Science.

Allison, M., and Kaye, J. (2005). *Strategic planning or nonprofit organizations: A practical guide and workbook.* Hoboken, NJ: John Wiley & Sons.

American Institute of Certified Public Accounting. (2008). Recruiting for small firms. *Journal of Accountancy, 206*(6), 40.

American Library Association. (2011). TEACH Act best practices using Blackboard. Accessed January 2011. *www.ala.org/ala/issuesadvocacy/copyright/teachact/teachactbest.cfm.*

Andors, Alice. (2005). Tech smarter. *HRMagazine, 50*(10), 66–71.

Andriole, Stephen. (2010). Business impact of Web 2.0 technologies. *Association for Computing Machinery, Communications of the ACM, 53*(12), 67.

Anglin, G.J. (1995). *Instructional technology past, present, and future.* Englewood, CO: Libraries Unlimited, Inc.

Anonymous. (2009). How to select HRIS software—defend your planned purchase. *HR Focus, 86*(9), 3–4.

Anonymous. (2010). The Qtel Group announces collaboration with Microsoft to boost Mobile Education at Mobile World Congress. *Al Bawaba*, Feb 18, London.

Arbaugh, J.B. (2000). Virtual classrooms versus physical classrooms: An exploratory study of class discussion patterns and student learning in an asynchronous Internet-based MB course. *Journal of Management Education, 24*(2), 207–227.

Arnold, Jennifer Taylor. (2010). Ramping up onboarding. *HRMagazine, 55*(5), 75–78.

Auroville Health Services. (2010). [April 28, 2011] *www.auroville.org/health/avhs_old.htm.*

Baker, Tim. (2010). Does the HRD industry have a future? *Training and Development in Australia, 37*(3), 12–13.

Bandura, A. (1977). *Social learning theory.* Englewood Cliffs, NJ: Prentice-Hall.

Bandura, A. (1986). *Social foundations of thought and action: A social cognitive theory.* Englewood Cliffs, NJ: Prentice-Hall.

Baun, John T., and Scott, Thomas. (2010). Business education under the microscope: Applying Six Sigma to workplace training. *T+D, 64*(8), 63–67.

Beaman, K., ed. (2002). *Boundaryless HR: Human capital management in the global economy.* Austin, TX: IHRIM Press Book.

Bedell, M.D., Canniff, M., and Wyrick, C. (2009). Systems considerations in the design of an HRIS. In *Human resource information systems: Basics, applications, and future directions,* edited by M.J. Kavanagh and M. Thite, 45–76. Thousand Oaks, CA: Sage Publications, Inc.

Bernard, R.M., Abrami, P.C., Lou, Y., and Borokhovski, E. (2004). How does distance education compare with classroom instruction? A meta-analysis of the empirical literature. *Review of Educational Research, 74*(3), 379–440.

Bersin, Josh, and O'Leonard, Karen. (2005). Performance support systems. *T+D, 59*(4), 67–70.

Billings, D. (2005). From teaching to learning in a mobile, wireless world. *Journal of Nursing Education, 44*(8), 343.

Bingham, Tony, and Conner, Marcia. (2010). *The new social learning: A guide to transforming organizations through social media.* Alexandria, VA: ASTD & Berrett-Koehler.

Boland, Joe. (2010). The case (studies) for social media. *Fundraising Success, 8*(8), 18–27.

Bolman, L., and Deal, T. (2009). Battles and beliefs: Rethinking the roles of today's leaders. *Leadership in Action, 29*(5), 14–18.

Bondarouk, T., and Ruel, H. (2010). Dynamics of e-learning: Theoretical and practical perspectives. *International Journal of Training and Development, 14*(3), 149–152.

Bonk, C., and Graham, C. (2006). *The handbook of blended learning.* San Francisco: Pfeiffer, 105–119.

Boyd, Dana, and Ellison, Nicole. (2008). Social network sites: Definition, history, and scholarship. *Journal of Computer-Mediated Communication, 13*(1), 210–230.

Brandenburg, Carly. (2008). The newest way to screen job applicants: A social networker's nightmare. *Federal Communications Law Journal, 60*(3), 597–626.

Britt, Phil. (2011). KM to the rescue—Helping companies help their customers. *KM World* April, 18 & 28.

Brooks, R. (2001). Online help for a busy HR staff. *Occupational Health Safety*, 70(2):26–29.

Brown, Tom H. (2005). Towards a model for m-learning in Africa. *International Journal on ELearning, 4*(3), 299–315.

Bughin, Jacques. (2009). How companies are benefiting from Web 2.0: Selected McKinsey Global Survey Results. *The McKinsey Quarterly, 4,* 84.

Carter, Sandy. (2007). *The new language of business: SOA and Web 2.0.* Upper Saddle River, NJ: IBM Press.

Casse, P. (1982). *Training for the multicultural manager.* Yarmouth, ME: Intercultural Press.

Cavanagh, T.B. (2004). The new spectrum of support: Reclassifying human performance technology. *Performance Improvement, 43*(4), 28–32.

Chapman, D.S., and Webster, J. (2003). The use of technologies in the recruiting, screening, and selection processes for job candidates. *International Journal of Selection and Assessment, 11,* 113–120.

Chermack, T.J. (2003). Decision-making expertise at the core of human resource development. *Advances in Developing Human Resources, 5*(4), 365–377.

Chute, Alan, Williams, David, and Hancock, Burton. (2006). Transformation of sales skills through knowledge management and blended learning. In *The handbook of blended learning,* edited by C. Bonk and C. Graham. San Francisco: Pfeiffer.

Cober, R.T., Brown, D.J., Blumental, A.J., Doverspike, D., and Levy, P. (2000). The quest for the qualified job surfer: It's time the public sector catches the wave. *Public Personnel Management, 29,* 479–496.

Conley, Curti, and Zheng, Wei. (2009). Factors critical to knowledge management success. *Advances in Developing Human Resources, 1*(3), 334–348.

Cornelius, J., and Lawrence, J. (2009). Receptivity of African-American adolescents to an HIV-prevention curriculum enhanced by text messaging. *Journal for Specialists in Pediatric Nursing, 14*(2), 123–131.

Crosbie, Vin. (2011). *What Is New Media* [URL]. Vin Crosbie, July 19, 2010 [cited April 26 2011]. Available from *http://www.vincrosbie.com/tag/new-media/*.

Davenport, T., De Long, D., and Beers, M. (1998). Successful knowledge management projects. *Sloan Management Review, 39*(2), 43–57.

Davidovich, Michael. (2011). *Web EDI, Internet Browsers, Windows, Mac, Web 2.0 and latest technologies* [Blog]. Direct EDI, July 23, 2010 [cited April 29, 2011]. Available from *http://www.directedi.com*.

de Burgh, Robyn. (2008). Second Life and the Australian Open. *The Licensing Journal* (September 2008), 16–19.

Derven, Marjorie. 2010. Managing the matrix in the new normal. *T+D, 64*(7), 42–47.

Desisto, R.P. (June 21, 2010). Four steps to get in front of the SaaS curve. *www.gartner.com/technology/media-products/reprints/netsuite/article4/article4.html.* Access date October 29, 2010. *www.gartner.com*.

Desouza, Kevin, and Awazu, Yukika. (2003). Knowledge management. *HRMagazine, 48*(11), 107–113.

Detlor, B. (2000). The corporate portal as information infrastructure: Towards a framework for portal design. *International Journal of Information Management, 20*(2), 91.

Dick, Walter, and Carey, Lou. (1996). *The Systematic Design of Instruction,* 4th ed. New York: HarperCollins.

Dillman, Don. (2000). *Mail and Internet surveys: The tailored design method,* 2nd ed. New York: John Wiley & Sons, Inc.

Dobbs, Rita L. (2006). Development phase of systematic training: New technology lends assistance. *Advances in Developing Human Resources, 8*(4), 500–513.

Dobson, Sarah. (2009). Virtually speaking—employee avatars. *Canadian HR Reporter, 22*(21), 15–18.

Doherty, Jacqueline. (2001). Telecom tightrope. *Barron's, 81*(2), 17–18.

Duffy, T.M., and Jonassen, D.H., eds. (1992). *Constructivism and the technology of instruction, a conversation.* Hillsdale, NJ: Lawrence Erlbaum Associates, Publishers.

Fay, C.H., and Nardoni, R. (2009). Performance management, compensation, benefits, payroll, and the HRIS. In *Human resource information systems: Basics, applications, and future directions,* edited by M.J. Kavanagh and M. Thite, 338–360. Thousand Oaks, CA: Sage Publications, Inc.

Foster, D. (2002). *The global etiquette guide to Africa and the Middle East.* New York: John Wiley & Sons, Inc.

Fountain, Christine. (2005). Finding a job in the Internet Age. *Social Forces, 83*(3), 1235–1262.

Fox, Adrienne. (2003). HR makes leap to strategic partner. *HRMagazine, 48*(7), 34.

Fox, Adrienne. (2010). At work in 2010. *HRMagazine, 55*(1), 18–24.

Fox, Adrienne. (2010). Newest social medium has recruiters a-Twitter. *HRMagazine.* SHRM's 2010 HR Trend Book (Staffing Management), 30.

Frankola, Karen. (2001). Why online learners drop out. *Workforce, 80*(10), 52–60.

Freeman, Lee. (2010). Using social media—Twitter. *Printing News,* February 1.

Gagne, R.M. (1965). *The conditions of learning.* New York: Holt, Rinehart & Winston.

Gagne, R.M., Wager, W.W., Golas, K.C., and Keller, J.M. (2005). *Principles of instructional design,* 5th ed. Belmont, CA: Wadsworth/Thomson Learning.

Galanaki, E. (2002). The decision to recruit online: A descriptive study. *Career Development International, 7*(4), 243–251.

Gannon, Martin. (1994). *Understanding global cultures.* Thousand Oaks, CA: Sage Publications, Inc.

Garavan, T.N. (2007). A strategic perspective on human resource development. *Advances in Developing Human Resources, 9*(1), 11–30.

Gardenswartz, Lee, Cherbosque, Jorge, and Rowe, Anita. (2009). Coaching teams for emotional intelligence in your diverse workplace. *T+D, 63*(2), 44–49.

Garvin, David. (1993). Building a learning organization. *Harvard Business Review,* *71*(4), 78–91.

George, Mike, Rowlands, Dave, and Kastle, Bill. (2004). *What is Lean Six Sigma?* New York: McGraw-Hill.

Gery, G. (1995). Attributes and behaviors of performance-centered systems. In *EPSS revisited: A lifecycle for developing performance-centered systems,* edited by G.J. Dickelman, 4–50. Silver Spring, MD: International Society for Performance Improvement.

Gery, G. (2003). Ten years later: A new introduction to attributes and behaviors and the state of performance-centered systems. In *EPSS revisited: A lifecycle for developing performance-centered systems,* edited by G.J. Dickelman, 1–3. Silver Spring, MD: International Society for Performance Improvement.

Gery, Gloria. (1991). *Electronic performance support systems.* Boston: Weingarten Publications.

Glynn, Christopher E. (2008). Building a learning infrastructure. *T+D, 62*(1), 38–43.

Guerin, Lisa. (2009). *Smart policies for workplace technologies: E-mail, blogs, cell phones, and more.* NOLO's Human Resources Essentials. Berkeley, CA: NOLO.

Gueutal, H.G., and Stone, D.L., eds. (2005). *The brave new world of eHR.* San Francisco: Jossey-Bass.

Gurchiek, Kathy. (2006). 10 steps for HR to earn its seat at the table. *HRMagazine, 51*(6), 44.

Hall, Sue O., and Hall, Brandon. (2004). A guide to Learning Content Management Systems. *Training, 41*(11), 33–37.

Halliday, Josh. (2011). *Tablet sales poised for spectacular growth* [Online Journal]. The Guardian 2011 [cited April 12, 2011]. Available from *http://www.psfk. com/2011/04/tablet-sales-poised-for-spectacular-growth html.*

Halls, Jonathan. (2010). Give learning a listen: Audio podcasting and learning. *T+D, 64*(10), 92–93.

Harris, M.M., Van Hoye, G., and Lievens, F. (2003). Privacy and attitudes toward Internet-based selection systems: A cross-cultural comparison. *International Journal of Selection and Assessment, 11,* 230–236.

Harris, Philip Robert. (2005). *Managing the knowledge culture: A guide for human resource professionals and managers in the 21st century workplace.* Amherst, MA: HRD Press, Inc.

Hearn, Greg, Foth, Marcus, and Gray, Heather. (2009). Applications and implementations of new media in corporate communications, an action research approach. *Corporate Communications: An International Journal, 14*(1), 49–61.

Hoffman, C., and Goodwin, S. (2006). A clicker for your thoughts: Technology for active learning. *New Library World, 107*(9/10), 422–433.

Hofman, P. (2008). ERP is dead, long live ERP. *IEEE Internet Computing,* (July/August), 84–89. Accessed May 5, 2011.

Hofstede, G. (1980). *Culture's consequences: International differences in work related values*. Beverly Hills, CA: Sage Publications, Inc.

Hofstede, Geert, Hofstede, Gert Jan, and Minkov, Michael. (2010). *Cultures and organizations: software of the mind*, 3rd ed. New York: McGraw-Hill.

Individual Software, Inc. (2009). *Typing instructor*, platinum edition. Pleasanton, CA: Individual Software, Inc.

International Telecommunications Union. (2002). *ITU Internet report 2002: Internet for a mobile generation*. Geneva: ITU.

Isenhour, L.C. (2009). HR administration and HRIS. In *Human resource information systems: Basics, applications, and future directions*, edited by M.J. Kavanagh and M. Thite, 211–250. Thousand Oaks, CA: Sage Publications, Inc.

Kavanagh, M.J., and Thite, M. (2009). *Human resource information systems: Basics, applications, and future directions*. Thousand Oaks, CA: Sage Publications, Inc.

Kazemi, Mostafa, and Allahyari, Maral Zafar. (2010). Defining a knowledge management conceptual model by using MADM. *Journal of Knowledge Management, 14*(6), 872–890.

Ketter, Paula. (2010). Six trends that will change workplace learning forever. *T+D, 64*(12), 34–40.

Kim, Min Kyu. (2011). Technology-enhanced learning environments to solve performance problems: A case of a Korean company. *TechTrends, 55*(1), 37–41.

Knowles, M.S. (1970). *The modern practice of adult education: Andragogy vs. pedagogy*. New York: Association Press.

Kramer, R. (2008). How to learn: Action learning for leadership development. In *Innovations in public leadership development*, edited by R. Morse, 296–326. Washington DC: Sharpe and National Academy of Public Administration.

Krell, Eric. (2006). Notable by its absence. *HRMagazine, 51*(2), 50–57.

Lamont, Ian. (2007). *Harvard's virtual education experiment in Second Life* [Blog]. Computerworld, May 21, 2007 [cited May 5, 2011]. Masie, E. (2002). Blended learning: The magic is in the mix. In *The ASTD e-learning handbook: Best practices, strategies, and case studies for an emerging field*, edited by A. Rossett, 58–63. New York: McGraw-Hill.

Leggatt, Helen. (2011). *What's the difference between Gen X and Gen Y?* [Online news]. BizReport July 24, 2008 [Accessed April 28, 2011]. Available from *http://www.bizreport.com/2008/07/whats_the_difference_between_gen_x_and_gen_y.html*.

Leidner, D.E., and Jarvenpaa, S.L. (1995). The use of information technology to enhance management school education: A theoretical view. *MIS Quarterly, 19*(3), 265–291.

Lemmergaard, Jeanette. (2008). Roles in the ISD process: A collaborative approach. *Journal of Enterprise Information Management, 21*(5), 543–556.

Letza, S., Kirkbride, J., Sun, X., and Smallman, C. (2008). Corporate governance theorising: Limits, critics and alternatives. *International Journal of Law and Management, 50*(1), 17–32.

Liker, J.K., Haddad, C.J., and Karlin, J. (1999). Perspectives on technology and work organization. *Annual Review of Sociology, 25*, 575–596.

Linderman, Kevin, Schroeder, Roger, and Sanders, Janine. (2010). A knowledge framework underlying process management. *Decision Sciences Journal, 41*(4), 689–719.

Love, Janice. (2004). Speaking to the big dogs. *Training, 41*(12), 84.

Lukaszewski, K.M., Dickter, D.N., Lyons, B.D., and Kehoe, J.F. (2009). Recruitment and selection in an Internet context. In *Human resource information systems: Basics, applications, and future directions*, edited by M.J. Kavanagh and M. Thite, 277–306. Thousand Oaks, CA: Sage Publications, Inc.

Lyncheski, John. (2010). Social media in the workplace. *Long-Term Living, 59*(10), 32–35.

MacLeod, Calum. (2010). Microblogging spreads in China, even without Twitter. *USA Today*, January 12. [cited April 26, 2011]. Available from *http://www.usatoday.com/news/world/2010-01-12-china-microblogging_N.htm*.

Mager, R.F. (1988). *Making instruction work*. Belmont, CA: David S. Lake Publishers.

Marler, J., and Floyd, B. (2009). Database concepts and application in HRIS. In *Human resource information systems*, edited by M.J. Kavanagh and M. Thite, 25–44. Thousand Oaks, CA: Sage Publications, Inc.

Marquardt, Michael. (2011). *Building the Learning Organization*. 3rd Ed. Cambridge: Nicholas Brealey Publishing.

Marquardt, Michael. (2011). *Optimizing the power of action learning*, 2nd ed. Boston: Nicholas Brealey Publishing.

Marquardt, Michael, and Berger, Nancy O. (2003). The future: Globalization and new roles for HRD. *Advances in Developing Human Resources, 5*(3), 283–295.

Marquardt, Michael, and Engel, D. (1992). *Global human resource development*. Englewood Cliffs, NJ: Prentice-Hall.

Marquardt, Michael, and Kearsley, Greg. (1999). *Technology-based learning*. Boca Raton, FL: St. Lucie Press.

Marquardt, M., and Yeo, R. (2011). *Breakthrough problem solving with action learning*. Palo Alto: Stanford University Press.

McCormack, J. (2004). Compliance tools. *HRMagazine, 49*(3), 95–99.

McManus, M.A., and Ferguson, M.W. (2003). Biodata, personality, and demographic differences of recruits from three sources. *International Journal of Selection and Assessment, 11*, 175–183.

Meade, J.G. (2003). *The human resources software handbook: Evaluating technology solutions for your organization*. San Francisco: Jossey-Bass/Pfeiffer.

Mellina, Edmond. (2010). The short-term future of HR. *Canadian HR Reporter, 23*(10), 13–17.

Merriam, S.B., and Caffarella, R.S. (1999). *Learning in adulthood*, 2nd ed. San Francisco: Jossey-Bass.

Meyer, G. (2001). eWorkbend: Real-time tracking of synchronized goals. *HRMagazine, 46*(4), 115–118.

Miller, G., and Veiga, J. (2009). Cloud computing: Will commodity services benefit users long term? *ITPro* (1520–9202/09), 57–59.

Mittleman, Daniel, and Briggs, Robert. (1999). Communication technologies for traditional and virtual teams. In *Supporting work team effectiveness: Best management practices for fostering high performance*, edited by E. Sundstrom. San Francisco: Jossey-Bass.

Morrison, Scott. (2009). A second chance for Second Life—Northrop, IBM use virtual world as setting for training, employee meetings. *Wall Street Journal*, Aug 19, 2009, 5.

Morse, Judith, Ruggieri, Margaret, and Whelan-Berry, Karen. (2010). Clicking our way to class discussion. *American Journal of Business Education, 3*(3), 99–108.

Murray, Sarah. (2002). High-tech solution eases cost pressures. *Financial Times* Surveys edition (April 4), 8.

Naran, Juggie. (2010). Online study aid brings lessons to life. *Sunday Tribune*, September 12, 2010.

Neff, M.D. (2002). Online knowledge communities and their role in organizational learning. In *Handbook of online learning: Innovations in higher education and corporate training*, edited by K.E. Rudestam and J. Schoenholtz-Read, 335–352. Thousand Oaks, CA: Sage Publications, Inc.

Nguyen, Frank. (2009). The effect of performance support and training on performer attitudes. *Performance Improvement Quarterly, 22*(1), 95–114.

Nguyen, Frank, and Hanzel, Matthew. (2007). LO + EPSS = Just-in-time reuse of content to support employee performance. *Performance Improvement, 46*(6), 8–14.

Nguyen, Frank, and Woll, Craig. (2006). A practitioner's guide for designing performance support systems. *Performance Improvement, 45*(9), 37–48.

Nikandrou, I., Apospori, E., and Papalexandris, N. (2005). Changes in HRM in Europe: A longitudinal comparative study among 18 European countries. *Journal of European Industrial Training, 29*(7), 541–560.

Nonaka, Ikujiro. (2008). The knowledge-creating company. *Harvard Business Review, 69*(6), 96–104.

Nonaka, I., and Takeuchi, H. (1995). *The knowledge-creating company*. New York: Oxford University Press.

Nunamaker, Jay, Briggs, Robert, Mittleman, Daniel, Vogel, Douglas, and Balthazzard, Pierre. (1997). Lessons from a dozen years of group support systems research: A discussion of lab and field findings. *Journal of Management Information Systems, 13*(3), 163–207.

O'Driscoll, Tony, and Cross, Jan. (2005). In her own words: Gloria Gery on performance. *Performance Improvement Journal, 44*(8), 5–7.

Osberg, C. (2002). How to keep e-learners online. *T+D, 56*(10), 45–46.

Paino, Marci, and Rossett, Allison. (2008). Performance support that adds value to everyday lives. *Performance Improvement, 47*(1), 37–44.

Patel, Laleh. (2010). Overcoming barriers and valuing evaluation. *T+D, 64*(2), 62–64.

Pelofsky, Jeremy, and Ross Colvin. (2010). *U.S. to tighten security after WikiLeaks disclosure* [Online newspaper]. Reuters, Nov 29, 2010 [Cited April 28, 2011]. Available from *http://in.reuters.com/article/2010/11/29/idINIndia-53217920101129.*

Perry, Bill. (2009). Customized content at your fingertips. *T+D, 63*(6), 29–31.

Pfieffelmann, B., Wagner, S., and Libkuman, T. (2010). Recruiting on corporate websites: Perceptions of fit and attraction. *International Journal of Selection and Assessment, 18*(1), 40–47.

Phillips, J.J., Phillips, P.P., and Hodges, T. (2004). *Make training evaluation work.* Alexandria, VA: ASTD Press.

Pincher, Michael. (2010). Big ERP is dead, long live agile. *Computer Weekly,* (May 18–May 24), 24–25.

Piskurich, George M. (2004). Preparing instructors for synchronous e-learning facilitation. *Performance Improvement, 43*(1), 23–29.

Pollitt, D. (2005). Testing graduates at Lloyds TSB: How the bank selects the people who will lead it into the future. *Human Resource Management International Digest, 13*(1), 12–14.

Porter, Michael, and Kramer, Mark M. (2006). Strategy and society: The link between competitive advantage and corporate social responsibility. *Harvard Business Review, 84*(12), 78–92.

Prensky, M. (2005). What can you learn from a cell phone? Almost anything. *Innovate, 1*(5), 1–8.

Presby, L., and Zakheim, C. (2006). Enhancing student learning with only a click. *The Business Review, Cambridge, 6*(1), 153–156.

Raelin, Joseph A. (1998). Work-based learning in practice. *Journal of Workplace Learning, 10*(6/7), 280–283.

Raybould, Barry. (2000). Building performance-centered web-based systems, information systems, and knowledge management systems in the 21st century. *Performance Improvement, 39*(6), 32–39.

REACH. (2009). New media for newbies. *Challenge* March/April, 9 [Cited May 5, 2011]. Available from *www.ps21.gov.sg/challenge/archives/pdf/200903.pdf.*

Reynolds, D.H., and Weiner, J.A. (2009). *Online recruiting and selection: Innovations in talent acquisition.* West Sussex, UK: Wiley-Blackwell.

Ribbens, E. (2007). Why I like clicker personal response systems. *Journal of College Science Teaching, 37*(2), 60–62.

Rienties, B., Tempelaar, D.T., Pinckaers, M., Giesbers, B., and Lichel, L. (2010). The diverging effects of social network sites on receiving job information for students and professionals. *International Journal of Sociotechnology and Knowledge Development, 2*(4), 39–53.

Robb, D. (2004). Building a better workforce. *HRMagazine, 49*(10), 86–94.

Robbins, S. (2002). Evolution of the Learning Content Management System. *ASTD Source for Learning*. Accessed January 15, 2010. *www.astd.org/LC/2002/0402_robbins.htm.*

Roberts, Bill. (2003). Are you ready for biometrics? *HRMagazine, 48*(3), 95–99.

Roberts, B. (2006). New HR systems on the horizon. *HRMagazine, 51*(5), 103–108.

Roberts, B. (2008). Hard facts about soft-skills e-learning. *HRMagazine, 53*(1), 76–79.

Roberts, B. (2009). Open-source solutions for HR. *HRMagazine, 54*(3), 69–72.

Roberts, B. (2008). Teaching tech. *HRMagazine, 53*(7), 83–87.

Roberts, Bill. (2010). Developing a social business network. *HRMagazine, 55*(10), 54–61.

Roberts, Mary Rose. (2010). Biometric scanner reduces EMS on-scene time. *International Wireless Communications*. Accessed April 26, 2011. Available from *http://urgentcomm.com/mobile_data/news/biokey-mychoice-20100506/index. html.*

Rosenberg, M.J. (2001). *E-learning: Strategies for delivering knowledge in the digital age.* New York: McGraw-Hill.

Rosman, P. (2008). M-learning as a paradigm of new forms in education. *E&M Ekonomic and Management, 1*, 119–125.

Rossett, A. (2000). Confessions of a web dropout. *Training, 37*(8), 100.

Rossett, A., ed. (2002). *The ASTD e-learning handbook: Best practices, strategies, and case studies for an emerging field.* New York: McGraw-Hill.

Rossett, A., and Marshall, J. (2010). E-learning: What's old is new again. *T+D, 64*(1), 34–38.

Rossett, Allison, and Schafer, Lisa. (2007). *Job aids and performance support: Moving from knowledge in the classroom to knowledge everywhere.* San Francisco: Pfeiffer.

Rudestam, K.E., and Schoenholtz-Read, J., eds. (2002). *Handbook of online learning: Innovations in higher education and corporate training.* Thousand Oaks, CA: Sage Publications, Inc.

Rungtusanatham, M., Ellram, L., Siferd, S., and Salik, S. (2004). Toward a typology of business education in the Internet age. *Decision Sciences Journal of Innovative Education, 2*(2), 101–120.

Russ-Eft, Darlene, and Preskill, H. (2001). *Evaluation in organizations.* Cambridge, MA: Basic Books.

Saba, F. (2000). Research in distance education: A status report. *International Review of Research in Open and Distance Learning, 1*(1), 1–9. Ed. New York: Nichols.

Safko, Lon. (2010). *The social media bible: Tactics, tools, and strategies for business success,* 2nd ed. Hoboken, NJ: John Wiley & Sons, Inc.

Savery, John R., and Duffy, Thomas M. (1996). Problem-based learning: An instructional model and its constructivist framework. In *Constructivist learning environments: Case studies in instructional design*, edited by B.G. Wilson. Englewood Cliffs, NJ: Educational Technology Publications.

Schein, Edgar H. (1992). *Organizational culture and leadership*. San Francisco: Jossey-Bass.

Schramm, J. (2004). Cybercrime and HR. *HRMagazine, 49*(2), 152.

Schramm, Jennifer. (2010). HR's challenging next decade. *HRMagazine, 55*(11), 96.

Schreft, Stacey. (2007). Risks of identity theft: Can the market protect the payment system? *Economic Review—Federal Reserve Bank of Kansas City, 92*(4), 5–42.

Schwandt, David R., and Marquardt, Michael J. (2000). *Organizational learning: From world-class theories to global best practices*. Boca Raton, FL: St. Lucie Press.

Scriven, Michael. (1991). *Evaluation thesaurus*, 4th ed. Thousand Oaks, CA: Sage Publications, Inc.

Shotsberger, P., and Vetter, R. (2002). The handheld web: How mobile wireless technologies will change web-based instruction and training. In *The ASTD e-learning handbook*, edited by A. Rossett, 175–181. New York: McGraw-Hill.

Slotte, V., and Herbert, A. (2007). Engaging workers in simulation-based e-learning. *Journal of Workplace Learning, 20*(3), 165–180.

Society for Human Resource Management. (2007). HR and business education: Building value for competitive advantage. *HRMagazine, 52*(6), 1–12.

Society for Human Resource Management. (2010). Hear what's happening in workplace law? *HRMagazine, 55*(5), 102.

Steele, Laura. (2007). Internet 2.0: The faster web. *Kiplinger Letters, 84*(5), 1.

Stewart, Thomas. (1997). *Intellectual capital: The new wealth of organizations*. New York: Doubleday.

Sullivan, Dan. (2004). *Proven portals: Best practices for planning, designing, and developing enterprise portals*. Addison-Wesley Information Technology Series. Boston: Addison-Wesley.

Sundstrom, Eric. (1999). *Supporting work team effectiveness: Best management practices for fostering high performance*. The Jossey-Bass Business and Management Series. San Francisco: Jossey-Bass.

Swan, K., and Shea, P. (2005). The development of virtual learning communities. In *Learning together online: Research on asynchronous learning networks*, edited by S.R. Hiltz and R. Goldman. Mahwah, NJ: Lawrence Erlbaum Associates Publishers.

Swanson, R.A., and Dobbs, R.L. (2006). The future of systemic and systematic training. *Advances in Developing Human Resources, 8*(4), 548–554.

Swanson, R.A., and Holton, E.F.I. (2001). *Foundations of human resource development*. San Francisco: Berrett-Koehler Publishers, Inc.

The Economist. (2011). United States: Still patchy; the recovery. *398*(8716), 32–33.

Thite, M., and Kavanagh, M.J. (2009). Evolution of human resource management and human resource information systems. *Human Resource Information Systems*, 3–24. Thousand Oaks, CA: Sage Publications, Inc.

Trehan, K. (2007). Psychodynamic and critical perspectives on leadership development. *Advances in Developing Human Resources, 9*(1), 72–82.

Tucker, M. (2005). E-learning evolves. *HRMagazine, 50*(10), 74–79.

Unneberg, L. (2007). Grand designs for e-learning—can e-learning make the grade for our biggest corporations? *Industrial and Commercial Training, 39*(4), 201–207.

Van Rooy, D., Alonso, A., and Fairchild, Z. (2003). In with the new, out with the old: Has the technological revolution eliminated the traditional job search process? *International Journal of Selection and Assessment, 11*(2–3), 170–174.

van Schaik, Paul, Pearson, Robert, and Barker, Philip. (2002). Designing electronic performance support systems to facilitate learning. *Innovations in Education and Teaching International, 39*(4), 289–306.

Velicanu, Manole, Litan, Daniela, and Mocanu, Aura-Mihaela. (2010). Some considerations about modern database machines. *Informatica Economica, 14*(2/2010), 37–44.

Vygotsky, L.S. (1978). *Mind in society: The development of higher psychological processes*. Cambridge, MA: Harvard University Press.

Waddill, Deborah, Banks, Shannon, and Marsh, Catherine. (2010). The future of action learning. *Advances in Developing Human Resources, 12*(2), 260–279.

Walden, V. M., Scott, I., and Lakeman, J. (2010). Snapshots in time: Using real-time evaluations in humanitarian emergencies. *Disaster Prevention and Management, 19*(3), 283–29.

Watkins, Ryan. (2007). Designing for performance, part 3: Design, develop, and improve. *Performance Improvement, 46*(4), 42–48.

Weatherly, L. (2005). HR technology: Leveraging the shift to self-service—it's time to go strategic. *HRMagazine, 50*(3), A1–12.

Weinstein, Margery. (2010). Sizing up simulation. *Training*, November/December 2010, 46–47.

Welsh, E.T., Wanberg, C.R., Brown, K.G., and Simmering, M.J. (2003). E-learning emerging issues, empirical results, and future directions. *International Journal of Training and Development, 7*, 245–258.

Wenger, E. (1998). *Communities of practice: Learning, meaning and identity*. Cambridge, UK: Cambridge University Press.

Wenger, E., McDermott, Richard, and Snyder, William M. (2002). *Cultivating communities of practice*. Boston: Harvard Business School Press.

Wesner, Marilyn, and Miller, Tammy. (2008). Boomers and Millennials have much in common. *Organizational Development Journal, 26*(3), 89–96.

Wexler, S. (2008). RSVP to e-learning 2.0. *Training*, September 2008, 14–21.

Whitney, L. (2010). Cell phone subscriptions to hit 5 billion globally, *Mobile World Congress*. 2011, February 16, 2010 ed., vol 2011: Mobile World Congress.

Wiig, K. (1997). Role of knowledge-based systems in support of knowledge management. In *Knowledge management and its integrative elements*, edited by J. Liebowitz and T. Beckman. Boca Raton, FL: CRC Press.

Wiley, D.A., ed. (2002). *The instructional use of learning objects*. Bloomington, IN: Agency for Instructional Technology.

Wiley, D.A. (2002). Learning objects need instructional design learning theory. In *The ASTD e-learning handbook*, edited by A. Rossett, 115–126. New York: McGraw-Hill.

Woodward, N. (2008). Seamless relocation. *HRMagazine, 53*(3), 57–63.

Wright, Aliah D. (2009). Thwarting lawsuits—one fingerprint at a time. *HRMagazine*, SHRM's 2009 HR Trend Book, 57–59.

Wright, Aliah D. (2009). Dive into clean water. *HRMagazine, 54*(6), 76–80.

Wright, Aliah D. (2010). More employees visit social sites while working. *HRMagazine, 55*(9), 20.

Yang, J.F. (2006). The discussion of media selection and accessible equity in distance education. *Journal of American Academy of Business, Cambridge, 10*(1), 126–130.

Yoo, Y., Kanawattanachai, P., and Citurs, A. (2002). Forging into the wired wilderness: A case study of a technology-mediated distributed discussion-based class. *Journal of Management Education, 26*(2), 139–163.

Zeidner, Rita. (2005). Building a better intranet. *HRMagazine, 50*(11), 99–104.

Zeidner, Rita. (2009). The tech effect on Human Resources. *HRMagazine* SHRM's 2009 HR Trend Book (January 1), 49–53.

Zielinski, D. (2009). Be clear on cloud computing contracts. *HRMagazine, 54*(11), 63–66.

Zielinski, D. (2010). Make your HR portal a destination location. *HRMagazine, 55*(6), 107–112.

Zweifel, Thomas. (2010). *Culture Clash: Managing the Global High Performance Team, The Global Leader*. NY: Select Books Incorporated.

Index